Charitable Words

Recent Titles in Contributions in Women's Studies

Frances Trollope and the Novel of Social Change
Brenda Ayres, editor

Women Among the Inklings: Gender, C. S. Lewis, J.R.R. Tolkien, and Charles Williams
Candice Fredrick and Sam McBride

The Female Body: Perspectives of Latin American Artists
Raysa E. Amador Gómez-Quintero and Mireya Pérez Bustillo

Women of Color: Defining the Issues, Hearing the Voices
Diane Long Hoeveler and Janet K. Boles, editors

The Poverty of Life-Affirming Work: Motherwork, Education, and Social Change
Mechthild U. Hart

The Bleeding of America: Menstruation as Symbolic Economy in Pynchon, Faulkner, and Morrison
Dana Medoro

Negotiating Identities in Women's Lives: English Postcolonial and Contemporary British Novels
Christine Wick Sizemore

Women in Iran: Gender Politics in the Islamic Republic
Hammed Shahidian

Women in Iran: Emerging Voices in the Women's Movement
Hammed Shahidian

Rebecca West: Heroism, Rebellion, and the Female Epic
Bernard Schweizer

Adventures Abroad: North American Women at German-Speaking Universities, 1868–1915
Sandra L. Singer

Adrienne Rich: Poetry of the Possible
Cheryl Colby Langdell

Charitable Words

Women, Philanthropy, and the Language of Charity in Nineteenth-Century Dublin

MARGARET H. PRESTON

Foreword by Maria Luddy

Contributions in Women's Studies, Number 202

Westport, Connecticut
London

Library of Congress Cataloging-in-Publication Data

Preston, Margaret H. (Margaret Helen)
Charitable words : women, philanthropy, and the language of charity in nineteenth-century Dublin / Margaret H. Preston ; foreword by Maria Luddy.
p. cm. — (Contributions in women's studies ISSN 0147–104X ; no. 202)
Includes bibliographical references and index.
ISBN 0–275–97930–X (hardcover : alk. paper)
1. Women in charitable work—Ireland—Dublin—History—19th century. 2. Women philanthropists—Ireland—Dublin—History—19th century. 3. Charities—Ireland—Dublin—History—19th century. 4. Dublin (Ireland)—Social conditions—19th century. I. Title. II. Series.

HV541. P74 2004
361.7′082′0941835—dc22 2004012296

British Library Cataloguing in Publication Data is available.

Library of Congress Catalog Card Number: 2004012296
ISBN: 0–275–97930–X
ISSN: 0147–104X

First published in 2004

Praeger Publishers, 88 Post Road West, Westport, CT 06881
An imprint of Greenwood Publishing Group, Inc.
www.praeger.com

Printed in the United States of America

The paper used in this book complies with the Permanent Paper Standard issued by the National Information Standards Organization (Z39.48–1984).

10 9 8 7 6 5 4 3 2 1

Dedicated to Helen and Robert Preston
and in memory of
Adele M. Dalsimer

Contents

Foreword by Maria Luddy ix

Acknowledgments xv

Abbreviations xvii

Introduction 1

1 Setting the Stage: Dublin and Ireland in the Nineteenth Century 13

2 Race, Class, and Religion in the Language of Dublin's Charities 41

3 Conversion amidst Compassion: Saving the Souls of the Poor 67

4 An Inner Light: The Charitable Work of Dublin's Quakers 101

5 The Good Nurse: Women Philanthropists and the Creation of a Career 127

Conclusion 175

Select Bibliography 181

Index 201

Foreword

An account of Dublin, published in 1822, while extolling the virtues of those of rank and fortune in the city, also noted that it ". . . contain[ed] a large mass of human beings in the most squalid and wretched conditions . . . it is not possible to walk in any direction half an hour without getting among the loathsome dwellings of the poor."[1] Eighty years later the Rev. Gilbert Mahaffy, in evidence before a parliamentary committee on street-trading children, observed that "Dublin is relatively the poorest [city] in the kingdom. There is a large number of people living on the absolute verge of poverty . . . there are large numbers of people living on such small sums of money that we who know them wonder how they keep body and soul together."[2] While it seemed as if the circumstances of the poor had altered little in those 80 years, what these observations hide is the extensive nature of philanthropic provision that had developed in the country, but particularly in Dublin, throughout the nineteenth century. The provision of charity in Dublin, the subject of this book, had grown so extensive that it took almost 300 pages of a guidebook, published in 1902, to describe the charitable organizations in existence, their facilities, and the clientele they served. G. D. Williams's *Dublin Charities* lists hundreds of charitable organizations operating in the city. "Dublin," he noted, "like all other large cities and towns, has a very large poor population; it has also a noble army of Christian workers, who are constantly devoting whole-hearted energy in doing all they can to alleviate sickness, suffering and poverty."[3] There was one major problem with all this charitable activity, a lack of cooperation between the different charitable groups. "Surely," Williams asked, "if there was more co-operation, closer scrutiny, and in some cases amalgamation, much saving could be effected and more effectual work carried out."[4] The call for unity was naïve. Philanthropic provision in nineteenth-century Ireland was denominational provision. Few charitable workers of any particular religious denomination could see the benefit in amalgamating their resources. For many philanthropists the provision of relief was a material and spiritual battle, and it was often the souls of the poor that were the prize.

Three major religious denominations functioned in Ireland in the nineteenth century, Catholicism, Anglicanism, and Presbyterianism. The most reliable early figures for affiliation to a particular congregation come from the census of 1861, which showed that Catholics made up almost 78 percent of the total population, members of the Church of Ireland (Anglicans) made up 12 percent, and Presbyterians 9 percent, the remainder being divided among nonbelievers, Methodists, Congregationalists, Unitarians, Baptists, Jews, and Quakers, among others.[5] It is to be remembered also that the Church of Ireland was the Established Church in Ireland until 1869. Religion shaped the lives of Irish men and women in many ways, but for women it had a profound effect, at once limiting and defining their place to the domestic sphere but also, ironically, in pursuing the demands of "Christian duty" to help the less well-off in society, ushering them into the public domain of charity work. The Protestant charity network was well developed in Ireland from the late eighteenth century. The scriptural basis for charitable involvement was much invoked in the reports of the various charitable institutions formed in the period. Protestant women such as Mary Mercer, who established Mercer's hospital in Dublin in 1734, played an important role in funding charitable enterprises.[6] Also in the eighteenth century numerous almshouses, particularly for widows, were established and funded by men and women. Religion was a primary motivating factor in engaging in charitable work in the eighteenth century, as it was in the nineteenth century. Good works were a means toward spiritual salvation and were expected from members of all religious denominations.

The establishment of institutions that catered to the poor and destitute of all religious denominations took place against a backdrop of state provision, often viewed as inadequate by many philanthropists. Numerous government commissions were appointed to inquire into the causes of, and possible solutions for, Irish poverty in the first part of the nineteenth century. Attempts to alleviate poverty and destitution were made through the introduction of statutes and institution building. By the mid-1830s, for instance, government had initiated the construction of 41 county infirmaries, 70 fever hospitals, nearly 600 dispensaries, and 10 lunatic asylums around the country.[7] Ireland, as a result, was the first country in the western world with a system of public asylums for the insane. However, the existence of these institutions did not mean the poor and sick were entitled to aid, because the principal subscribers controlled who could or could not be assisted through these foundations. With the rise in population, many of these medical institutions were under severe strain in terms of finances and capacity by the 1830s. Government concern with the increasing costs and level of Irish destitution allowed the initiation of a number of parliamentary committees and a Royal commission to suggest what was to be done about Irish poverty.

While the Irish authorities were always reluctant to take responsibility for the Irish poor, they were continually concerned with the possibility of political upheaval in Ireland. Throughout the eighteenth and into the nineteenth century there was a general perception that Ireland was a land of disorder and violence, and that the causes of Irish misery were to be found most often in the character of the Irish themselves. Ireland, in the prefamine period, was continually disturbed by agrarian outrages, while the mobilization of the Catholic masses by Daniel O'Connell in his Catholic emancipation and Repeal campaigns frightened the government. Poverty was seen by the government, and by many commentators, as one of the prime factors in the disorder that plagued the country in this period. The government accepted the view that the causes of disorder were to a large extent the consequence of social and economic conditions for which Irish landlords were much to blame. There was a strong belief that Irish landlords had some responsibility for the state of the country, and the government was willing to intervene to ensure that the Irish were awarded some degree of justice. In 1838 when the Tipperary magistrates requested the government to introduce more coercive legislation, the chief secretary's famous reply revealed the government's feeling toward landlords: "Property," Thomas Drummond stated, "has its duties as well as its rights."[8]

The development of a policy to deal with the Irish poor was eventually to mirror the establishment of the new poor law in England and was also to reflect government belief that the landowning class in Ireland had to share the responsibility for the poor of the country. The Irish Poor Law, which was introduced in 1838, divided the country into 130 administrative divisions, designated unions, each of which constructed its own workhouse. Relief was to be made available only within the confines of the workhouse, although the distress caused by the Great Famine led boards of guardians to institute outdoor relief beginning in 1847. The principles upon which the workhouses were run were intended to deter people from seeking relief and to ensure that only the truly destitute would enter. Government had thus essentially centralized the provision of poor relief, directing local boards of guardians and holding them responsible for the successful management of the workhouses. The poor law provided some rights to the mass of Irish poor; however, the inadequacy of this poor relief system was demonstrated by its inability to cope with the crisis of the Great Famine (1845–1850), and by the rise in private philanthropic societies throughout the century.[9] One of the features of Dr. Margaret Preston's study is the use made of poor law records, particularly those of the

North Dublin Union. These records are a much neglected resource among historians of Ireland, and Dr. Preston uses them to illuminate the relationship between workhouse managers and the individuals who sought shelter and sustenance under their roofs.

Protestant men of the wealthier classes had a monopoly on political power at the local and national level throughout the eighteenth and into the nineteenth century. Power and authority came to some extent from the control of charitable and public institutions, such as those funded by the government. Protestant prosperity also allowed the development of charitable initiatives. Thus we see Protestants funding hospitals and asylums and sitting on committees of charitable enterprises. Protestant charities were well supported by the Protestant community, and many charitable initiatives became the concern of individual families who raised funds and sat on managing committees. Charitable initiatives were sponsored by the rising middle classes.

Dr. Preston focuses particularly on the charitable work of lay Protestant women in the nineteenth century. Like most philanthropists of the period, these women sought, through their endeavors, to create an industrious poor, who could support themselves, know their place, and remain loyal subjects to the Crown. Some of these women also became involved in proselytizing work, although it appears that the rates of conversion were low enough to dent the most enthusiastic missionary zeal.[10] Significantly, Protestant women appear to have been more independent of clerical authority in their philanthropic work than their Catholic counterparts. However, their institutions and societies operated on a much smaller scale than Catholic charities in the care of nuns. The minority position of Protestants in Irish society allowed a sense of community to develop among these philanthropic women, and at the least charity work allowed them a more active social life. For many there must have been a feeling of excitement and danger attached to dealing with the "rougher" elements of society.

Quaker women and men were at the fore in organizing the most innovative of the charities of the nineteenth century. Dr. Preston focuses on their work during the Great Famine and on their charitable work in Dublin. Making up less than one percent of the city's population, the Quakers were involved in business and philanthropy out of all proportion to their actual numbers.

Class homogeneity and personal relationships kept many Protestant charities afloat. Organizational charity work for the Protestant community was a means of maintaining its identity and separateness from the Catholic masses. For many, their charitable activities complemented their role as legislators and administrators.

Catholic women, although not a central focus of this study, also engaged in philanthropic effort, but for Catholics the most extensive welfare provision was made by nuns. The expansion of convent networks throughout the century affected the extent to which lay Catholic women became involved in charity work. It was primarily Irish women who promoted the growth of the conventual movement in Ireland from the late eighteenth century to throughout the nineteenth century. Up to the 1850s convents were concentrated in the south and east of the country, the area recognized as the land of the Catholic gentry and emerging middle classes. Founders of these religious congregations were women of wealth and means, and their followers also had substantial incomes. It was these women who were to have a profound impact on Irish society, in terms of socializing the Catholic majority to a revitalized Catholic Church and teaching the tenets of the Catholic faith to a population that, in prefamine times at least, tended to pay little heed to the doctrines of the church. Congregations of nuns expanded from the early nineteenth century and by mid-century managed an increasing number of lay Catholic charitable enterprises. In consequence, many lay Catholic women, while remaining active as fund-raisers, were removed from the public arena of institutional charity work.[11] Whatever their role in charitable enterprises it is clear that, whether Catholic or Protestant, women helped to consolidate church power by evangelizing and developing the social function of religion.

It is evident that a key element of philanthropy in Ireland was the denominational nature of its development. One of the consequences of this denominational aspect was its divisive impact. Charities of different religions competed not only for resources, but also for clients. This had a profound impact on the provision of welfare for the poor, and particularly for children. Chapter 3 of this study, which examines the work of the Protestant Ellen Smyly and the Catholic Margaret Aylward, affords a superb example of interdenominational rivalry and of the collision that occurred in the battle for the souls of children. The bitterness revealed in the study of Smyly and Aylward provides a glimpse of the deeply sectarian nature of much of the philanthropic work in nineteenth-century Ireland. But even in these battles it is clear that Aylward had a different understanding of the nature of poverty than many other philanthropists. Her religious enthusiasm did not blind her to the fact that it was poverty, rather than an internal predisposition to idleness, that led to ignorance and destitution.

While there is a growing literature on philanthropic work in nineteenth-century Ireland, Dr. Preston highlights new areas of research. She extends our knowledge of charitable activity in nineteenth-century Dublin, focusing more deeply than has been done previously on the meanings of race, class, and religion in charitable provision. We have, for the first time, a detailed study of the development of nursing and the integral role played by philanthropic women in the formation of nursing as a career for women. There is a sustained analysis of the work done by Quakers, both during the Great Famine and in the innovative charities they established in Dublin throughout the century. Philanthropists constantly sought to provide relief only to the "deserving" poor. In order to ascertain who were deserving, it was essential always to make inquiries. Questions had to be asked about employers, places of work, places of worship, earnings before the application for relief, references, whether relatives could assist, debts, marital status, and other issues. These inquiries were to provide a basis for further investigation into the individual's circumstances. While some argued that such prying into the lives of the poor was unnecessary and uncharitable, others suggested that it was ". . . true charity, because we want to do much better than merely provide a meal or two, we want to cure the disease, apply a proper remedy, and remove, if possible its cause."[12] Without detracting from the laudable aspirations of philanthropists, it is clear that it was in the investigations of cases, in home visitations, in dealing with the poor in institutions that the drama of philanthropic work was evident. It was this that made the work exciting, interesting, and attractive to so many women.

Maria Luddy
University of Warwick

NOTES

1. "Dublin in 1822," *New Monthly Magazine and Literary Journal* 4 (1822), pp. 503–11.

2. *Report of the Committee on Street Trading Children*, House of Commons (H.C.) (1902), xlix (cd. 1144).

3. George C. Williams, ed., *Dublin Charities: A Handbook* (Dublin: Association of Dublin Charities, 1902), p. 1.

4. Ibid.

5. Sean Connolly, *Religion and Society in Nineteenth-Century Ireland* (Dundalk: Dundalgan Press, 1985).

6. See chapter 5.

7. *Report of the Poor Law Commission on Medical Charities (Ireland)*, H.C. (1841), xi, pp. 1–7.

8. *A Copy of the Correspondence Which has Recently Taken Place Between Her Majesty's Government and the Magistrates of County Tipperary, Relating to the Disturbed State of the Country*, H.C. (1837–38), xlvi, p. 571.

9. See Maria Luddy, "Religion, Philanthropy and the State in Late Eighteenth and Early Nineteenth-Century Ireland," in *Charity, Philanthropy and Reform from the 1690s to 1850*, ed. Hugh Cunningham and Joanna Innes (New York: St. Martin's Press, 1998), pp. 148–67.

10. See chapter two.

11. See Maria Luddy, *Women and Philanthropy in Nineteenth-Century Ireland* (New York: Cambridge University Press, 1995); and Mary Peckham Magray, *The Transforming Power of Nuns: Women, Religion and Cultural Change in Ireland 1750–1900* (New York: Oxford University Press, 1998).

12. Williams, *Dublin Charities*, pp. 3–5.

Acknowledgments

My particular thanks must go to Kevin O'Neill (Boston College), Peter Weiler (Boston College), and Mrinalini Sinha (Pennsylvania State University), all of whom gave me support, advice, and insightful criticism. The Boston College History Department, staff, and postgraduate friends were always ready with a kind word for the project. The Irish Studies Program of Boston College is where I found my greatest source of encouragement. In particular, the late Adele Dalsimer was an important mentor. I must also thank Seamus Connolly, Ruth-Ann Harris, Kevin Kenny, Vera Krielcamp, Catherine McLaughlin, Kristen Morrison, Philip O'Leary, Robert Savage, and Jim Smith for their personal and professional friendship during my time in Boston.

For access to the archives I must thank the Convent of the Holy Faith, which permitted me to work with the records of the Ladies Association of Charity and St. Brigid's Orphanage. Thanks must also be given to David Sheehy, archivist of Dublin Diocesan Archives; Mary Shackleton and the Religious Society of Friends, Swanbrook Library; and Gregory O'Connor of the National Archives, who assisted with the records of the Royal Hospital, Kilmainham. Mary O'Doherty of Mercer's Library, Muriel Haire of the Irish Nurses Organization, Robert Mills of the Royal College of Physicians, Marylin Lesh of the Cottage Home for Little Children, Mr. Hodges of the Home for Aged Governesses and Other Unmarried Ladies, Arthur Moyse of the Atkinson House, Claire Dean of the St. John's House of Rest, and Julie Carville of the YWCA all provided needed source documents. The librarians and staff of the Augustana College Mikkelsen Library, Boston College O'Neill Library, Marsh's Library, Mercer's Library, National Library of Ireland, National Archives of Ireland, Representative Church

Body Library, and the Royal Irish Academy are generous professionals. I was able to spend time in Ireland because of a number of grants. These include the International PEO Organization, The Boston College Abbey Theater Summer School, The Meave O'Reilly Finley Scholarship, the Janet Wilson James Scholarship, the Boston College Women's Studies Research Incentive Grant, and the Augustana College Academic Research Grant.

Boston College's Irish Studies students are fortunate to have the Burns Visiting Scholar, and I give special thanks to Margaret MacCurtain (University College Dublin), Kevin Whelan (University of Notre Dame), and Alvin Jackson (Queen's University, Belfast). Each helped during the formation of this work and supported me during its completion. Other academic friends who provided support include Nancy Anderson (Loyola University), Sighle Bhreathnach-Lynch (National Gallery, Ireland), Geoffrey Dipple (Augustana College), Margaret Kelleher (NUI, Maynooth), Michael Mullin (Augustana College), Timothy O'Neill (University College Dublin), Gary Olson (Augustana College), Cormac Ó Gráda (University College Dublin), and my many new colleagues at Augustana College. There are many who offered moral support. I must thank Jane Biondi, Anne Butler, Mary Lou Connolly, Kathleen Fanning and her daughter Kathleen, Kathleen Finnan, Marta Geletkanycz, Christine Guerra, Gail Howe, Joseph Lennon, Niamh Lynch, Kitty Migaki, Ken Migaki, Nancy Marx, William Neenan, Meabh ni Fhuarthain, Robert Newton, Ciáran Ó hÓgartaigh, Fay Plohn, Bob Preston, Jim Preston, Richard Spinello, Elizabeth Tolman, Beatriz Valdés, James Zisk, and Molly Zisk.

In particular, I would to thank Margaret Ó hÓgartaigh for having twice read and commented on this work. Maria Luddy, in whose academic footsteps I have trod for years, has always been generous with source information, support, and encouragement. Kate Costello Sullivan, Enda Delaney, and Robert Preston all read and provided important feedback. Finally, a special remembrance for Hugh O'Meagher, who traveled with me in spirit each time I returned to Ireland.

Abbreviations

AVH	Association for Visiting Roman Catholics in Hospital
BNR	Bird's Nest Report
BSN	Belfast Society for Providing Nurses for the Sick Poor
CRC	Central Relief Committee of the Religious Society of Friends
DSH	Dr. Steevens Hospital
DVM	Dublin Visiting Mission
EHR	Elliot's Home Report
FRS	Friends' Ragged School
HHH	Helping Hand Home
ICM	Irish Church Missions
LAC	Ladies Association of Charity
NAI	National Archives, Ireland
NDU	North Dublin Union
NLI	National Library, Ireland
PGM	Prison Gate Mission
PRONI	Public Records Office, Northern Ireland
RBH	Ragged Boys' Home
RCD	Baggot Street Hospital (Royal City of Dublin Hospital)

RCP	Royal College of Physicians
RCS	Royal College of Surgeons
RGH	Ragged Girls' Home
RHK	Royal Hospital, Kilmainham
SBO	St. Brigid's Orphanage
SPD	Sir Patrick Dun's
SPI	Sick-Poor Institute
SPN	St. Patrick's Nurses Home and Bible Woman Association
SSI	Strand Street Institute
TCD	Trinity College Dublin

Introduction

Of women philanthropists, Matthew Davenport Hill suggested that, "in addition to the intelligence, firmness, judgment and kindly disposition," they actually attained impressive influence "derived from the refined manners and the chastened habit of command which belong to their social position—an influence gently enforcing the prompt obedience of all who have the good fortune to be under their control."[1] Hill described the image of the nineteenth-century lady philanthropist that many in the middle class envisioned. Key to the evolution of women's involvement in philanthropy was the unfolding of the industrial revolution, which fostered the growth of the middle class throughout Western Europe and North America.[2] This middle class sought to emulate the aristocracy, and as such, middle-class women found that there were few public roles into which they could respectably enter.[3] One of a handful of activities open to women was philanthropy, and through their volunteer efforts, these women believed that they could be role models to the poor.[4] The women of charity were to be experts on right living, particularly because they spent a lifetime perfecting their knowledge of domestic economy, sanitary practice, and honest behavior. Thus, as Hill stated, the poor should have been grateful to come under the control of the lady philanthropist, for it was she who could guide the indigent out of poverty.

This project, from its beginning, has sought to focus upon women who did not take religious vows, but it instead is about Irish lay women.[5] As such, this research will further our knowledge of the work of Irish women philanthropists, suggesting similarities with their Western European and

North American sisters while alluding to unique qualities attributable only to an Irish cultural context.[6] While Irish women chose the same causes as their philanthropic sisters, including establishing orphanages, homes for distressed gentlewomen, Magdalene asylums, and ragged schools for poor children, in particular they faced the sectarian tensions, sometimes violent, that often characterized social and political relationships within Irish society.

While religion played an important role, it was the stereotypes of class and strict roles for both genders that dominated social relationships in Victorian society. The upper classes believed that they were superior in all ways. Intellectually and morally more advanced, they had earned their position in the power structure. However, this authority was not without responsibility, and Victorian society also ordained that it was the Christian duty of those with so much to provide assistance and guidance to those with so little. In response, the poor were to deferentially accept the benevolence of their betters.[7] Although not always successful, this was the dynamic that the upper classes hoped to achieve, thereby creating an ordered, functional, and peaceful society.[8]

Just as the classes had their roles, so too did the genders, and historians have argued that Victorian society created separate spheres.[9] The male inhabited the world outside the home where he earned an income, participated in politics, and contributed to the governing of the nation in a very public way.[10] He was responsible for the financial well-being of family and home. Ideally, in the female sphere, women were to be the "angels of the house," spiritual protectors of and caregivers to the family.[11] Universally, women's defining role was to be supportive: as mother, nurse, peacekeeper, and spiritual guide.[12] Such women had cultivated "social and pious affections, namely, gentleness of temper, kindness of heart, and resignation to the will of God."[13] Nevertheless, through charitable endeavors, upper-class women used their role of moral guardian and spiritual sentinel to legitimize their entrance into that public space from which they were shunned. These women negotiated the limits of the social order by involvement in nonsalaried activity.

Women's experience of organizing their own homes helped them to establish the charities in which they were involved. Not only the day-today activities but also fund-raising often became woman's sphere.[14] Records reveal that women raised funds through fancy bazaars or musical concerts as well as habitual activities including Mother's Meetings, sewing exhibits, tea parties, and prayer meetings.[15] Despite their exceptional goals, charities could only contribute to society if they could sustain themselves financially. Thus, while donations were essential, many organizations earned income through providing such services as making, washing, and mending clothes or selling handmade goods. Establishing and maintaining a charity involved much preparation: funds to be raised, meals to be planned, curricula to be established, and training to be determined. The women of philanthropy were equipped for such tasks because they were already doing many of them in their own homes.

One role that the women of philanthropy were particularly prepared for was that of nursing. Taking advantage of society's expectation that females were innately caregivers, the women of philanthropy first sought to integrate nursing into their charitable work. Soon enough, however, they realized that, naturally, the next step was a campaign to reform nursing.[16] The records of local Dublin hospitals, sick-poor charities, and visiting nurse organizations show how philanthropists worked to construct the role of the nurse into a respectable profession. By the nineteenth century, Ireland had developed a complex hospital system in which the poorest found aid. In addition, nurses were housed on hospital premises—and between patients and nurses, the ladies of charity had two captive groups upon which they could impose reforms. In particular, philanthropists hoped they could turn nurses into moral role models for their patients. Not only interested in hospital nurses, philanthropists were also involved in creating visiting nurse programs, which were particularly important to Ireland's rural communities. While philanthropists sought to turn nursing into a respectable career, at the same time they created an occupation that supplied women with a measure of independence, authority, and intellectual stimulation that could not be found in other employment opportunities open to them.

Regardless of whether they brought medical aid to the poor, worked to reform prostitutes, or founded homes for orphans, most charities advocated that imparting the Christian message was essential to bringing about personal change. As one Dublin charity, the Girls' Training Home, noted, while it sought to "protect girls from the temptations of the city," it also hoped to "bring them under religious influences."[17] Hence, Bible classes, tracts, and scripture meetings were almost always included in the reform process. Women involved with the philanthropic movement were adamant about "instilling of faith," and volunteers could be unrelenting in their attempts to have the poor repent for their sins.[18] Thus, while promoting the themes of hard work, sobriety, and sanitary practice, reformers also called upon the poor to attend religious services.[19]

Another theme that appears within charitable pamphlets is the desire to create hardworking citizens and loyal subjects. To train a person to work and then find her a job was to end her dependence upon the benevolence of others, particularly the state. The Protestant Orphan Society, which placed children with those industrious families who had been recommended by a local minister, argued that by living in respectable homes, orphans would then become "the happy fruits of honest industry."[20] In addition, a child would learn "laborious [*sic*] habits" and would, over time, be "trained to hate his sin."[21] Sin, many philanthropists believed, contributed to indigence.

In particular, it was the homes of the poor that charitable workers believed to be dens of iniquity. Thus, philanthropists advocated visiting in order to present themselves as moral role models as well as teachers of home economy and sanitary techniques.[22] Hence, Dublin's charitable women became sanitary missioners to the poor as they fanned out into the city's slums in order to bring all manner of relief. To sing the theme of cleanliness helped to wash away the stain of poverty. In addition, not only did women volunteers go to the homes of the poor, but they also imparted their know-how in local hospitals, workhouses, and prisons.

While charitable records make clear the philanthropists' belief that sin contributed to poverty, what is also revealed is that issues of race and class actually played an important role in how charitable volunteers viewed the poor. Within philanthropic publications and other primary source documents can be found a similar theme: that the poor were inferior but, with the help of their superiors, their status in society could be somewhat improved although never completely changed. The failings of the impoverished, philanthropists believed, were the result of both nature and nurture.[23] This was the age of Darwin, and hypotheses about the evolutionary state of humans bled into theories regarding the characteristics of class.[24] Thus, in the same way that the middle classes argued that there were superior and inferior races, they applied these same ideas to class, resulting in a hierarchy where class characteristics were not dissimilar to those of race. Ultimately, what charitable records suggested was that those in the upper classes believed that members of the working class were lower on the scale of evolution.

In addition, for Ireland, historic religious divisions often characterized social and political relations and were disruptive. In nineteenth-century Dublin, rhetoric, fear, and loathing between Catholics and Protestants inhibited charitable giving. This situation was made worse by the few Protestant charities that labored to convert Roman Catholics. Hostility between charities was intense, and evidence shows that due to sectarian animosity, many Irish charities limited their aid to members of the denomination to which the charity was affiliated. However, this does not mean that Ireland was bereft of charities providing aid to the poor regardless of religious affiliation. One of the best examples was the Religious Society of Friends, a Protestant sect that spread the Christian message but did not impose religious restrictions upon those to whom they brought assistance.[25]

While this work focuses upon charities both collectively and individually, what thematically will link the chapters together is a discussion of the language contained in the records of charitable workers and social reformers alike. The language within the primary evidence mirrored the paternalism informing the relationship between middle- and upper-class philanthropists and Dublin's poorer classes. This paternalism, based on contemporary conjecture regarding class, race, and religion, led philanthropists to believe that by imposing strict rules upon the poor, teaching them sanitary techniques, and encouraging frugality of lifestyle, they could mold the poor into model employees and loyal subjects.

Dublin's women philanthropists established a variety of charities focusing particularly on children, poor women, prostitutes, and the elderly. There was the Clergy Daughter's School for the education of the children of poor clergy; the Asylum for Aged and Infirm Female Servants; the Seaton Association Fund, which provided aid to wives and widows of Crimean War veterans; and the Rescue Mission Home for young women of a better social class. The Managing Committee of the Association for the Suppression of Mendacity in Dublin aided the "unobtrusive classes of the meritorious poor," while the volunteers for Dublin By Lamplight searched for prostitutes by candlelight, gathering them into the mission, giving them tea and biscuits, all while trying to convince them of the error of their ways.[26]

While many women reformers attempted to relieve the personal hardship of the poor, they rarely inquired into what led to such hardship.[27] Few philanthropists questioned the political system that permitted wealth to be concentrated among a few, leaving one-third of the population to live in poverty.[28] Most reformers spent their days in the streets among the poorly fed, clothed, and housed, but went home each night to comfortable surroundings and a warm bed. While private institutions, hospitals, missions, and other charity organizations relieved much misery, generally, it appears that most reformers failed to reflect upon their own wealth or question the political and economic policies that contributed to poverty.

This research will show that charity work in nineteenth-century Dublin was more than simply just the wealthy trying to help the poor. The women of charity were both manipulators of social mores and tools of social control. They were actors who were being acted upon. Charity was an occupation for intelligent women through which they accepted their sphere as domestic while challenging that domestic did not simply mean their own homes. Ultimately, this research evaluates and represents the contributions and the impact of many of Ireland's philanthropic women.

This book will proceed in the following manner. Chapter 1 will set the stage upon which philanthropists worked by focusing particularly on Ireland's central city, Dublin. Dublin was a growing metropolis at the end of the eighteenth century, and this legacy is reflected in the city's beautiful Georgian architecture. However, Dublin suffered along with much of the island as the relationship between Britain and Ireland remained inequitable. After the Napoleonic wars, when the price of grain dropped but the charge for rent did not, Ireland's population, most of whom lived on the land, increasingly grew dependent upon the potato as their sole source of food. When a fungus struck the potato, the impact was immediate and many began to starve. By mid-century, Dublin was reeling under the pressure of migrants forced into the city by the devastation wrought by famine. Little improved in the postfamine era, as Dublin's political leadership was unable to effect many enhancements to the city's slums due to corrupt practices that were aggravated by sectarian divisions and chronic deficits. The once proud capital was staggered by the needs of an ever-increasing poor population. The city came to depend heavily upon private charity, as both women and men braved unimaginable conditions to bring aid to the most destitute.

Chapter 2 focuses upon the ideology behind the nineteenth-century charitable agenda. This chapter proposes that, in relation to poverty, Dublin's philanthropists adopted the same attitude regarding race, class, and religion as their Victorian counterparts elsewhere, and such opinions were revealed within the records of Dublin charities. Philanthropists believed poverty not only to be the result of a degenerate evolutionary state but the consequence of sin, laziness, and, for many, an adherence to a dissenting faith. Thus, within their records, philanthropists called for the poor to live morally, work hard, and practice their religion. This effort was not about changing the poor's class status but instead sought to improve their circumstances in an effort to make them contributing subjects of the state. Behind this overt desire to create a model working class was the fear of the crowd. The upper classes were well aware of the potential violence of which the poor were capable, and they hoped that by supplying aid and encouraging good behavior, the poor might provide the ruling classes with a measure of deference. This chapter examines the hidden incentives of charity cloaked behind the philanthropists' sincere desire to provide for those who had so little.

Chapter 3 brings to light the religious divisions that hindered cooperation between Ireland's Catholic and Protestant communities. Not only in the private sector, sectarian divisions also affected state-run institutions, and evidence from the records of the North Dublin Union reflect this pervasive problem. An in-depth discussion of two local charities will reveal how serious the discord between aid organizations was. Ellen Smyly's charitable network desired to convert Catholic children to the Protestant tradition while Margaret Aylward and the Ladies Association of Charity sought to combat proselytizers. This chapter gets to the heart of Dublin's religious tensions and argues that historic sectarian animosities influenced the behavior of Dublin's charities and limited their effectiveness. In addition, by focusing on the language of charity, this chapter reveals that there was a minority of philanthropists who held a divergent attitude toward poverty. While most philanthropists believed that, at minimum, indigence was the result of sinful behavior, the work here will show that Margaret Aylward's writings suggest that she was one among a minority who believed that poverty led to sin.

Chapter 4 highlights the work of the Religious Society of Friends. In contrast to the organizations discussed in chapter 3, while the Society clearly stated its Christian mission, Friends offered aid to all in need regardless of religious denomination. The Religious Society of Friends began in England as a revolutionary sect that was openly critical of the government's political authority. In addition, Friends were expected to shun the trappings of a consumer society but, ironically, this did not preclude them from establishing profitable businesses. By the nineteenth century, Ireland's Quakers were well established and Dublin Friends could be found among the prominent business leaders of the city. The Friends' financial success was aided by the changing political climate, which adopted laissez-faire economic theories in relation to the operation of industry and trade. As a result, Friends increasingly interacted with a mainstream society from which they had originally sought to be separate. Hence, this chapter proposes that, as the Society slowly lost its revolutionary nature, Friends steadily transformed their radical discourse into the direct action of philanthropy. Nevertheless, chapter 4 will show that the discourse contained within the Society's records revealed the same class prejudices that marked much of nineteenth-century charity. As such, the Friends' language reflected their move away from their traditionally more radical rhetoric and suggested an acceptance of the dialogue of the Victorian social and political authority.

Chapter 5 offers new information on how the women of charity worked to establish a modern nursing system for Ireland and make it a career for working-class women. This chapter shows how the language of charity was put into practice. For upper-class women, nursing was the key to their sanitary mission. While the women of philanthropy could not respectably become nurses, they desired to see their working-class sisters enter the hospitals and homes of the poor and bring with them the message that sanitary practice was important to good health. In order to effect this agenda, women who were involved in nursing reform worked to enforce highly restrictive regulations, hoping to turn working-class women into nurses who would be models of respectable behavior to their patients. Chapter 5 proposes that nursing reformers created opportunities that provided women with a career that offered greater authority, independence, and financial reward. The chapter goes on to discuss that due to Ireland's rural nature, the visiting nurse became an important figure upon the island's late nineteenth-century landscape. Here, with the help of the ladies of charity who established district nursing programs, Irish women benefited from the opportunities offered by rural nursing. District nurses, who were much more independent than their hospital sisters, were often the only medical personnel for miles, and evidence shows that their responsibilities were great. In looking at Ireland's nursing history, we find the clear involvement of the women of philanthropy, who sought to improve the role of women in medicine.

A variety of sources was consulted in order to emphasize the unique nature of Irish charity. Contemporary pamphlets offer insight into the work as well as economic viability or "profitability potential" of many of these organizations. Some philanthropic associations did not publish pamphlets but instead kept minutes or similar records that included day-to-day details, income generated, and numbers aided. This evidence is supplemented by the commentary of the day that was coming from local and national social reform advocates and contained in privately published pamphlets or other publications, including *Transactions of the National Association for the Promotion of Social Science* and the *Journal of the Dublin Statistical Society*. Such work also offers anthropological insight into nineteenth-century Dublin.

This work does not seek to be a comprehensive discussion of the charity work of women in nineteenth-century Ireland but aspires to provide a better understanding of the middle-class philanthropists' agenda. What becomes clear is that philanthropy was an industry. The women who involved themselves in charity raised impressive amounts of money while endeavoring to ensure that particularly the worthy received their largesse. Yet, the philanthropists' understanding of poverty was also complicated by their belief that it was the result of not only personal irresponsibility, but also an essentialism that the poor could not escape. This work seeks to add to our understanding of the world of Irish charity, while at the same time revealing its many complexities. Finally, it hopes to be another contribution to the canon of women's history in Ireland.[29]

NOTES

1. Matthew Davenport Hill, "A Paper on the Irish Convict Prisons" (London: J. W. Parker and Son, 1857), pp. 22–23. Hill (1792–1872) was a lawyer and prison reform advocate and worked much of his life in his hometown of Birmingham, England.

2. See Philippa Levine, *Feminist Lives in Victorian England: Private Roles and Public Commitment* (Oxford: Basil Blackwell, 1990); Julia Parker, *Women and Welfare: Ten Victorian Women in Public, Social Service* (London: St. Martin's Press, 1989); F. K. Prochaska, *Women and Philanthropy in 19th Century England* (Oxford: Oxford University Press, 1980); and Patricia Branca, *Silent Sisterhood: Middle-Class Women in the Victorian Home* (Pittsburgh: Carnegie-Mellon University Press, 1975).

3. "Rigid social rules ensured the safety of the bourgeois family; within the home women were assigned a special position as caretakers of morality and religion, for their unique sensibility made them alone capable of child care and domestic responsibilities." Martha Vicinus, *Independent Women: Work and Community for Single Women, 1850–1920* (Chicago: University of Chicago Press, 1985), p. 2.

4. See Kathleen D. McCarthy, ed., *Lady Bountiful Revisited: Women, Philanthropy, and Power* (New Brunswick, N.J.: Rutgers University Press, 1990); Lori D. Ginzberg, *Women and the Work of Benevolence: Morality, Politics and Class in the Nineteenth-Century United States* (New Haven, Conn.: Yale University Press, 1990); and Peter Mandler, ed., *The Uses of Charity: The Poor on Relief in the Nineteenth-Century Metropolis* (Philadelphia: University of Pennsylvania Press, 1990).

5. While there is still much to be done, there has been a good deal of research on Irish women who entered the convent. For example, see Jacinta Prunty, *Lady of Charity, Sister of Faith: Margaret Aylward, 1810–1889* (Dublin: Irish Academic Press, 1999); Mary Peckham Magray, *The Transforming Power of Nuns: Women, Religion and Cultural Change in Ireland, 1750–1900* (New York: Oxford University Press, 1998); Margaret MacCurtain, "Late in the Field: Catholic Sisters in Twentieth-Century Ireland and the New Religious History," *Journal of Women's History* (Winter/Spring 1995), pp. 49–63; and Catriona Clear, *Nuns in Nineteenth Century Ireland* (Dublin: Gill & MacMillan, 1987).

6. See Maria Luddy, *Women and Philanthropy in Nineteenth Century Ireland* (Cambridge: Cambridge University Press, 1995); and Alison Jordon, *Who Cared? Charity in Victorian and Edwardian Belfast* (Belfast: Queen's University of Irish Studies, Institute of Irish Studies, 1993).

7. Jessica Gerard, "Lady Bountiful: Women of the Landed Classes and Rural Philanthropy," *Victorian Studies* 30 (Winter 1987), pp. 183–210; E. P. Thompson, "The Moral Economy of the English Crowd in the Eighteenth Century," *Past and Present* 50 (1971), pp. 76–136; and Gareth Stedman Jones, *Outcast London: A Study in the Relationship between Classes in Victorian Society* (Oxford: Clarendon Press, 1971).

8. There was a measure of cooperation from both above and below. See, among others, F.M.L. Thompson, "Social Control in Victorian Britain," *Economic History Review* 34, 2 (May 1981), pp. 189–208; Gareth Stedman Jones, "Class Expressions vs. Social Control," *History Workshop* IV (1978), pp. 163–70; and Jennifer Hart, "Religion and Social Control in the Mid-Nineteenth Century," in *Social Control in Nineteenth Century Britain,* ed. A. P. Donajgradzki. (London: Croom Helm, 1977), pp. 108–37.

9. See Leonore Davidoff and Catherine Hall, *Family Fortunes: Men and Women of the English Middle Class, 1780–1850* (Chicago: University of Chicago Press, 1987).

10. "The masculine guardians represent the state in the function of providing the money—the raw material, as it were, of shelter, food, clothing and teaching. The ladies, now occupying a recognized place as feminine guardians, must represent the state in the function of seeing that money properly used, and in so doing seeing also that the wants of the heart and soul are supplied likewise." Isabella Tod, "Boarding-out of Pauper Children," *Statistical and Social Inquiry Society of Ireland* VII, 5 (August 1878), p. 298. Tod (1836–1896), a resident of Belfast, worked to improve educational opportunities—particularly for middle-class girls. See Maria Luddy, "Isabella M. S. Tod," in *Women, Power and Consciousness in 19th Century Ireland,* ed. Maria Luddy and Mary O'Dowd (Dublin: Attic Press, 1995), pp. 197–230.

11. See Priscilla Robertson, *An Experience of Women: Pattern and Change in Nineteenth-Century Europe* (Philadelphia, Pa.: Temple University Press, 1982), pp. 488–89.

12. Barbara Welter, "The Cult of True Womanhood, 1820–1860," *American Quarterly* 18 (Summer 1966), p. 152.

13. Catherine Cappe suggested that all women, regardless of class, had such qualities. Catherine Cappe, *Extracts from Observations on Charity Schools and Other Subjects Connected with the Views of the Ladies Committee* (Dublin: William Watson, 1807), p. 8.

14. Not only married but many unmarried women added to the charitable coffers. Prochaska, *Women and Philanthropy*, p. 41. See also F. K. Prochaska, "Charity Bazaars in Nineteenth-Century England," *Journal of British Studies* 16, 2 (Spring 1977), pp. 62–84.

15. Prochaska, *Women and Philanthropy*, pp. 44–45. See also F. K. Prochaska, "A Mother's Country: Mothers' Meetings and Family Welfare in Britain 1850–1950," *History* 74 (October 1989), pp. 379–99.

16. Regina Markell Morantz, "Making Women Modern: Middle Class Women and Health Reform in 19th Century America," *Journal of Social History* 10, 4 (1977), pp. 490–507; and Brian Abel-Smith, *A History of the Nursing Profession* (London: Heineman, 1960).

17. George C. Williams, ed., *Dublin Charities: A Handbook* (Dublin: Association of Dublin Charities, 1902), p. 222.

18. "Severity went hand in glove with their conception of love. By instilling a sense of shame, or criminality, in their charges, they prepared the ground for conversion and reformation." Prochaska, *Women and Philanthropy*, p. 156.

19. "Armed with the paraphernalia of their calling—bibles, tracts, blankets, food and coal tickets, and love—these foot soldiers of the charitable army went from door to door to combat the evils of poverty, disease and irreligion." Prochaska, *Women and Philanthropy*, p. 98.

20. Third Annual Report of the Protestant Orphan Society founded A.D. 1828 (1832), p. 34.

21. Protestant Orphan Society (1832), p. 34.

22. See Gertrude Himmelfarb, "Manners into Morals: What the Victorians Knew," *The American Scholar* 57 (Spring 1988), pp. 223–32.

23. "The poor conspired in their tragic fate, their manners and customs making them particularly susceptible to misery and vice." Gertrude Himmelfarb, *The Idea of Poverty: England in the Early Industrial Age* (London: Alfred A. Knopf, 1984), p. 106.

24. Perry Curtis, Jr., *Apes and Angels: The Irishman in Victorian Caricature* (Washington, D.C.: Smithsonian Institution Press, 1997); Floya Anthias, "Race and Class Revisited—Conceptualizing Race and Racisms," *The Sociological Review* 38, 1 (February 1990), pp. 19–42; Douglas Larimer, "Nature, Racism and Late Victorian Science," *Canadian Journal of History* 25 (December 1990), pp. 369–85; and Christine Bolt, *Victorian Attitudes to Race* (London: Routledge & Kegan Paul, 1971).

25. See Helen Hatton, *The Largest Amount of Good: Quaker Relief in Ireland 1654–1921* (Montreal: McGill-Queen's University Press, 1993).

26. 17th Report Managing Committee of the Association for the Suppression of Mendacity in Dublin (1833), 10; (1834), 14. Dublin By Lamplight aided former prostitutes in earning money via the charity's laundry, which allowed them to then acquire "habits of punctuality, diligence, and self-respect, e'er they go out

again into the perilous paths of life." Thirteenth Annual Report, Dublin By Lamplight (1867), p. 7.

27. Prochaska, *Women and Philanthropy*, p. 219.

28. Parker, *Women and Welfare*, pp. 145–46 and 151.

29. For discussion of women's experience in Irish history, see Bernadette Whelan, ed., *Women and Paid Work in Ireland 1500–1930* (Dublin: Four Courts Press, 2000); Maryann Gialanella Valiulis and Mary O'Dowd, eds., *Women & Irish History* (Dublin: Wolfhound, 1997); Mary Cullen and Maria Luddy, eds., *Women Power and Consciousness* (Dublin: Attic Press, 1995); Mary O'Dowd and Sabine Winchert, eds., *Chattel, Servant or Citizen: Women's Status in Church, State and Society* (Belfast: Institute of Irish Studies, 1995); Mona Hearn, *Below Stairs: Domestic Service in Dublin and Beyond 1880–1922* (Dublin: Lilliput Press, 1993); Margaret MacCurtain, Mary O'Dowd, and Maria Luddy, "An Agenda for Women's History in Ireland, 1500–1900," *Irish Historical Studies* 28, 109 (May 1992), pp. 1–37; Margaret MacCurtain and Mary O'Dowd, *Women in Early Modern Ireland* (Edinburgh: Edinburgh University Press, 1991); Maria Luddy & Cliona Murphy, eds., *Women Surviving: Studies in Irish Women's History in the 19th and 20th Centuries* (Dublin: Poolbeg Press Ltd., 1989); Hasia Diner, *Erin's Daughters in America* (Baltimore, Md.: Johns Hopkins University Press, 1983); and Margaret MacCurtain and Donncha O'Corrain, eds., *Women in Irish Society: The Historical Dimension* (Westport, Conn.: Greenwood Press, 1978).

CHAPTER 1

Setting the Stage: Dublin and Ireland in the Nineteenth Century

> The streets of Dublin stare the vacant and helpless stare of a beggar selling matches on a doorstep, and the feeble cries for amusement are like those of a child beneath the ragged shawl for the red gleam of a passing soldier's coat. On either side of you, there is a bawling ignorance or plaintive decay. Look at the houses! Like crones in borrowed bonnets some are fashionable with flowers in the rotting window frames—others languish in silly cheerfulness like women living on the proceeds of the pawnshops . . . And the souls of the Dubliners blend and harmonise with their connatural surroundings.
>
> —George Moore (1886)

Here was Dublin of George Moore's *A Drama in Muslin,* a story about the coming of age of five young Irish girls during the late nineteenth century.[1] Moore vividly captured the nation's tarnished capital. The resplendent Dublin of the late eighteenth century had, due to neglect during the nineteenth, become old and inelegant.[2] Throughout the nineteenth century Dublin steadily suffered, particularly because it was a port through which the poorest moved. While many were fleeing the devastating potato famine of the mid-century, all were seeking assistance, hoping to find a job or, more likely, the opportunity to emigrate. Dublin offered no relief as it was a city that was already overcrowded, unsanitary, and impoverished.[3] In the long term, the famine left Dublin with an extensive indigent population who found little in the way of employment, housing, or help. The city, mismanaged by a local authority that was both unwilling and unable to solve Dublin's problematic infrastructure, lacked the needed industrial development to provide employment for the many. However, undaunted by these extreme economic hardships, many of Dublin's residents, both rich and poor, attempted to provide some relief to those in need.

It is important to understand the conditions under which philanthropists worked because not only Dublin, but all of Ireland steadily declined throughout the nineteenth century. In truth, Dublin's charitable workers, in spite of overwhelming conditions, attempted, by supplying education, training, food, clothing, housing, and other necessities, to improve the lives of the thousands who flocked to the city in search of relief. These men and women sought to bring succor to extensive suffering as they quietly worked their way through the alleyways and back lanes that made up the maze of Dublin's slums. Their records tell of the horrible conditions into which charity workers forged and provide greater understanding of the many challenges faced by both private and state charity. For example, in 1854, when volunteers from Dublin's Ladies Association of Charity of St. Vincent De Paul went to visit a poor, sick woman, they found her "lodged in a most wretched place; with difficulty we made our way up to her room, the stairs being in total darkness . . . entering into a large waste room, we saw a figure leaning against the wall; about a handful of straw was strewn behind her."[4]

Dublin's decline in the nineteenth century actually followed years of progress for the city that, by the late eighteenth century, was the second largest metropolitan area in Britain and Ireland. Dublin enjoyed a well-developed medical system of both hospitals and medical schools and, because of its capital status, was ensured the year-round presence of a wealthy population who contributed to Dublin's financial health.[5] The capital of Irish banking, Dublin was home to British insurance companies, an active stock exchange, a burgeoning port and railway infrastructure, and Trinity College, one of the largest universities in Britain or Ireland.[6] Throughout the eighteenth century, Dublin saw impressive change to its skyline. Architects such as James Gandon, designer of the Customs House and Four Courts, joined colleagues in creating Dublin's Georgian character, which featured wide streets lined with beautiful homes.[7] Nevertheless, in 1800, Dublin's Parliament voted itself out of existence and Ireland became part of the United Kingdom. The impact of this loss, as wealthy politicians transferred to London, was not immediately apparent as Dublin's economic status actually improved in the years immediately following the Union.[8] Like Dublin, during the early part of the century, Ireland also made gains as it increased its grain, textile, and livestock exports to England, and some, particularly medium to large farmers, benefited.

Increasingly, however, in the years following the end of the Napoleonic wars, Dublin was unable to compete. Technological advances in shipping made it less expensive to move supplies by way of ship to other Irish cities rather than via rail from Dublin.[9] This loss of revenue contributed to the port's failure to modernize and it quickly began to lose business. While the city was home to such enterprises as brewing and paper manufacture, Dublin was not a major industrial center, and scant existing ventures hired too few and often only temporary employees.[10] The lack of diversification in industry hampered the nation as a whole, which experienced economic decline in the third and fourth decades of the century, and with it Dublin's circumstances also deteriorated.[11]

To add to the island's difficulties, between 1600 and 1845 Ireland saw its population swell from 1 million to 8.5 million—with, impressively, between 1801 and 1845, Ireland's population increasing by approximately 50 percent.[12] Where and how were these growing numbers surviving? The land question in Ireland is a topic that has received much attention from scholars who have shown that a small number of landlords, many of whom were absentee, controlled much of Ireland's land. Generally, these absentee landlords then leased management of the land to middlemen who often rented it themselves to farmers who did the same and so on, such that, as the famine approached, Ireland's land was extraordinarily subdivided, particularly in the western counties.[13] The statistics were stunning. On the eve of the Great Famine, 75 percent of the Irish lived on 20 acres or less with almost 25 percent surviving off of 5 acres or less.[14] In addition to persons who leased land, there were cottiers who, in exchange for their labor, were given a small plot of land for potatoes and a cabin. Finally, there were at least 100,000 persons who owned no land at all but instead worked as farm help.[15]

Nevertheless, after the first decades of the nineteenth century, and the end of the Napoleonic wars, as Ireland's economy began to weaken, absentee landlords continued to exact ever-higher rents from the island's burgeoning population.[16] In addition, the postwar slump resulted in increased unemployment for Ireland's textile industry, compelling even more of the population to depend upon agriculture.[17] By the eve of the famine, three quarters of all employed males worked the land.[18] Because landlords resisted lowering rents, small to medium farmers used more of what they grew to pay the rent, leaving them increasingly dependent upon the potato for daily sustenance, and, all the while, the impoverishment of the nation steadily increased.[19]

Some years prior to the first signs of famine, the issue of dealing with the administration of poverty was a problem that Parliament had sought to tackle for the whole of the United Kingdom. Westminster's decisions were very much guided by an acceptance of the economic models laid down by the political economists of the day. Adam Smith's theory of laissez-faire economics led the way. Smith proposed that an invisible hand regulated the market and, when it came to the activities of that market, the government should seek to interfere as little as possible. In addition, as Smith's theories gained acceptance, others used his model to argue that the government must complement its nonintervention in the nation's economic life with a similar strategy toward the nation's social needs. Hence, increasingly, Britain's leaders believed that an unregulated economy would provide jobs for all, and, ultimately, extensive governmental relief of poverty was counterproductive.[20] In 1834, Britain introduced the New Poor Law that redesigned a relief system that had been in existence in England since the reign of Elizabeth I.

For Ireland, in 1838, Westminster passed the Irish Poor Relief Act.[21] Prior to 1838 Ireland had no state-funded poor relief, but the New Poor Law now organized all of the United Kingdom's relief under a central authority.[22] In particular, the Imperial Treasury made it clear that it expected Ireland, and specifically Irish landlords, to pay for the majority of Irish relief. The British government had long believed that many of Ireland's problems were due to careless landlords who failed to pay attention to their land and permitted extensive subdivision that only further impoverished the people. Hoping to force landlords to begin to take some responsibility for their estates, the government made the tax burden a local charge.[23] Thus, for example, throughout the famine, Charles Trevelyan, the Assistant Secretary of the Treasury, spent much of his time wrangling with Ireland's poor law administrators about how the imperial treasury could spend less on Irish relief, while demanding that poor law administrators collect ever greater amounts of money from local taxpayers—particularly Ireland's large landowners. This resulted in continual internal strife, and poor law administrators became increasingly frustrated at the government's efforts to force even the poorest parts of Ireland to pay for its own famine relief.[24]

The Irish Poor Relief Act divided Ireland into 130 geographic divisions called unions: each was to have a workhouse that was located near a city or town.[25] The government appointed poor law commissioners who then implemented the Irish Poor Law Act. Commissioners issued orders and supplied guidance to on-site poor law guardians, but generally commissioners did not get involved in individual cases.[26] The guardians, who voluntarily administered the workhouse, were, in the system's early years, wealthy landowners or businessmen living in the same district as the workhouse. Since local taxes paid for the operation of the workhouse, this provided the guardians with incentive to be as frugal as possible. Finally, unlike England or Scotland, before Ireland's local guardians could supply outdoor relief, they had to show that the workhouse was filled to capacity.

In order to avoid achieving capacity while discouraging the poor from relying upon government assistance, the designers of the poor law sought to ensure that conditions inside the workhouse were worse than those outside.[27] Husbands and wives were separated as they entered, and children were not allowed to be with either parent.[28] In addition, mobility was restricted, accommodations were unpleasant, and food was purposely bland and simple. Poor relief in Ireland was therefore limited in scope and impact because, while the government acknowledged it must provide some relief, it hoped that its aid would be ever diminishing.[29]

It seems such conditions did result in the workhouse becoming a place of fear and dread; when in need of charity, the poor often sought out private organizations. Many of the poor chose to remain outside of the workhouse and, "when it is sometimes thoughtlessly suggested to [the poor], that . . . if all fail, they can go to the Union, the answer is quick and to the point—'it were better to go back to the old trade than do that!' "[30] As Dublin philanthropist Margaret Aylward suggested, "on talking with these unfortunate creatures in their homes, we found their dread of the poor-house so great, that for the morsel of dry bread doled out to them in the Sunday school, they pledged their immortal soul."[31] Thus, philanthropists were often the first line of defense for the poor who resisted entering the grim confines of Ireland's workhouses. Soon enough, however, most of Ireland's workhouses would be filled beyond capacity.

In 1845, the arrival of phytophthora infestans on the Atlantic wind currents would trigger a catastrophe of unimaginable proportions. By the eve of the famine, dependence upon the potato had become so high, and the population's living circumstances so reduced, that the ability to purchase an alternative food had all but disappeared. Evidence suggests that over three million were living solely off the potato and almost five million were relying upon it as an essential part of their diet, while only fewer than one million could be considered free of dependence upon the root crop.[32]

Although in the fall of 1845 there was only a hint of what was to come as the potato failed sporadically, nevertheless it became increasingly clear that suffering would soon be widespread. It was not long before Sir Robert Peel, Britain's Prime Minister, privately acknowledged that, in Ireland, a potential disaster was in sight.[33] As a result, in November of 1845, Peel ordered £100,000 worth of corn to be sent to Ireland—both to feed the people but, in particular, to keep down the price of grain.[34] In addition, the government established a relief committee in Dublin that included government representatives and set in motion the establishment of public works.[35]

The entire crop of 1846 was ruined; the crisis was now clearly widespread and demand for aid rapidly escalated. Written records from those who witnessed the growing catastrophe made it apparent that in short order the devastation was unimaginable. In 1846, Belfast's *The Vindicator* quoted that "fever, dropsy, diarrhoea, and famine rioting in every filthy hovel, and sweeping away whole families."[36] At the same time, American Aesnith Nicholson was traveling through Ireland and in her diary she related the case of a poor widow who went into the field of her landlord to take some potatoes. When the landlord saw her, he sent a magistrate to the cabin. There, he discovered "three children in a state of starvation and nothing in the cabin but the pot, which was over the fire. He demanded of her to show him the potatoes. She hesitated; he inquired what she had in the pot—she was silent; he looked in, and saw a dog, with the handful of potatoes she had gathered from the field."[37]

By midyear of 1846, the government decided to implement public works on the principle that those who needed it could work for their relief provisions. The public works program was to begin in September of 1846 and included such activities as road reconstruction, harbor and pier construction, and drainage implementation. However, there were delays. The guardians of the North Dublin Union Workhouse (to be discussed later) wrote to the poor law commissioners and expressed clear frustration:

> [we] cannot but regret the great delay that has taken place in the employment of the Poor on Public works and still more deplore the Principle of Political Economy adopted and acted upon by them in leaving the supply of food wholly to private enterprise, at a time when the energies of Government should be exercised to the fullest extent in providing a starving population with the means of subsistence at such a rate as would enable them by their earnings to support their families.[38]

Despite such complaints, the government did implement a massive public works program on a widespread scale with impressive speed.[39] And, at first, the wages provided would likely have enabled a worker to feed his family.

However, by late 1846, the resulting market demands had caused the cost of food to rise to such a level that this was no longer the case—and the government failed to either raise wages or place a limit on grain prices.[40] Despite this, the demand for work rose by impressive degrees. By late summer of 1846, public works already employed close to 100,000 persons, quickly rising to some 600,000 per week by January of 1847, and peaking at over 700,000 during one week in March of that year.[41] Obviously, the public works system was soon overwhelmed, and local administrators began complaining that they could not handle the numbers. As time progressed, it became clear that many of those who applied for employment on public work schemes were too weak from malnourishment to work so intensively at such physically demanding labor.[42] As one observer remembered, "poor men sitting on heaps of stones, breaking them for a certain number of hours after walking five and six miles to their work in rags and tatters, more like specters than able-bodied."[43]

In the first months of 1847, the government acknowledged the increasing problems posed by public works.[44] It now began to consider doing what it had to date resisted: supplying food directly to the starving population. Hence, in March, the government began to end public works and open up soup kitchens.[45] Yet, the transition was not always so smooth, nor did it occur concurrently, leaving many without any aid for months.

For example, at the Ballina Union in County Mayo, the soup kitchen was not immediately opened after public works ended, and for two months there was no government relief at all.[46] By June of 1847, when all soup kitchens did open, they were feeding over three million persons per day, including areas of the west where almost all of the population appeared in order to receive soup.[47]

Not surprisingly, local relief committees and poor law unions were buckling under escalating costs. While the government recognized that many of the poor law unions were financially strapped, it continued to hold firm in its expectation that Irish property should be made to pay for Irish poverty. However, Parliament acknowledged that, temporarily, it needed to supply more financial aid to much of the nation.[48] In order to provide the needed monies, Westminster, under the Temporary Relief Act of 1847, subsidized loans to Ireland's poor law unions with the money being recouped out of taxes placed upon the harvest of 1848.[49]

In the spring of 1848, when the government began to ask for repayment, guardians expressed doubt regarding their ability to repay. For example, in a letter to the Lord Lieutenant of Ireland, the North Dublin Union guardians expressed great surprise, and even anger:

> While we do not by any means repudiate the debt we cannot but express it as our opinion, that it is a most impolitic measure at such a time as the present when the citizens have to pay for the support nearly double the number of Poor that they had in the early part of last year, and while business of every kind is standing still, to be called upon to discharge a debt, a great portion of which, as has been stated, was incurred by the indefinite, and in many instances, uncalled for measures of the Government itself.[50]

The guardians went on to provide a subtle warning: "we have assumed that if at the present moment we are compelled to levy a rate . . . a feeling of discontent & disapprobation will be engendered in the minds of the citizens, which may ultimately lead to very unpleasant results."[51] In the fall of 1848, it was clear that the harvest would again be at less than normal levels.[52]

By this stage, while certainly much of the island was reeling from the famine, its effects were not experienced evenly throughout. The rural areas, particularly in the west, were hardest hit, while urban sectors and the northeast and east felt the crisis to a lesser degree.[53] In Dublin, the crisis manifested itself through higher food costs and food shortages. Nevertheless, the experiences of poor urbanites may have been comparable to those of their rural cousins because, well before the famine, Dublin's poorest were already in dire straits, "probably less well fed and less healthy than country people."[54] Dublin's poor were housed in slum conditions that offered little in the way of clean water or sanitation and, effectively, were incubators of disease.[55] Thus, in the first instance, what the famine did to the least of Dublin's inhabitants was to further reduce their ability to purchase food. In addition, the incidence of disease and death increased dramatically, as the already weakened slum dwellers were joined by famine-stricken migrants in the desperate search for assistance.[56] In the city, while private charities struggled to provide some aid, government assistance was limited to the poor law and workhouse system.

The city of Dublin was home to two workhouses. The North and South Dublin Unions were opened in March of 1840. As their names denote, the South Dublin Union was located on the city's south side, which was also the city's wealthier district. The North Dublin Union, located closer to the port and the army barracks, was in a district where most property was of lesser value. The General Valuation of Ireland (1852–1854) estimated the north's ratable property at £265,586 while the south's was almost double at £402,516.[57]

In spite of the lower valuation, the North Dublin Union's guardians argued that the NDU was at a greater disadvantage than the South Dublin Union, and the NDU's records revealed this to be a very sore point for its guardians.[58] First, because of the higher property values of the South Dublin Union district, the south's workhouse received more money from taxes. Second, the NDU's guardians believed that it was to the North Dublin Union that a majority of Irish citizens sent home from England eventually arrived.[59] In a letter to the poor law commissioners, the guardians complained that all the arriving ships carried "these destitute persons broken down in constitution, and whose labor has not enriched this country . . . sent home to Ireland when of no further use (by reason of their being born maybe sired or lived here) become at once chargeable on the North . . . sad disappointment is their lot, they find nothing but distress & destitution."[60] Conditions in the North Dublin Union deteriorated as a result of massive overcrowding. The crisis of the famine can be easily followed in the Union's records. The enrollment of the north's workhouse, which was built to house a maximum of 2,000, leapt from 1,655 in September of 1845 to 2,853 in April 1847 with the numbers remaining high well into the next decade.[61] It appears, however, that the poor law commissioners made few attempts to respond to the guardians' complaints, while both of Dublin's workhouses continued to be crowded with the poor of the city.

What the workhouse records also provide is a glimpse at the relationship between those who worked in the Union and those who sought its shelter. Historians have recorded the many abuses that inmates suffered at the hands of workhouse employees: "they were often accused of many irregularities, total lack of interest in their jobs . . . of professional incompetence, laxity and deliberate cruelty."[62] Indeed, the conditions in the NDU, like all workhouses, were harsh. Nevertheless, what is surprising is that among the recordings of the bimonthly meetings, the NDU guardians showed a measure of empathy toward the workhouse inmates.[63] For example, in 1845, the NDU guardians asked the poor law commissioners ". . . whether it may not be advisable to associate themselves into parochial or electoral divisions to visit and distribute private relief amongst the struggling and worthy objects whom sickness and misfortune or other causal circumstances have rendered necessarily dependent upon such persons."[64]

This compassion was also suggested by the guardians' efforts to convince the poor law commissioners to provide more autonomy and, in particular, more money to the North Dublin Union. From the beginning, the north's guardians railed against the injustices of the poor law system and complained that they had no authority over how they spent the money for which the government taxed them. "We protest against an unlimited power of taxation being vested in any commission the expenditure of such funds being uncontrolled by those from whom they are to be levied, and equally arbitrary and unaccounted for."[65] As the famine raged on, the guardians continued to complain about the actions of the government. In 1848, the guardians wrote a letter expressing their unhappiness with the government's plan to move persons from Galway's workhouses to Dublin's. The guardians sought "to prevent a proceeding which would be most injurious to the City of Dublin and oppressive to the rate payers."[66] As with this episode, generally, guardians' efforts proved fruitless. In the end, little relief was forthcoming and conditions improved only when the potato crop recovered after 1851; but by this time it seems at least a million were dead and many more had emigrated.

In an effort to alleviate overcrowding in the workhouses, the government also sanctioned emigration. In 1847, the government, with the cooperation of Australian authorities, developed a scheme to ship young women, who generally outnumbered young men, from British workhouses to Australia, where males greatly outnumbered females.[67] In May of 1848, the poor law commissioners wrote to the North Dublin Union stating that "only Female Orphans, between the ages of 14 and 18 years, will be sent to Australia from the Workhouse-no males."[68] Although workhouses helped others to emigrate, between 1840 and 1870 Irish workhouses assisted over 50,000 women to depart the island.[69]

From 1845 to 1851, historians estimate that some 1.2 million persons emigrated while over 1 million died; by 1855, total emigrant numbers had risen to 2.1 million.[70] The vast numbers that left the country had extensive impact on Ireland's economy, agriculture, and ultimately the population's psyche. Irish emigration was often a family affair and, unusually, almost as many women as men emigrated.[71] For the families who remained, land consolidation became the norm, as fewer fathers subdivided the land among their children, but instead willed it to the eldest male—leaving the rest with few alternatives but emigration.

After the famine, Ireland's farming economy began to shift from tillage to pasture, spurred on as the price of grain rose only between 20 and 40 percent while payments for meat and dairy products increased between 80 and 140 percent.[72] Overall, there was impressive land consolidation, except in the west where land remained divided among small landholders.[73] Nevertheless, the end of the famine did not mark a cessation of potato infestation.[74] The years 1860–1862 were particularly wet, causing extensive crop loss, while the potato failure of 1879–1880 was so widespread that local authorities feared that the devastation could equal that of the 1840s.[75] The economic impact of the famine upon the nation would last for years and Ireland would remain an island of emigrants until the latter half of the twentieth century. Heavy reliance upon agriculture would continue, while widespread poverty, particularly in the west, would characterize the country's future.

While the worst of Ireland's famine was reserved for the west where the poor existed on too little land, the east had been subjected to its own share of problems. Dublin's experience of the famine was not as drawn out as in the west, but the crisis certainly visited the city. Throughout the nineteenth century, Ireland lurched from agricultural crisis to political outrage, and all the while the nation and its capital sank deeper into economic ruin. With each episode there came a regular influx of impoverished persons who traveled to Dublin in search of solace. In the first half of the century, cholera visited the city almost every decade, and this is just one example of the epidemics that regularly haunted its slums.[76] Dublin had too little housing for too many people with much of it lacking in proper sanitation, further contributing to unremitting disease and high mortality. It is on this stage that Dublin philanthropists worked trying to bring some relief to the suffering. While government aid continued in the form of the poor law into the twentieth century, most sought to avoid entering the confines of the workhouse and instead went in search of private charity. In the early twentieth century, Dublin would once again become the capital of Ireland; it was still a tarnished capital that had made little progress in improving the overcrowded, dirty, and impoverished slums that characterized its inner city.

NINETEENTH-CENTURY DUBLIN: BUREAUCRATIC MISMANAGEMENT AND ENDEMIC POVERTY

In the post-famine era, Dublin experienced a surge of philanthropic activity, and increasingly women made their way into the public sphere to become activists for Dublin's poor. Yet, little federal relief was forthcoming either for the poor or for those who helped them, and the job of the philanthropist in Dublin was a daunting one. For the city's poorest neighborhoods, Dublin's local leadership proved to be ineffective at improving the unsanitary state of the streets, clearing the city of uninhabitable tenement housing, or penalizing local industries that polluted the municipality's waterways and thoroughfares. Local projects were hampered by some of the tightest revenue constraints in the United Kingdom, while corrupt politicians and sectarian tensions hindered cooperation by Corporation members.[77] Indeed Dublin Corporation would remain so ineffective that late into the nineteenth century a Royal Commission advised "that unity of administration over the whole of Dublin would conduce to better administration."[78] Thus, to understand the state of the city is to know the hurdles faced by those who sought to bring relief to its poorest.

To begin, the fact that slaughterhouses and dairy yards were located within crowded, poor neighborhoods greatly contributed to Dublin's unsanitary state. While the city's administration established laws to remove slaughterhouses from highly populated areas, it does not appear that the Corporation strictly enforced the new rules.[79] Butchers were a powerful force, and the municipality's efforts to pass regulations were contentious. Even late into the nineteenth century, there still remained a great number of slaughterhouses and dairy yards within the city proper, with most being located in the poorest neighborhoods.[80]

Another problem that Dublin Corporation knew it needed to tackle was the city's thoroughfares. This was the result of the fact that what sewage was not dumped into Dublin's poorly-planned sewer system was strewn onto the roadways, thereby contaminating any accessible running water.[81] In addition, evidence shows that the cleansing of Dublin's streets was a haphazard and unsuccessful affair. The city made little progress in surfacing streets, building sewers and drains, or penalizing those who dumped filth in public roadways.[82]

By 1853 the Liffey River was the primary location into which Dublin's sewer system filtered.[83] The river's notorious stench was the result of its being a raw sewage dumping ground, "at low water edges of the bed of the river are uncovered, and the sewage putrefies and emits for many months the most pestilential vapors."[84] Although, some ten years later, the Corporation's greatest success may have been the Vartry Water Scheme (1863–1868), which daily brought over 13 million gallons of fresh water into the city, Dublin's poorer neighborhoods saw little of the water as they did not have the indoor plumbing to support such a system. In addition, there was the Liffey Drainage Act of 1871, which was designed to pipe sewage outside the city limits, but Dublin Corporation was unable to afford the cost of the project and did not complete it until 1906.[85]

In an effort to try to improve Dublin's many sanitation problems, in 1874 the government passed the Public Health (Ireland) Act in order to regularize sanitation legislation. Four years later, Dublin Corporation imposed more comprehensive policies that increased the power of the Sanitary Authority.[86] The Corporation charged this authority with inspecting sewage conduits and the water supply, as well as imposing fines upon those who practiced public dumping or failed to maintain sanitary conditions in the city's dairies and slaughterhouses.[87] Finally, under the 1878 amendment, the North Dublin Union became the Sanitary Authority for those areas north of the River Liffey.

The NDU's records reveal that it encountered the same difficulties that the Corporation met with while seeking to enforce the cleansing of the city's streets and lanes.[88] For example, Blackhorse Lane, near the city's Phoenix Park, came under the NDU's particular scrutiny due to its uninhabitable state.[89] In March 1879, the NDU minutes noted that "as a general rule there are no privies attached to the cabins, & where 2 or 3 do exist, they are placed over the running stream where the soil not only pollutes the water which the people use a little further down, but is exposed to public view in the most objectionable manner."[90] The North Dublin Union quickly hired someone to clean the street at 15s. per week, and it appeared that the lane saw improvements, "with all necessary provisions for sanitary purposes & that the roadway so far is also rendered quite safe."[91] However, less than six months later complaints resurfaced and the guardians issued a summons against Margaret Kennedy of Blackhorse Lane for "erecting three new houses . . . without any privy or rear accommodation . . . she was fined for the first offence [and] a seven days order was made to have the nuisances abated."[92] Margaret Kennedy appears not to have been frightened by the fines and was given a further penalty of £2 due to "Mrs. Kennedy's being almost impassable with bricks, carts, & *channels* obstructed with manure."[93] In truth, because there were few options, people continued to dump their refuse in Dublin's streets without serious prosecution, and late into the nineteenth century landlords were still erecting buildings without proper plumbing, thereby leaving tenants to live in squalor.[94]

Insight into the extent of the city's unsanitary state, and particularly the overcrowded and uninhabitable condition of tenements, can be found in the published work of social statisticians who walked the streets of the inner city.[95] Throughout the century, their findings revealed a city that had long been in dire condition. Dublin contained hundreds of congested, uninhabitable tenements such as those described in a survey of Plunkett Street late in the eighteenth century. There, investigators found 32 houses that contained "917 inhabitants, which gives an average of 28.7 to a house, and the entire liberty averages from about 12 to 16 persons to each house."[96] These people lived in unimaginable filth and degradation. In one incident, one investigator found a home swamped by "putrid blood alive with maggots, which had, from an adjacent yard, burst the backdoor, and filled the hall to the depth of several inches . . . the sallow looks and filth of the wretches . . . indicated their situation though they seemed insensible to the stench."[97]

Throughout the nineteenth century, local government had little success in improving the conditions within the city's slum neighborhoods.[98] By mid-century, a description of a Dublin tenement revealed the continued dilapidated state of the city's housing. "There are nine three-story houses; the roofs are broken, the windows are boarded for more than half their space . . . there is but one yard for all, and in this, until last year, there was a hovel about 8 square feet and 10 feet high in which three adults were huddled."[99] Late in the century, in 1883, Francis White in *Report and Observations on the State of the Poor of Dublin* wrote of the continuing overcrowded and unsanitary state of the homes in a number of the city's parishes. For example, in St. Luke's Parish he had found 65 houses that contained 1,763 persons, "amongst the entire of whom scarcely fifty blankets could be found."[100] In 1893, the *Dublin Builder* detailed that "there are thousands in this small city, living in an atmosphere that is slowly but assuredly poisoning their blood, living in habitations totally unfit to shelter human beings—thousands huddled together in sweltering masses."[101]

Dublin's Corporation made little progress in improving the condition of inner-city housing. Between 1868 and 1880 the Corporation passed a series of acts that sought to require tenement owners to improve their housing. However, these amendments contained a loophole that compelled Dublin Corporation to buy tenements if owners could not afford enhancements.[102] Thus, Dublin Corporation was increasingly left with uninhabitable slums that the city could also not afford to repair. In addition, Dublin offered few alternative accommodations for families left homeless when the city condemned tenements. Even philanthropists could see the problem, as Rosa Barrett, in her *Guide To Dublin Charities,* noted in her conclusion that even in 1881, "in Dublin nothing has yet been done for the lowest classes. That in 7,234 houses in Dublin 32,303 families live, and one house was found to have 78 tenants."[103] By 1882, some thirty percent of Dublin homes were inhabited by almost sixty percent of its families "at the rate of 1.5 rooms per family."[104] Between 1879 and 1882, 1,345 houses had been closed though not, however, destroyed and rebuilt. The houses could be reopened if the sanitary improvements were enacted, although, as the Royal Commission's Housing Inquiry Act of 1885 stated, there were numerous houses that were reopened without the required enhancements.[105]

The poor, expensive, and limited housing in inner-city Dublin aggravated the overcrowded and unsanitary state of its neighborhoods. Certainly Dublin's expensive rents did not reflect the quality of the accommodation, because in truth there were too few places for too many. As early as the eighteenth century, the cost of rents resulted in three and four families being forced to live together in small rooms that soon became unsanitary.[106] Contributing to the problem, Dublin Corporation permitted most new housing to be built for either skilled artisans or the lower-middle classes, and therefore new accommodations were too expensive for the poorest workers.[107] In 1875, the Iveagh Trust and the Dublin Artisans Dwelling Corporation began to buy derelict sites and establish well-constructed homes, but these too were unaffordable to unskilled laborers.[108]

Not surprisingly, Dublin had many fewer skilled workers than unskilled. In postfamine Dublin, the traditional industries of brewing and distilling remained, while few other large businesses developed. Dublin's port generally offered only temporary employment that became even more precarious if bad weather ruined crops. Late into the century, the city continued to supply more opportunities to casual laborers who could be quickly dismissed when business slowed. Women had even fewer opportunities and rarely could their earnings alone support a family.[109] Thus, many women supplemented any income with begging while hoping that local charities also could provide additional succor.[110]

Ultimately, while Dublin's poorest faced unsanitary living conditions and chronic unemployment, it was made all the worse by high food prices, which resulted in a limited diet and increased incidence of illness for most slum dwellers.[111] The poor did not consume enough vitamins to strengthen the body and ward off disease, particularly because most of Dublin's poorest consumed bread as the main staple of their diet.[112] For instance, a half loaf given at the end of the day or bread and water served for lunch was the menu for many. An entry concerning the ragged school of the Quaker-run Strand Street Institute provided an example of the poor nutritional value of the meals supplied: "many of them [children] gladly give their half-pennies for cocoa and bread and jam, often sharing it with those who are not so rich."[113] Writing at the turn of the century, George D. Williams, in his *Dublin Charities: A Handbook,* stated that the South Dublin Union's outdoor relief per week for a family of four generally consisted of "4 ounces of tea, two pounds of sugar and from 8 to 14 loaves of bread."[114] In the Meath Place Infant School during the year 1900, children received a lunch consisting of bread and cocoa or a stirabout and milk. Though these "meals" were likely all that these charities could provide on their minimal funds, the body could not fight off disease when sustained on bread alone, and inadequate diet contributed to the high mortality rate of poor Dubliners, particularly the youngest.[115]

Late into the century, the mortality of all of Dublin's poorest remained shockingly high. In 1879, Dublin's overall mortality rate was 35.7 per 1,000 while London's was 23.6, Glasgow 22.4, and Edinburgh 21.3.[116] At the turn of the century, Dublin had only dropped to 31.9 while London was now at 19.7, with Glasgow at 21.6, and Edinburgh 19.6.[117] By noting death figures on a social scale, it becomes clear that Dublin's unskilled workers had the highest mortality. By the late 1870s, children under five had a mortality rate of 82.5 per 1,000 in Dublin compared with 69.7 per 1,000 in London, although obviously both numbers are stunning.[118] Dublin's Registrar General noted in 1889: "the death-rate of young children in Dublin is startlingly different in different classes of the community. Thus, while it is only 18 per 1,000 in the professional and independent classes, it rises to 117 per 1,000 in the general service and workhouse class."[119] This sustained high mortality rate at the turn of the century reflected Dublin's other ongoing problems, including the continued endemic outbreak of infectious diseases. As noted earlier, the majority remained poorly housed with few employment opportunities. Dublin's mortality would not improve until it could provide both regular employment as well as enough housing to its citizens; and this would not occur at any significant rate until the early twentieth century. (See Tables 1.1 and 1.2.)

Throughout the nineteenth century, Dublin's charities did what they could to alleviate the suffering. Many of Dublin's middle-class citizens, just as those in London, led a life of leisure, residing in their beautiful Georgian homes in such areas as Fitzwilliam Square, Merrion Square, and St. Stephen's Green.[120] At the same time, many were not indifferent to the squalor that existed not far from their homes, and Irish women joined men in charity work. In addition, these women quickly realized that philanthropy was not only an opportunity for them to get out of the house, but their chance to expand upon one of the few options open to women in the public sphere.

The records of Dublin's charities not only give insight into the conditions in which the poor lived, many contain the home addresses of the

Table 1.1
Deaths per 1,000

	1883–90	1891–1900	1901–1910
Professional and Independent	14.50	20.62	19.82
Middle Class	26.98	20.40	16.16
Artisan and Shopkeeping	22.73	23.00	18.10
General Service and Workhouse	34.71	35.20	33.38

Source: Mary E. Daly. *Dublin: The Deposed Capital* (Cork: Cork University Press, 1984), p. 270.

Table 1.2
Population of Dublin City and Suburbs

Year	Dublin City	Dublin Suburbs
1821	224,000	
1831	232,362	32,954
1841	232,726	48,480
1851	258,369	59,468
1861	254,808	70,323
1871	246,326	83,410
1881	249,602	95,450
1891	245,001	102,911
1901	290,638	90,854
1911	304,802	99,690

Source: Mary E. Daly. *Dublin: The Deposed Capital* (Cork: Cork University Press, 1984), p. 3.

Note: City boundaries changed in 1900, and the 1901 numbers reflect this change.

persons who volunteered their time. Similar to enjoying the patronage of a member of the aristocracy, provision of the addresses of the elite of Dublin was an incentive for potential donors to join in and thus associate with persons of similar, if not better social status. By comparing this information with Dublin's housing valuations and mapping the locations of a handful of these addresses, the disparity that existed between Dublin's rich and poor citizens becomes clear.

In 1854, Robert Griffith administered and published a valuation of Dublin housing.[121] Griffith's work highlighted the extensive poverty of Dublin, which was compounded by the fact that inner-city property valuation decreased as lower suburban taxes tempted away those who could afford to move.[122] The names in Table 1.3 are some of the women who volunteered their time to the Elliott Home for Waifs and Strays and the Training School for Female Servants. By matching their names to Griffith's valu-

Table 1.3
Charitable Records: Home Addresses and Valuation

Elliott Home for Waifs and Strays (1883), 167 Townsend Street

Names and Addresses	Approximate Home Valuation
Miss Franks, 21 Lower Fitzwilliam Square	£60–100
Mrs. Smyly, 35 Upper-Fitzwilliam Square	£60–100
The Misses Smyly, 35 Upper-Fitzwilliam Square	£60–100
Miss Staples, 23 Upper Merrion Street	£60–100
Mrs. Fishe, 55 South Richmond Street	£30–60

Training School for Female Servants (1857) 135 Townsend Street

Names and Addresses	Approximate Home Valuation
Mrs. Saurin, 32, Stephen's Green, North	£60–100
Mrs. Webber, 12, Pembroke Place	£60–100
Mrs. Vesey Nugent, 19, Merrion Square North	£100
Miss C. Crampton, 14, Merrion Square, North	£100
Miss M. Brownlow, 29, Merrion-Square, South	£100
Miss Hawkins, 17, Lower Baggot-street	£30–60
Miss M. Whately, Palace, Stephen's-Green, North	£100
Mrs. Ball, 20, Hatch-street	£30–60
Miss Emily Foster, 4, Fitzwilliam Place	£60–100

ation it is clear that most of these women's homes were located in the upper valuation areas between £50 and £100 per annum, while the bulk of Dublin's citizens lived in houses valued at under £30—with the majority of these at less than £10.[123] All of these volunteers' addresses were located in the wealthier district of the southeastern corner of the city, showing that they lived among Dublin's exclusive Georgian Squares, and all not far from the most fashionable site in Dublin, St. Stephen's Green.[124]

Dublin's nineteenth-century home valuations reveal the great chasm between the haves and the have-nots.[125] While women volunteers were the beneficiaries of enormous wealth, the resulting social restrictions placed upon upper-class women by Victorian society created a void in their lives that many sought to fill with charity work. Despite the unpleasant conditions they found, many of these women consistently ventured into Dublin's tenements to provide all forms of aid. While it appears few questioned the reasons behind the economic disparity that they encountered, they were willing to donate impressive amounts of time and money to those who had so much less.

What this chapter has sought to provide is an understanding of the daunting tasks that most of Dublin's philanthropic activists confronted when trying to aid the poor. Dublin faced ever-growing problems during the nineteenth century that continually constrained its ability to function properly. Dublin Corporation was ineffective in legislating improvements due to sectarian divisions, political corruption, and fiscal limitations. Its finances were further circumscribed when members of the middle and upper classes moved to the suburbs outside of Dublin's tax base. The housing accommodations for the poorest were substandard and remained so because the city's finances were never such that extensive improvements could be implemented. Dublin did not have sufficient industries, and along with the city's failure to modernize the port, unskilled laborers had very few employment options. Dublin harbored large numbers of irregularly employed persons who looked to public and private charities for aid. The city's charities were numerous and their services various as philanthropists worked amidst terrible poverty and unimaginable conditions.

NOTES

1. George Moore, *A Drama in Muslin* (Gerrard's Cross: Colin Smythe, 1981), p. 158.

2. Mary E. Daly, *Dublin: The Deposed Capital* (Cork: Cork University Press, 1984), p. 54.

3. In 1833 Francis White, social statistician, described that upon entering a house in Dublin he "saw three women lying on dung, with scarcely a covering, and four more of them sitting opposite to an open hearth without fire, eating some

broken potatoes off the earthen floor." White's report would have been published just after a major cholera epidemic swept through the city killing thousands. Francis White, *Report and Observations on the State of the Poor of Dublin* (Dublin: J. Porter, 1833), p. 14.

4. Report of the Ladies Association of St. Vincent De Paul, henceforth LAC (1854). These records are held in the Dublin archives of the Sisters of the Holy Faith.

5. As Dickson notes, by the early eighteenth century, "no European capital apart from London and possibly Copenhagen combined such a range of urban functions as the Irish capital." David Dickson, "The Demographic Implications of Dublin's Growth, 1650–1850," in *Urban Population Development in Western Europe from the late Eighteenth Century to Early Twentieth Century*, ed. Richard Lawton and Robert Lee (Liverpool: Liverpool University Press, 1989), p. 180.

6. Daly, *Dublin: The Deposed Capital*, p. 5.

7. Maurice Craig, *Dublin, 1660–1860* (London: Penguin, 1952), pp. 238–40. Gandon completed the Customs House in 1791 and finished the Four Courts in 1803.

8. Cormac Ó Gráda, *Black '47 and Beyond: The Great Irish Famine in History, Economy and Memory* (Princeton, N.J.: Princeton University Press, 1999), p. 158.

9. Kevin B. Nolan, *Travel and Transport in Ireland* (Dublin: Gill & MacMillan, 1973), p. 98.

10. See John Lynch, *A Tale of Three Cities: Comparative Studies in Working-Class Life* (Houndmills: Macmillan Press, 1998), pp. 14–15; and Joseph V. O'Brien, *"Dear Dirty Dublin": A City in Distress, 1899–1916* (Berkeley: University of California Press, 1982), p. 11.

11. For a discussion of nineteenth-century Ireland, see Cormac Ó Gráda, *Ireland: A New Economic History 1780–1939* (Oxford: Oxford University Press, 1994); D. George Boyce, *Nineteenth-Century Ireland: The Search for Stability* (Dublin: Gill & MacMillan, 1990); W. E. Vaughan, *Landlords and Tenants in Ireland, 1848–1904* (Dublin: Economic and Social History Society of Ireland, 1984); and J. J. Lee, *The Modernisation of Irish Society 1848–1918* (Dublin: Gill & MacMillan, 1973).

12. Christine Kinealy, *This Great Calamity: The Irish Famine 1845–52* (Dublin: Gill & Macmillan, 1994), p. 9. It is important to note, however, as Ó Gráda shows, that the population was not expanding at the high rate historians have alleged. The increase in Ireland's population was "less rapid after 1821 than before, and closer to the European norm." Ó Gráda, *Ireland: A New Economic History*, pp. 69 and 71.

13. James S. Donnelly, Jr., *The Great Irish Potato Famine* (London: Sutton Press, 2001), p. 8. See also Ó Gráda, *Ireland: A New Economic History*, p. 123; and Peter Gray, *Famine, Land and Politics: British Government and Irish Society 1843–50* (Dublin: Irish Academic Press, 1999).

14. Donnelly, *The Great Irish Potato Famine*, p. 8.

15. By 1841, there were over one million cottiers and their dependents working the ground. Kevin Whelan, "Pre and Post-Famine Landscape Change," in *The Great Famine*, ed. Cathal Póitéir (Dublin: Mercier Press, 1995), p. 20. Briefly, much of Ireland's land division, particularly in the west, was based on the rundale and clachan system that, simply put, was community cooperation and familial rights to land. See Robert J. Scally, *The End of Hidden Ireland: Rebellion, Famine and Emigration* (Oxford: Oxford University Press, 1995), p. 13.

16. Donnelly, *The Great Irish Potato Famine*, p. 4. Nevertheless, Ó Gráda suggests that the rental increases were not as oppressive as historians have alleged. Ó Gráda, *Ireland: A New Economic History*, pp. 163–65.

17. Donnelly, *The Great Irish Potato Famine*, p. 7; and Whelan, "Pre and Post-Famine Landscape Change," p. 25.

18. Kevin Kenny, *The American Irish* (New York: Longman, 2000), p. 48.

19. Donnelly, *The Great Irish Potato Famine*, p. 4. On the eve of the famine some 2 million acres of land, or 1/3 of all the land being sowed, was dedicated to growing potatoes. Kinealy, *This Great Calamity*, p. 6.

20. For Irish poor relief, it seems that the government also relied on scientific arguments regarding the inherent inferiority of the poor combined with English racial stereotyping of the Irish to create a system that would be as punitive as possible so that the poor would not rely upon the state but instead find employment elsewhere. Peter Gray, "The Triumph of Dogma Ideology and Famine Relief," *History Ireland* 3, 2 (Summer 1995), p. 33; and "*Punch* and the Great Famine," *History Ireland* 1, 2 (Summer 1993), pp. 26–32.

21. Ireland's relief act was actually a more severe version of England's New Poor Law. In particular, the act prohibited relief to be provided outside the workhouse. Christine Kinealy, "The Administration of the Poor Law in Mayo, 1838–1898," *Cathair Na Mart: Journal of the Westport Historical Society* 6, 1 (1986), p. 98. See also John O'Connor, *The Workhouses of Ireland* (Dublin: Anvil Books, 1995); and Gerard O'Brien, "The Establishment of Poor-law Unions in Ireland, 1838–43," *Irish Historical Studies* 13, 90 (November 1982), pp. 97–120.

22. Kinealy, *This Great Calamity*, p. 18.

23. Kinealy, *This Great Calamity*, p. 24.

24. Kinealy, *This Great Calamity*, p. 231.

25. Kinealy, *This Great Calamity*, p. 24.

26. Helen Burke, *The People and the Poor Law In Nineteenth Century Ireland* (London: George Philip Services, 1987), p. 47.

27. Burke, *The People and the Poor Law*, pp. 22, 49.

28. However, as the records of the North Dublin Union show, parents were permitted brief meetings with their children when in 1847 it was ordered that parents "may have the privilege of seeing their female children on Sundays and Holidays as is the case with boys." North Dublin Union, henceforth NDU (5 May 1847). These records are located in the NAI.

29. "That relief might be so administered as not merely to relieve, but also to deter was incorporated into the Poor Law Act of 1834. Thus did the ruling class seek to drive the poor out of their poverty or failing this, to leave them to live as best they could." Kathleen Woodroofe, *From Charity to Social Work In England and the United States* (London: Routledge & Paul, 1966), p. 18. See also Kinealy, *This Great Calamity*, p. 25.

30. "Begin at the Beginning," *Irish Quarterly Review* 8 (January 1859), p. 1188.

31. LAC (1852), p. 23. See also Burke, *The People and the Poor Law*, p. 220; Dympna McLoughlin, "Workhouses and Irish Female Paupers, 1840–70," in *Women Surviving*, ed. Maria Luddy and Cliona Murphy (Dublin: Poolbeg Press, 1989), pp. 117–47; and Sarah Atkinson and Ellen Woodlock, "The Irish Poor in Workhouses," *Transactions of the National Association for the Promotion of Social Science* 6 (1861), pp. 645–51.

32. Austin Bourke, *Visitation of God? The Potato and the Irish Famine,* ed. Jacqueline Hill and Cormac Ó Gráda (Dublin: Lilliput Press, 1993), p. 52.

33. Kinealy, *This Great Calamity,* p. 34.

34. Peel took this action despite Britain's Corn Laws. These laws prohibited the importation of grain into the British markets until a set price was met. Eventually, Peel would achieve the repeal of the Corn Laws in 1846, but his actions killed his career and Lord John Russell became prime minister. Kinealy, *This Great Calamity,* pp. 36–37. See also Mary E. Daly, "The Operations of Famine Relief: 1845–47, " in *The Great Irish Famine,* ed. Cathal Póirtéir (Dublin: Mercier Press, 1995), p. 129.

35. After Russell took the helm, he proposed that local areas in Ireland take financial responsibility for the total cost of relief works, thereby avoiding "undue dependence upon the central government." Daly, "The Operations of Famine Relief," p. 129.

36. John Killen, ed., *The Famine Decade Contemporary Accounts 1841–1851* (Belfast: Blackstaff Press, 1995), p. 83. *The Vindicator* was quoting the *Cork Examiner.*

37. Asenath Nicholson, *Annals of the Famine in Ireland,* ed. Maureen Murphy (Dublin: Lilliput Press, 1998), p. 37.

38. NDU (4 November 1846).

39. Donnelly, *The Great Irish Potato Famine,* p. 72.

40. Daly, "The Operations of Famine Relief," p. 130. While not completely stopped, contrary to contemporary suggestions, exports of grain were reduced. Donnelly, *The Great Irish Potato Famine,* p. 61.

41. Kinealy, *This Great Calamity,* pp. 97 and 363–65. Increasingly women and children were seeking employment. "During the period from October 1846 to June 1847, the average daily number of labourers on the public works was 363,400, which was equivalent to 10.3 per cent of the total Irish labour force as enumerated in the 1841 Census." Kinealy, *This Great Calamity,* p. 99.

42. Kinealy, *This Great Calamity,* pp. 56–60; and Burke, *The People and the Poor Law,* pp. 108–9.

43. Eneas MacDonnell, Esq., *County Mayo Its Awful Conditions and Prospects and Present Insufficiency of Local Relief* (London: John Ollivier, 1849), p. 11.

44. The logistical problems were immense, with increasing evidence of corruption as well as outright theft. Daly, "The Operations of Famine Relief," p. 131.

45. Soup kitchens were modeled on the example already provided by the Religious Society of Friends, which established its first soup kitchens beginning in 1846. Rob Goodbody, *A Suitable Channel: Quaker Relief in the Great Famine* (Bray: Pale Publishing, 1995), p. 29; and Society of Friends, *Transactions of the Central Relief Committee of the Society of Friends during the Famine in Ireland 1846–7* (Dublin: Hodges & Smith, 1852), p. 53. See also Thomas P. O'Neill, "The Society of Friends and the Great Famine," *Studies* 39 (1950), p. 204.

46. Kinealy, *This Great Calamity,* p. 144.

47. Daly, "The Operations of Famine Relief," p. 133; and Burke, *The People and the Poor Law,* p. 118.

48. For example, by September of 1847, "the Ballinrobe union in Co. Mayo was so deeply in debt that the local sheriff seized the property of the workhouse and threatened to sell it. The neighbouring unions of Castelbar and Westport had also financially collapsed and were seeking assistance from the government." Kinealy,

This Great Calamity, p. 187. In the case of Westport, the Marquis of Sligo began to spend his own money to keep the workhouse open. Donald Jordan, *Land and Popular Politics in Ireland: County Mayo from Plantation to the Land War* (Cambridge: Cambridge University Press, 1994), p. 107.

49. Kinealy, *This Great Calamity,* p. 189.

50. NDU (12 April 1848). The Earl of Clarendon was Lord Lieutenant of Ireland from 1847 to 1852.

51. NDU (12 April 1848).

52. Kinealy, *This Great Calamity,* p. 194. Most of Ireland's Poor Law Unions remained deeply in debt.

53. Certainly, however, the northeast experienced the famine. See Christine Kinealy and Gerard Mac Atasney, *The Hidden Famine: Hunger, Poverty and Sectarianism in Belfast* (London: Pluto Press, 2000).

54. Ó Gráda, *Black '47 and Beyond,* p. 160.

55. Apparently, normally, Dublin had a higher incidence of fever and dysentery. Ó Gráda, *Black '47 and Beyond,* p. 166.

56. Ó Gráda shows that Dublin's population, between 1841 and 1851, increased by 11 percent. "Immigration was probably largely responsible for the rise in deaths from typhoid fever." Ó Gráda, *Black '47 and Beyond,* p. 173.

57. NDU (14 April 1847); Jacinta Prunty, *Dublin Slums 1800-1925* (Dublin: Irish Academic Press, 1997), p. 7.

58. The NDU guardians' complaints seem to be supported by the statistics—although the increase in demand upon north of the Liffey was only marginally greater than on the south. Ó Gráda, *Black '47 and Beyond,* p. 173.

59. NDU (2 October 1844). "We have, year after year, protested unanimously against the provisions of the poor law by which [an] aged and broken down Irish artisan is subject to the miseries of a forcible transmission from the manufacturing districts in England with an English wife and English children merely because he has been born in this country although his productive energies have been consumed amongst those whom the law now relieves from the burden of his support."

60. NDU (14 April 1847). "If they seek admission in the South Union they are refused as having no claim, and when they apply to the North the residence of one night in the asylum establishes a right to admission, and they then become chargeable on the North Electoral Division."

61. For example, in April of 1855, 2,826 people were registered in the Union. NDU (April 1855). The numbers would rise again, as for example during the famine of 1879–1881 when the North Dublin Union's numbers, after January of 1880, would again be over 2,000. See NDU (3 January 1880).

62. Dympna McLoughlin, "Superfluous and Unwanted Deadweight: the Emigration of Nineteenth-Century Irish Pauper Women," in *Irish Women and Irish Migration,* ed. Patrick O'Sullivan (London: Leicester University Press, 1995), p. 67.

63. As Guinnane and Ó Gráda note, among the harsh conditions and evidence of corruption in the workhouse, the guardians' minutes also offer "sentiments of economy and compassion." Timothy W. Guinnane and Cormac Ó Gráda, "Mortality in the North Dublin Union During the Great Famine," *Economic History Review* 55, 3 (2002), p. 493.

64. NDU (19 March 1845).

65. NDU (2 October 1844).

66. NDU (26 April 1848).

67. Kinealy, *This Great Calamity*, p. 316. The government charged the workhouses for the cost of transferring the females from the workhouse to the port from which the ship departed. Kinealy, *This Great Calamity*, p. 317.

68. NDU (17 May 1848).

69. McLoughlin, "Superfluous and Unwanted Deadweight," p. 66. See also Janet A. Nolan, *Ourselves Alone: Women's Emigration from Ireland 1885–1920* (Lexington, Ky.: University of Kentucky Press, 1989); Pauline Jackson, "Women in 19th Century Irish Emigration," *International Migration Review* 18 (1984), pp. 1004–112; and Hasia Diner, *Erin's Daughters in America* (Baltimore, Md.: Johns Hopkins University Press, 1983).

70. Kenny, *The American Irish*, pp. 97–98; Donnelly, *The Great Irish Potato Famine*, p. 178; Kinealy, *This Great Calamity*, pp. 315–27; and Burke, *People and the Poor Law*, p. 31.

71. David Fitzpatrick, "A Share of the Honeycomb: Education, Emigration and Irishwomen," *Continuity and Change* 1, 2 (1986), p. 224. In truth, so many women emigrated that throughout the twentieth century there was a surplus of Irish males in the nation. Given that women live longer than men, this male surplus was the result of consistent female emigration. Joy Rudd, "Invisible Exports: The Emigration of Irish Women This Century," *Women's Studies International Forum* 11, 4 (1988), p. 307.

72. K. Theodore Hoppen, *Ireland Since 1800: Conflict and Conformity* (New York: Longman, 1989), p. 86. Another incentive for farmers was the doubling of wages as the numbers of laborers went down. See Timothy Guinnane, *The Vanishing Irish: Households, Migration and the Rural Economy in Ireland, 1850–1914* (Princeton, N.J.: Princeton University Press, 1997), p. 40.

73. Gerard Moran, "Near Famine: The Crisis in the West of Ireland, 1879–82," *Irish Studies Review* 18 (Spring 1997), p. 14.

74. Timothy P. O'Neill, "The Persistence of Famine in Ireland," in *The Great Irish Famine*, ed. Cathal Póirtéir (Dublin: Mercier Press, 1995), p. 207.

75. See Thomas P. O'Neill, "From Famine to Near Famine 1845–1879," *Studia Hibernica* 14 (1974), pp. 161–71. As the Mansion House Committee wrote: "the harvest was the worst since the famine years. Two-thirds of the potato crop were rotted and gone, and 250,000 people, to whom it was the staff of life, would, by the beginning of the new year, be without food or the means of buying it; 500,000 people or more stood upon the verge of ruin." Mansion House Committee, *Relief of the Famine of 1880* (Dublin: Browne & Nolan, 1881), p. 5. The Mansion House Committee was originally formed in 1831 during agricultural distress. It worked during the Great Famine and included the support of Dublin's Mayor and Lord Lieutenant. Kinealy, *This Great Calamity*, p. 162.

76. Cholera was prevalent during 1818–1819, 1831–1832, 1848–1849, 1853–1854, and 1866.

77. "Dublin would seem to have been closer to Tamanny Hall than to Birmingham, or Leeds town hall." Daly, *Dublin: The Deposed Capital*, p. 220.

78. *Royal Commission on the Housing of the Working Class 1884*, p. 5, House of Lords (H.L.) 1885 (c. 4549–1), p. xxxi. As Daly notes, "where Dublin's small businessmen parallel their English counterparts is in lack of broader municipal concern, and tolerance of sanitary breaches, mainly because they and their allies

tended to be tenement landlords or proprietors of slaughter houses or dairy yards." Daly, *Dublin: The Deposed Capital*, p. 220.

79. Daly, *Dublin: The Deposed Capital*, p. 257.

80. Most dairy farmers worked within the city limits living in tenements where they stored milk, which, due to lack of refrigeration, spoiled. However, after realizing that it would be much more difficult to monitor dairy yards located in the countryside, the Corporation's enthusiasm for removing the yards from the city waned. Daly, *Dublin: The Deposed Capital*, pp. 263–64.

81. Dublin Corporation, in 1851, appointed a policeman as inspector of nuisance. Due to the size and nature of the problem, his efforts provided few results even after the Corporation supplied him with a support staff of three in 1859. Beginning in 1856, the Corporation paid for the construction of public urinals and passed the Adultery of Food Act in 1860, which charged a physician with inspecting the produce of the city's bakers, butchers, and grocers. In 1864, the Corporation appointed the first Medical Officer of Health. Two years later, during a cholera epidemic, Dublin passed the Sanitary Act (1866), which had limited impact because of its complicated rules and regulations. As Prunty bluntly states, "The 1866 Act did so little to increase the effective powers of the public health authority that the period 1849–1874 can be treated as one." Prunty, *Dublin Slums*, pp. 70 and 77.

82. Prunty, *Dublin Slums*, pp. 29–30. See also Parke Neville, "City of Dublin Sewerage," *Transactions of the National Association for the Promotion of Social Science* 6 (1861), pp. 524–35.

83. Daly, *Dublin: The Deposed Capital*, p. 250.

84. "The Nuisance from the Liffey," *Medical Press & Circular* (28 March 1866), p. 322. O'Brien's noting of the story of the man who attempted to commit suicide near the Liffey warrants an ironic laugh: "for his purpose he bought, rope, a pistol, and some poison, tied the rope [suspended from a lantern on Carlisle Bridge] around his neck, and fired the pistol at his head. The shot missed, severing the rope and causing him to fall into the river, which was so foul that it made him throw up the poison thus saving his life." O'Brien, *"Dear Dirty Dublin,"* p. 18.

85. Daly, *Dublin: The Deposed Capital*, p. 250.

86. Daly, *Dublin: The Deposed Capital*, p. 260.

87. Prunty, *Dublin Slums*, p. 97.

88. Prunty, *Dublin Slums*, p. 231.

89. Prunty, *Dublin Slums*, pp. 231–32.

90. NDU (1 March 1879).

91. NDU (26 March 1879). Blackhorse Lane was only one among many streets to receive complaints. "M. Byrne Esq., Rosemount Philopsburgh Avenue . . . stat[ed] he has repeatedly, but up to the present ineffectually complained of the continued existence of abominable nuisances both at the entrance to his house & in the yard attached to it there are at this moment some hundreds of tons of festering manure spread over the yard with pools of stagnant fluid filth & requesting immediate steps may be taken to abate the several nuisances & protect the health of his family." NDU (7 June 1879).

92. NDU (12 November 1879).

93. NDU (24 April 1880) (their emphasis).

94. Daly, *Dublin: The Deposed Capital*, p. 282.

95. This includes J. Cheyne's (1818) room occupancy study, Thomas Willis's (1845) life expectancy investigation, and William Wilde's (1841) mortality tables. Prunty, *Dublin Slums,* p. 18.

96. J. Warburton, J. Whitelaw, and R. Walsh, *History of the City of Dublin,* vol. 1, (London: T. Cadell and Davies, 1818), p. 443.

97. Warburton, Whitelaw, and Walsh, *History of the City of Dublin,* p. 444. Francis White argued that due to the absence of the wealthy aristocracy "there is nothing but the most deplorable destitution for the poor of the metropolis. In one parish, with a population of 23,918 there are no less than 17,000 paupers!!!" (his emphasis). Francis White, *Report and Observations on the State of the Poor of Dublin* (Dublin: J. Porter, 1833), p. 3.

98. In 1862, Nugent Robinson, a municipal employee, noted that the homes of the poor "are fitter for swine than human beings." Nugent Robinson, *Homes of the Working Poor* (Dublin: Goodwin, Son and Nethercott, 1862), p. 5. See also Charles Eason, "Housing of the Working Classes," *Social Service Handbook,* ed. J. P. Smyth (Dublin: Association for the Promotion of Christian Knowledge, 1901), p. 151.

99. Daly, *Dublin: The Deposed Capital,* p. 283, as quoted from E. D. Mapother, Lectures on Public Health, No. 12, *Dwellings of the labouring classes* (Dublin, 1867), p. 298.

100. White, *Report and Observations,* p. 9. St Luke's, a very poor parish, was located south of the river Liffey. See Prunty, *Dublin Slums,* pp. 22–23.

101. "The Dwellings of the Poor in Dublin," *Dublin Builder* (15 October 1863), p. 173. See also "The Dwellings of the Poor in Dublin," *Dublin Builder* (1 November 1863), p. 180.

102. Prunty, *Dublin Slums,* p. 83.

103. Rosa M. Barrett, *Guide to Dublin Charities* (Dublin: Hodges, Figgis, & Co., 1884), p. 79. "In 1881, 182,278 persons were still living in tenement houses, many of which were reported as unfit for human habitation."

104. Prunty, *Dublin Slums,* p. 135. As Daly notes, "During the month of August, 1881, alone a total of 48 houses, 22 rooms and 6 cellars were closed and an estimated 160 families or 800 persons were made homeless." Daly, *Dublin: The Deposed Capital,* p. 290.

105. Prunty, *Dublin Slums,* p. 139. See also Daly, *Dublin: The Deposed Capital,* p. 283. As the *Report of the Committee appointed by the Local Government Board for Ireland to Inquire into the Housing Conditions of the Working Classes in the City of Dublin* (London: AlexThom, 1914) noted, into the early twentieth century there was no "systematic or comprehensive inspection by the experts of the Engineering Department of the Corporation with a view of ascertaining whether buildings are in a dangerous condition" (p. 28).

106. "A single apartment, rates from 1–2/-per week; and to lighten this rent two, three or four families become joint tenants, hence at an early hour we may find ten to sixteen persons of all ages and sexes in a room of not fifteen feet square stretched on a wad of filthy straw." Warburton, *History of the City of Dublin,* vol. 1, p. 443.

107. Daly, *Dublin: The Deposed Capital,* p. 281. The homes were "let at a rental of 5/2 per week, which was approximately 40% of the wages of an unskilled worker." Daly, *Dublin: The Deposed Capital,* p. 297. In 1890, Parliament passed the Housing of the Working Classes Act that made a comprehensive report regarding the state

of Dublin. This report revealed that in 1900, the absolute number of tenements in Dublin was greater than the number had been in 1850. Prunty, *Dublin Slums*, p. 148.

108. In the late nineteenth century, the Guiness family (of the Guiness brewery) established the Iveagh Trust which sought to construct affordable homes for workers but since, generally, the homes only went to Guiness employees, the impact was limited. See Prunty, *Dublin Slums*, pp. 141–42.

109. Besides laundry or domestic service, there were even fewer other opportunities for women than men, and late into the century, "only 34% of Dublin female population was classified as occupied." Daly, *Dublin: The Deposed Capital*, p. 51.

110. Daly, *Dublin: The Deposed Capital*, pp. 77–79.

111. Lynch shows that compared to Bristol or Belfast the weekly food bill of a Dublin worker was considerably higher. Lynch, *A Tale of Three Cities*, p. 129.

112. Daly, *Dublin: The Deposed Capital*, p. 269. As Cormac Ó Gráda notes, "Dublin was a bread-eating as much as potato eating city." Cormac Ó Gráda, *Black '47 and Beyond*, p. 163.

113. Strand Street Institute Report (1896), p. 20. "Between twenty and thirty children partake of these meals each evening."

114. George D. Williams, ed., *Dublin Charities: A Handbook* (Dublin: Association of Dublin Charities, 1902), p. 8.

115. "An investigation of 3,000 poor families carried out in 1845 by Dr. Thomas Willis led him to conclude that 22% of children did not survive the first year of life, 52% died before their sixth year and only one-third of the working class as a whole survived beyond 20 years." O'Brien, *"Dear Dirty Dublin,"* p. 20.

116. Prunty, *Dublin Slums*, p. 75.

117. Prunty, *Dublin Slums*, pp. 75, 153.

118. Numbers from Daly, *Dublin: The Deposed Capital*, p. 245. See also "Mortality Amongst the Dublin Poor," *Dublin Builder* (15 September 1862), p. 230.

119. As quoted in the Annual Report of the Cottage Home for Little Children (Dublin, 1889), pp. 11–12.

120. Beginning in the early nineteenth century, excerpts from the diary of Dubliner Salina Crampton provide insight. Nellie Ó Cléirigh, *Hardship & High Living: Irish Women's Lives 1808–1923* (Dublin: Portobello Press, 2003), pp. 27–43.

121. Martin has furthered this study by mapping each of the city areas to provide an overall view of Dublin. John H. Martin, "The Social Geography of Mid-Nineteenth-Century Dublin City," *Common Ground: Essays on the Historical Geography of Ireland*, ed. William J. Smyth and Kevin Whelan (Cork: Cork University Press, 1988), pp. 173–88.

122. For example, a Dublin resident of Upper Leeson Street paid over 6s. while a suburban resident of the same street outside the city limits paid little more than 3s. O'Brien, *"Dear Dirty Dublin,"* p. 15.

123. Prunty, *Dublin Slums*, pp. 50–51.

124. This work was executed by Dr. Jacinta Prunty with the kind assistance of Gillian Fitzgerald of the Geography Department of University College Dublin. John Martin used census figures and a variety of maps to provide an economic picture of nineteenth-century Dublin neighborhoods. Of particular relevance was a map created by Sir Richard Griffith that was "derived from a composite map compiled for the commissioners from larger scale maps on which the rateable

valuation of every building was plotted," and valuation was defined as the "hypothetical annual rent of a property and the valuators were to take into account such factors as the construction cost of a building, its solidity, age, state of repair, capacity and relative location." Martin, "The Social Geography of Mid-Nineteenthth Century Dublin City," pp. 177–79.

125. "The average valuation in the prosperous wards was between two and three times higher than the average in the poorest wards: South city ward had an average valuation of £47.80 per premises compared with the average of only £14.60 in Arran Quay." Martin, "The Social Geography of Mid-Nineteenth Century Dublin City," p. 181.

CHAPTER 2

Race, Class, and Religion in the Language of Dublin's Charities

"The young savage wanderers in the haunts of vice, or . . . the dark burrows of poverty in our crowded cities; these will not convert to Christianity the heathens in our own land, nor even loosen the fetters of dense ignorance which chain the intellects of these children of misery."[1] Here, Mary Carpenter argued that education and charity alone would not civilize poor children, and she advocated that those youngsters who had fallen into sin be placed in a reformatory. Reformatories, she proposed, acted as moral hospitals that could save children from the "dens of filth" where they lived "in a manner more degraded than the brutes."[2] What Carpenter was suggesting was what many in the Victorian middle and upper classes believed: while the perceived immorality of the poor certainly contributed to their circumstances, poverty was inherent—a condition that could be improved but never overcome.

During the nineteenth century, the British upper classes gradually accepted some of the newly evolving scientific theories of racial superiority. The new sciences of ethnography and anthropology proposed that the races were not only physically but also intellectually different. Seeing themselves at the top of the evolutionary pyramid, Britain's middle and upper classes became convinced that as the Crown's influence around the globe proliferated, they were bringing civilization to savages and then turning them into loyal subjects.[3] Thus, they became confident that their innate superiority maintained them in a position of authority both at home and abroad.

In seeking to maintain their position at the pinnacle of power, Britain's elite adopted theories of class hierarchy that were not dissimilar to those of race, and descriptions of the classes took on essentialist qualities.[4] Hence, when debating the theoretical roots of nineteenth-century charity, discussion of race and class cannot be taken individually but must be considered together because, increasingly, they became fused and confused. For example, The First Report of the Philanthropic Society (1788) noted that the laboring poor were the "basis on which all the higher gradations rest."[5] Thus, the nineteenth-century class power structure became an almost permanent state and, just as race could not be changed, most in the working classes could not go up while few in the upper classes went down.[6] Therefore, as race and class became intertwined, similar to race, gradations appeared within class levels. For example, on an evolutionary scale the working-class Englishman was below his middle-class brother. Nevertheless, this same working-class man was above his Irish colleague, for the Irish had not only the strike of poverty against them but also that of race, because the Celt was seen as inferior to the Anglo-Saxon.[7]

As the industrial revolution contributed to demographic change, increasingly the poor made their way into Britain's towns and cities where generally the unskilled found poorly paid and often-unreliable employment in local factories. Here, in the expanding urban slums, where the need was greatest, charity played an important role as volunteers sought to enlighten the poor in their own homes. Using the themes of hard work, education, sanitary lifestyle, and moral living, philanthropists worked to improve the conditions in which the poor lived, while at the same time molding them into compliant subjects of the Crown.[8]

Many of the poor complied with philanthropists' efforts, but of course, few had other alternatives. Examples of the indigent's submission to upper-class notions of respectability not only appeared through deference but also when the working class mimicked the behavior of the upper classes.[9] Friendly societies and other working-class associations often adopted the upper-class "language of respectability."[10] They accepted middle-class values of sobriety, self-help, and thrift as an agenda.[11] While in many ways this effort can be seen as one route the poor took to empower themselves, it also bolstered an authoritarian society.[12]

Yet this does not mean that there was not a level of defiance, if not outright manipulation by the poor of organizations that supplied charitable relief. This defiance came in a variety of forms. From prostitutes who used Magdalen homes for only a few nights' rest to the indigent who refused to enter the workhouse or the destitute who went from parish to parish asking multiple sources for help, the poor could, and did, exploit the charity system.[13] At the same time, philanthropists also feared the poor, not just the potential that came with greater knowledge, but also the power in mob violence. In the age of Daniel O'Connell and the Chartists, workers among others were increasingly recognizing the power that came through combined effort. Thus, while the Association for the Suppression of Mendacity in Dublin argued that it certainly could not afford to train children for "mechanical employments," it also noted that such skills not "gained under the sanction of the rules of apprenticeship, and comformably to the additional restrains of combination, might only prove dangerous or a useless acquisition."[14] It seems that philanthropists feared that training the poor for higher skilled jobs could result in an attainment of power over their own lives and create a population of people that the upper classes could no longer control.

While philanthropists did fear educating or training the working classes too well, at the same time, the language within the records suggests that, regardless, volunteers believed that they could improve the poor but not change them. Thus, the intrinsic inabilities of the poor maintained them in the class status to which they were born. It was as though charities held that there was an impenetrable barrier between the poor and the upper classes, a glass ceiling to which the working class could approach but never break through. Social commentator John R. Fowler argued that the poor should not be taken away from the "circumstances and condition in which they were born" but made honest through work "by which their characters may be strengthened, and by which they may be enabled to do their duty in that state in which it pleased God to place them."[15] Delia Gleeson made the unchangeable nature of the poor explicit when she discussed poor children and suggested that any hint of an industrious inclination on their part is quickly lost because "[h]awkers they begin, and hawkers they remain, till they drift into the ranks of outcasts, drunkards, and paupers, and then disappear—no one knows where or how."[16] Thus, throughout charitable records, there is a clear message of permanent difference between givers and receivers.

Religion also found its way into the mix. As will be discussed in chapter 3, sectarian divisions deeply characterized Irish charity. Here, it becomes clear that while Protestant charities suggested that Catholicism contributed to the shortcomings of the Irish, it was only one factor that charity workers added to a stew of inferiority that included both race and class. Thus, while some Protestants may have thought that to convert poor Catholics was to improve them intrinsically, upper-class Catholics sought to strengthen faith and encourage religious practice by poor Catholics in an effort to lessen their sin—not, however, to change their nature. Nevertheless, while upper-class Irish Catholics may not have seen the Irish poor as innately different, they applied the same descriptors that upper-class Protestants used. In this way, it becomes clear that while middle- and upper-class Irish Catholic philanthropists may have known well that some Protestants saw them as innately inferior, many of these Catholics sought to achieve equal social footing by adopting the language used by those perceived to be in positions of social and political authority.[17] Ultimately, however, for most of Ireland's charitable workers, it seems that it was the essentialist qualities of racial inferiority as applied to the perceived characteristics of class that dominated their thinking about the nature of the Irish poor.

"THE MISSING LINK": RACIAL STEREOTYPES

In 1892, Beatrice and Sidney Webb on a trip to Ireland wrote to a friend that "the people are charming but we detest them, as we should the Hottentots . . . Home Rule is an absolute necessity in order to depopulate the country of this detestable race."[18] This, from leading members of the Fabian Society and famous social reform and trade union activists, suggests that British prejudice against the Irish was deep-seated and, even for the most liberal minded, acceptable.[19] Relying on Darwin's *Origin of Species,* British anthropologists established a "racial" hierarchy that was shaped as a pyramid and placed the morally superior middle class on top with a gradation that then sloped slowly downward.[20] The Irish or Jews were portrayed as "inherently degenerate 'female races' within the white male gender, approaching the state of apes."[21] Peoples with darker skin tones came after the lowest whites followed by the Africans, with the female Khoisan (a.k.a. Hottentots or Bushmen) located at the very bottom, between human and beast.[22] Then, these variations were also applied to class. As a result, while Britain's upper classes described themselves as intelligent, level-headed, rational, masculine, predictable, and civilized, they labeled the darker races and the lower classes with the opposite descriptors including unintelligent, scatterbrained, irrational, spiritual, feminine, unpredictable, and savage.[23] Hence, while, the Irish were white, first, they were Celts; next, many were poor and, of course, most were Catholic. Through fusion and confusion of race, class, and religion the Irish, particularly poor Irish, were, whether at home or abroad, described as inferior.[24]

The British had long believed the Irish to be a distinct race from the Anglo-Saxon. As Celts, the Irish were labeled with such descriptions as "White Negroes" or "Celtic Calibans."[25] By the nineteenth century, British popular culture was portraying the Irish as somewhere between ape and human, as *Punch* and *The Times,* among others, published editorial cartoons with the simian-featured Irish people staring out from the newsprint.[26] *Fraser's Magazine,* in 1847, detailed that "of all the Celtic tribes, famous everywhere for their indolence and fickleness as the Celts everywhere are, the Irish are admitted to be the most idle and the most fickle."[27] In 1851, *Punch* described the native Irish as "the missing link between the gorilla and the Negro."[28] In 1860, on a visit to Sligo, Cambridge historian Charles Kingsley reinforced the idea that the Irish were not only of a different race but also of a different species, closer to ape than to human.[29] Irish philanthropists among others followed suit and compared the savagery of the Irish with other peoples that they believed to be heathens. For example, the Dublin Visiting Mission called poor Catholic boys "wild street Arabs."[30] Or, when discussing the Irish poor, physician Henry McCormack noted, "As many as 40 to 50 'Arabs' sometimes sleep in one room, boys and girls promiscuously. At fifteen or sixteen years of age, the male 'Arab' is mated, but not with the wife."[31] Newspapers, scholarly works, novels, and even charity pamphlets reinforced the prejudice that the Irish were inherently inferior.

Such criticism was not limited to the United Kingdom, and the Irish were described as other even beyond their own shores. For example, in North America where the Irish were grouped with Native Americans, both were considered at the far edge of civilization.[32] Eighteenth-century traveler Thomas Morton wrote that the natives construct their houses very similar to those of the "wild Irish."[33] Morton's contemporary William Strachey noted, "some [Indians] lie stark naked on the ground from six to twenty in a house, as do the Irish and the married women wear their hair all of a length shaven, as the Irish, by a dish."[34] Writing about how to cure Ireland of its poverty, one anonymous author focused on the "three phases of savage life" and discussed the Eskimos, North American Indians, and the natives of South America. Sounding very Swiftian, the author proposed that one solution for the many Irish poor was to "sell all the in and out-door paupers, male and female, to whomsoever will purchase them."[35]

India, another of Britain's colonial territories, was considered a proper model for Ireland, not only because the two countries had comparable agricultural systems, but also impoverished populations, sectarian divisions, and peasant economies.[36] Yet, the British did not necessarily believe Indians to be a completely different race.[37] Indians, some British anthropologists argued, were degenerate members of the Aryan race, and they suggested that Indians had deteriorated because of cultural and environmental factors such as mild winters, extremely hot summers, and monotonous surroundings.[38] Nevertheless, at times, Indians were placed "above" the Celt, as when in 1855, J. W. Jackson, a British anthropologist writing in the *Anthropological Review,* suggested that Ireland was "a moral fossil, like India, the only difference being that India is a civilized, while Ireland is a barbarous fossil."[39] However, due to the linguistic similarity of ancient texts, anthropologists asserted that Indians were from the same "tribe" as the Anglo-Saxon, although scholars maintained that their "language had been degraded by idolatry and lack of progressive Christian religion."[40] Ultimately, however, scientists theorized that the tribe had split with one going west to Europe and the other east to India.

The question of whether the British could rehabilitate the Indian was fodder for much debate. Many speculated that, with time, Indians could become civilized by following the example set by the British. In particular, if they imposed their "progressive religion upon India and at the same time, respect, purify and rebuild native Aryan religious traditions" they would establish a firm groundwork for Christian morality.[41] Believing that Indians came from the same stock, however, did not mean that the British perceived them to be equal. The descriptions of Indians and Irish suggest that the British upper classes accepted a racial classification based not on skin color alone but including other random factors used to legitimize race theories.[42]

In order to further legitimize their authority, British characterizations also used feminized descriptions suggesting that Indian males were physically and emotionally weaker than their British counterparts.[43] For example, Hindus were described as having "reserve and docility, gentleness, pity and procrastination (while the British virtues of determination, fearlessness and veracity simultaneously were lauded)."[44] The *Saturday Review* indicated that it was difficult for the Englishman to understand Hindus because their character was that of a "childish, impulsive, and preeminently vain Eastern race, fond of display, amusements, decorations and pomp of all kinds."[45] Seeing the Indian as childlike or effeminate, the British upper classes believed the colonies warranted a strong hand in order to be protected and guided toward maturity.[46]

By the same token, Britain often pictured Ireland as inferior, thereby reinforcing the justification for British rule.[47] Thus, for example, as a female, Ireland needed protection, and Brittania, the tall, healthy, broad-shouldered mother, or elder sister, carefully cared for Hybernia, or Erin, her petite, weak, and skittish younger sibling.[48] When imagined as a male, England was John Bull, the strong, manly, father figure while Ireland was characterized as "Paddy" or, less often, "Teague," the perennially drunk, perpetually belligerent (Fenian), potato-eating, Irish male. John Bull's manly strength, steadiness, intelligence, and rationality were contrasted with Paddy's dullness, violence, irrationality, and heightened spirituality. In addition to Brittania and Erin as sisters, England was also placed in the role of man to Ireland as woman, husband to Ireland as wife, or father to Ireland as son: "John Bull may occasionally have been a harsh parent, but we are sure the old fellow means well. It is too bad to see father and son at daggers drawn in this way. When will Ireland be a good boy and learn to remain quiet at home?"[49] Such questions reinforced Britain's efforts to maintain authority over the Irish, many of whom throughout the nineteenth century were seeking to reverse the Union.[50]

The pamphlets and published broadsheets that survive from Dublin's charities illustrate how the city's elite accepted the contemporary Victorian upper-class race ideology and then applied it to the poor. As *The Philanthropist* noted, it was "not afraid to tell our friend Paddy that he *is* lazy, and that sloth and apathy are uniformly the national attributes of an uneducated peoples."[51] However, while for some Protestants, religion was an added strike against poor Irish Catholics, in the language of philanthropy—regardless of denomination—it was the essentialist nature of class that was expressed most clearly. Whether Protestant or Catholic, Dublin's upper-class philanthropists often suggested that the sin of poverty was the result of nature, not nurture.

PHILANTHROPISTS, POVERTY, AND THE CREATION OF A LOYAL WORKING CLASS

The language within nineteenth-century charitable records show how stereotypes of race, class, and religion became conflated and confused. Some Irish philanthropists conceived of the poor as intrinsically inferior, capable of only a minimum of improvement. By perceiving working-class characteristics as inherent, philanthropists discussed the Irish poor as other and applied the same traits to the poor as they affiliated with other races.[52] The following examples contain common themes that can be found within the publications of many nineteenth-century charities: poverty was intrinsic, the poor were dirty and diseased, their inherently sinful nature contributed to their plight; the most to be hoped for with the working classes was minimal training or emigration, and hardened sinners and persistent beggars could not be saved. Ultimately, one clear goal, and a theme that runs throughout the language of charity, was the philanthropists' desire to create a hard-working subject who contributed to the well-being of the state.

One example of the inherent nature of poverty was revealed in the records of children's charities. Philanthropists believed poor children to be a reflection of their parents' degradation. Philanthropist Isabella Tod warned ladies of the difficulties that volunteers would encounter while aiding Dublin's poor children, because these children "will have to face discouragements arising not only from the ordinary difficulties of life, but from the tendencies of disease, drink, vice, and insanity, which many . . . inherit."[53] Or, for example, the First Report of the Philanthropic Society described poor children as malignant crops that "grow to maturity . . . in their turn to shed their seed, and perpetuate the baneful vegetation."[54] Hence, reformers suggested that, like Mendel's peas, the poor were genetically designed and it would take years of evolution to eliminate their malignant characteristics.

However, at the same time, women philanthropists particularly sought to save poor children because they believed them to be more easily reformed than hardened, adult sinners. The St. Joseph's Reformatory School for Catholic Girls noted that if young, poor girls could be separated from older ones, they would be saved from being contaminated by them.[55]

Mary Carpenter held out hope for young children when she wrote that she wanted to civilize and teach them "and to let them know practically that they were not regarded as the offscourings of the earth, the refuse of society—that there were those who cared for their souls."[56] Yet, while poor children had greater potential for becoming law-abiding subjects, philanthropists suggested that they could never escape the class into which they were born.

In addition, women philanthropists also set their sights on saving poor females. Yet, similar to their belief about poor children, charities reinforced their understanding of the inherent deficiencies of poor women by describing them as other. The Dublin Female Penitentiary alleged that such women could be found "herding among the lowest orders of profligate and abandoned characters."[57] Similarly, the House of Protection, which trained needy women at the laundry in the hope of attaining for them future employment, aspired to limit the numbers of "unhappy women who infest our streets and infect society."[58] The Dublin Female Penitentiary characterized poor Irish women as the lowest on the ladder and called them "hardened, unworthy, outcast, degraded, rejected and despised."[59] Although one author advocated for poor Irish females to be educated, she nevertheless characterized them as "but one degree removed from a savage state. Ferocious, idle, drunken and revengeful, they are the chief instigation of every outrage . . . taking an active part in the disturbance."[60] Thus, while the charities sought to aid poor women, they suggested that there could be only minimal improvements.[61]

Regardless of what philanthropists thought of poor women, finding them work was difficult in Dublin, a city with few employment options open to poor women. In Dublin, females constituted 40 percent of those arrested, and the numbers of women that police detained for vagrancy and public intoxication was quite high. In 1855, for example, women made up 45 percent of committals, which by the next year was up to 47 percent.[62] Generally referred to as "fallen women," the majority of crimes committed by females were not of a violent nature, and the courts primarily convicted them of "morality offenses" such as prostitution, drunkenness, disorderly conduct, or vagrancy.[63] In truth, it seems that when arrested, most women were charged with solicitation. For example, over 60 percent of the women arrested in 1871 were accused of being prostitutes.[64] After release, it was very difficult for women—especially those involved in prostitution—to find employment.[65] Another hurdle for poor females was the common assumption that women were more moral and if a woman sinned, she sank much lower in depravity than a man because she had so much further to fall. That is, a woman had acted in direct contradiction of her instincts.[66] Not surprisingly, due to harsh public attitudes and mistrust of those who had been incarcerated, there was a high rate of recidivism among former female prisoners.[67] The Discharged Female Roman Catholic

Prisoners' Aid Society was well aware that former female prisoners were rejected by society and "if unaided ran a great risk of relapsing into crime."[68] Thus by assisting them to emigrate, which this charity sought, it allowed these women to start over in a new community that was unaware of past indiscretions.

Charities suggested that if caught early, the young woman was "redeemable"—unlike the experienced sinner for whom philanthropists felt there was little hope.[69] The House of Refuge for Industrious and Distressed Females of Good Character tried to save young women from that extensive "class of misery" who were "unprotected" and "reduced to distress" and then it trained them in washing, mangling,[70] plain-work, and "other branches of Female Industry."[71] The Discharged Female Roman Catholic Prisoners' Aid Society adopted the theme that it only wanted to help those persons it deemed "saveable" from the sinful path upon which they had begun to walk. The society noted that it did not help those whose reformation appeared to be "humanly speaking, hopeless, but principally with those prisoners who have for a short time gone astray."[72] Many Magdalen homes noted that they would only work with a young woman after a "first fall."[73] The Dublin Female Penitentiary noted that it was not "a refuge to the *hardened and unworthy*."[74] The Penitentiary's 1813 report stated that it accepted "unfortunate females plunged in sin, but, from conviction, willing to quit the paths of vice," and thereby eventually able to legitimately earn an income.[75] Once this honest subsistence was established, they would no longer be the "pests of their respective stations in society."[76]

Another message that also becomes clearly evident within the records is that charities desired to turn the poor into hard-working, compliant employees and thus lead them "from the evil ways upon which they were beginning to walk, and become good and useful members of society."[77] The House of Refuge for Industrious and Distressed Females of Good Character was very proud of its work in saving destitute females and in helping the women to attain "improved habits of virtue and industry, which will render them more certainly useful to those who shall hereafter employ them."[78] By training them to be better servants, Dublin's reformers hoped to transform the city's indigent into proper, loyal, and obedient subjects.[79] The Managing Committee of the Association for the Suppression of Mendacity in Dublin taught young women lace making, not because it thought they would find employment in that field but because they wanted to train the girls in the "habits of cleanliness, neatness, dexterity, and patient diligence."[80] The association stated that it believed that the young girls, upon whom the charity conferred many benefits, would more likely become "useful servants."[81] It wanted them to avoid anything that "might possibly unfit them for that humble and laborious station in society" which the committee hoped to "prepare them to fill with respectability."[82] In addition to creating good subjects in order to engender their "fidelity to the State," the Providence (Row) Night Refuge and Home noted that it was also seeking to ensure a good, if not deferential, relationship between "rich and poor."[83] Ultimately, as a more valuable employee, a woman would, the charity hoped, also be more faithful to God and thus less inclined to sin. Nevertheless, wanting the poor to become respectable did not mean that charities wanted the poor to forget their station in society.

On the other hand, it seems that some reformers, particularly of prostitutes, attempted to completely erase their past and change their identity.[84] What linked these two apparently contradictory routes of reform was the philanthropists' overwhelming desire to eradicate a penitent's individuality and proscribe her ability to act independently.[85] Magdalen asylums, as the charities that worked with prostitutes were called, believed that by stripping the prostitute of any independence, she was more easily disciplined.[86] Instead of using her name, reformers would call a penitent by the name of a saint or by a number as did the Magdalen Asylum on Leeson Street, which "resolved that [numbers] 12 [and] 13 be dismissed from this Asylum for unruly conduct and discontent."[87] While this practice may have been enacted because it was both efficient and ensured confidentiality, it also may have been the case that Magdalen homes hoped they could completely erase a woman's past and mold her into the obedient servant reformers desired.[88] As part of this process, Magdalen asylums (and this was true of many charities) kept penitents under a strict regimen of work and reflection, hoping to keep them busy, docile, and obedient.[89] By stifling their singularity, disciplining them through a strict daily schedule, and training them for service-oriented positions, Dublin's reformers, in effect, furthered the conservative, hierarchical nature of Ireland by attempting to create a docile, uniform population of workers.

Wrapped up in the process of creating obedient employees was the effort to create loyal subjects to the Crown. It seems that loyal subjects were certainly those who were hard-working and law-abiding and did not live off the largesse of the state. As philanthropist Rosa Barrett noted, "to put him in the way of earning his dinner may be a more difficult task, but surely it is the truest charity."[90] In this way, charities took their cue from the Irish Poor Relief Act of 1838, which Parliament had designed to discourage the poor's continued reliance upon state aid. Charitable records show clear evidence that philanthropists feared fostering a class of dependents. In particular, charities emphasized the need to only help those allegedly deserving of aid.[91] Organizations aspired to have the poor only rely upon assistance until such time as they found employment or other opportunities. The report for the Cottage Home for Little Children noted that it was proud to have assisted many poor women to overcome difficult circumstances and avoid having to enter the workhouse where "ratepayers would have to support them."[92] Those "deserving" included the elderly, children, and those willing to work but who had fallen on hard times.

Dublin's charities used colorful descriptions for the "deserving" poor. In 1833, the Managing Committee of the Association for the Suppression of Mendacity in Dublin called them "praiseworthy [for] desir[ing] to establish a certain decency of appearance" and "well-disposed and orderly."[93] As St. Mary's Industrial Institute noted, it hoped to benefit the "distressed, but truly deserving portion of the community, viz., the Industrious Poor."[94] The Strangers' Friend Society for Visiting and Relieving Distressed Strangers and the Resident Sick Poor stated:

> Its benevolent operations are still more extended embracing a most deserving class of the community. It will at once be seen that they are not the noisy importunate beggars, who impede our progress in the streets, hang about our doors, taking every opportunity to exhibit their misery—nor are those who, with begging letters, fabricated testimonials and well-concerted tales of apparently genuine distress, go about, endeavouring to impose upon the kindness and credulity of the unsuspecting charitable and humane.[95]

While children and the deserving poor were worthy of assistance, philanthropists firmly believed that there were those who were unworthy of society's benevolence. Charities proposed that the "undeserving," such as beggars, alcoholics, and adults who appeared unwilling to work, should remain unassisted and thereby left to their own means. Philanthropists and social commentators alike frowned upon indiscriminate aid provided to beggars and "wandering mendicants." The homeless were stamped with names such as "wretched class" or "dangerous" or "neglected" persons. Philanthropists argued that contributions by private charities must be carefully administered because they were certain to only weaken any industrious tendencies held by the poor, causing them to become more entrenched in their status. As the Philanthropic Society noted, "charities to the poor may be compared to cordials administered to the sick: everyone knows the danger of their habitual use."[96] This was further emphasized by Dublin's Female Orphan House, which argued that indiscriminate giving only served to "encourage and confirm the most degrading profligacy of a number of the worst characters in the city."[97] Social statistician Francis White, in 1833, discussed indiscriminate aid to the poor Irish as the "perverted bounty of individuals [that] serves also to increase the difficulty of obtaining subscriptions for established public charities."[98] The Strangers' Friend Society recommended "*caution* and *careful* investigation" before providing any assistance, thereby making the greatest attempts at ensuring that the "truly poor" received aid.[99]

In Ireland, begging was seen as a particular scourge and described as "infesting the whole society . . . with a plague greater and more pernicious than any which crawled over ancient Egypt."[100] The Report of the Association for the Suppression of Mendacity noted that beggars in Dublin inhabited every door and found within their "garments the seeds of contagious disease; themselves the victims of idleness, their children were taught to depend on begging."[101] The upper classes believed that indiscriminate gifts of money would preserve the poor as parasites upon public and state aid. As such, philanthropists convinced themselves that provision of gratuitous charity was actually a selfish act. By providing the unworthy poor with assistance, the philanthropist was only furthering the indigent's dependence upon others, particularly the state, and thus failing to encourage the ultimate goal of self-reliance.

Finally, philanthropists suggested that through charitable work, they themselves received benefits since the "advantages they confer on society" secured them everlasting blessings.[102] In 1884, Dublin's Roman Catholic Archbishop McCabe was quoted by the Dublin Discharged Female Roman Catholic Prisoners' Aid Society as saying that "by every soul they were endeavouring to save they were helping him to save his own."[103] The Dublin Female Penitent Asylum encouraged inmates to petition God for their immortal soul and "to weep incessantly over their sins, and pray without intermission for their pious benefactors."[104] The annuals of the Ladies Association of Charity noted that the poor's spirits were improved when those "above" visited.[105] Margaret Aylward, author of the Ladies Association of Charity pamphlets, often wrote of the important mission of a lady of charity. She frequently noted that many of the poor were very grateful for assistance given. As one poor woman said to a lady of charity, "May the heavens bless you, dear Lady. May God and His Holy Mother protect you."[106] Certainly, those that expressed grateful deference were also the deserving poor and thus worthy of a philanthropist's attention.

"THE DISEASE OF POPERY": THE LANGUAGE OF CONVERSION

As will be discussed, sectarian tensions characterized Irish charity and hindered relationships between philanthropists. While many Protestants may have argued that Catholicism contributed to the poverty of the Irish, in particular, this argument is made most explicit by Protestant charities that sought to convert Catholics. Here again, it was alleged that Catholicism contributed to the inferiority and sinful nature of the Irish poor. For example, missionary Daniel Foley linked Catholicism and criminality when he stated that, "thefts, murders, seditions, &c. have thrown out the disease of Popery to the view of the most superficial observer."[107]

Certainly Ireland's Catholic charities were well aware of and sought to combat those Protestant organizations that worked for conversion. Nevertheless, as shown above, upper-class Roman Catholic philanthropists often adopted the same descriptors as upper-class Protestants when discussing the Catholic poor. Dublin's St. Joseph's Reformatory School for Catholic Girls suggested that volunteers doubted that the girls they assisted could overcome their poverty: "As a body we find them very difficult to be taught, or when taught, to retain what they have learned, having, from their past lives, imbibed unsettled volatile habits, and a great dislike for study."[108] The House of Protection for Distressed Young Women of Unblemished Character wrote that it offered aid to "poor [Catholic] young women of unblemished reputation who might be . . . rendered useful to society."[109] By saving a young woman from the mean streets, and providing her with some instruction, the House of Protection stated that it taught her "to walk to a more perfect way, and thereby render her more dear to God, and more valuable to her employers."[110] The Committee of the Catholic Ragged Schools noted that it had special affection for that class of children who because of their poverty and "the indolence or vice of their parents" must resort to begging to receive assistance or "attend those schools opened for their perversion by the enemies of our holy faith."[111] However, the committee went on to make the same argument as their Protestant colleagues would have, but from a Catholic perspective. Thus, the committee argued that if poor children were exposed to the "enemy" (i.e., Protestant proselytizers) then they would "grow up in ignorance, vice and irreligion, and as they approach maturity, are liable to get so inured to crime, so hardened to infamy, as to become pests to society, a disgrace and reproach to their country."[112] Ultimately, while Catholic philanthropists may not have added religion into the mix of intrinsic inferiority, nevertheless, in seeking to place themselves on an equal footing as those perceived to be in a position of authority, they adopted the same language that Protestant charities used. In addition, such examples also revealed that it was upper-class conviction about the essentialist characteristics of the classes that united most of Ireland's charitable volunteers.

The rhetoric used by those philanthropists who combined aid with religious conversion reinforced a belief that Catholicism could be equated with poverty, criminality, and idol worship. Missionaries desired to convert poor Irish Catholics because they believed it would put them on the route to both civilization and heaven.[113] As the Dingle and Ventry Mission reported, those who converted to Protestantism clearly showed signs of becoming more civilized, and this was not only exhibited in cleanliness and good conduct, but also Dingle had become "free from crime, or even agrarian or political outrage."[114] In another example, the Dublin Visiting Mission in Connection with the Society for Irish Church Missions sent missionaries into the streets of the city particularly seeking out Roman Catholics whom the mission described as idolaters needing to be saved from the clutches of Romanism in order to reach heaven.[115] Similarly, the

Report of the Ladies Irish Association described how a member wanted recipients of their largesse to be grateful for being shown that there was no need to offer worship to "dumb idols, and . . . bog water."[116]

Conversion was not a simple assignment, and a good missionary was not easily deterred from the task at hand. The 1885 report of the Dublin Visiting Mission noted that if missionaries met with "rough treatment" during a house-to-house visit, "they mark the place not to be avoided but for more frequent visits and more determined effort."[117] Missionary charities did not always meet with quiet success. For example, when one of the Dublin City missionaries attempted to talk to some Roman Catholic women about becoming "true Christians," the women began to curse at him and, as he suggested, "*they appeared like savages in human shape.* May the Lord change their hearts."[118]

Protestants who desired to convert Catholics often used the imagery of darkness to which conversion would bring light. This was not dissimilar to the image of Britain bringing the light of civilization to its colonies. As Sarah Davies wrote, "our missionaries tell Roman Catholics that this is darkness . . . they shew the people what error is, and what truth is."[119] Davies included one poem:

> Dark as the heathen, in sin they roam;
> Their school the wide world, the streets their home;
> No voice to warm them, no hand to guide,
> How should they know that the Lord hath died?[120]

Davies legitimized the conversion of Roman Catholics boys in one orphanage and asked, "Are we to train them in the way which they have begun to walk, the way of ignorance and superstition? Are we to hide from them that light which hitherto has only been exhibited to them in a dark lantern?"[121] The Rev. Alexander Dallas, who established the Irish Church Missions, stated, "It is not to be supposed that there were not constant efforts made to bring the light of the truth to bear upon Roman darkness."[122] Fellow missionary Rev. J. N. Griffin noted that the work of the proselytizing Irish Church Missions had brought, ". . . bright spots [to] the darkness."[123] Both the Irish Society for Promoting the Education of the Native Irish through the Medium of Their Own Language and the Ladies Irish Association for Promoting the Religious Instruction of the Native Irish, Partially Through the Medium of Their Own Language attempted to convert poor Irish Catholics by appealing to them through the Irish language, and, as the Ladies Irish Association stated, they hoped that they would know the truth "and that Ireland may once again be called the 'Isle of Saints' instead of being a reproach amongst the nations."[124]

Ultimately, evidence suggests that, statistically, the number of Catholics that converted to Protestantism was quite small.[125] For what little they may have actually accomplished, however, proselytizers made enough noise in Ireland to greatly worry Catholics. Thus, what becomes clear in the records is that much of the charitable activity in Ireland was inhibited by fears that each group was seeking to seduce the other into changing their religious adherence. In the end, to avoid accusations of proselytism, charities limited their assistance to those of their own denomination. Nevertheless, while conversion, some reformers thought, could result in self-improvement, it would not lead to equality with the most civilized class, only a closer association. In many ways, even in Ireland, the ideology of the "white woman's burden" was active as Christian women played an important role in attempting to civilize the native.

Whether in homes, hospitals, or the workhouse, philanthropists sent the message that sinful behavior contributed to poverty. Yet, charity workers also suggested that escaping that poverty was nearly impossible because it was passed down from generation to generation. Thus, the only hope was to improve one's circumstances. Many charity workers sought to find employment for the poor not only in order to assist them to escape from poverty but because philanthropists believed that an employed person was a more worthy and loyal subject of the state. Nevertheless, while most charities could not afford to train the poor for skilled occupations, at the same time, there is an insinuation that to educate the poor too well was to empower them. Here, philanthropists also imparted a message that charity was a cooperative endeavor, and while the upper classes would supply aid, the needy were to express gratitude in the form of deference.

This chapter has sought to show that nineteenth-century ideologies of race and class cannot be discussed individually. Many charity workers saw themselves at the top of a racial pyramid complicated by class and argued that the poor were destitute because of their inherent moral and intellectual mediocrity. In addition, there was a small but vocal group that clearly argued that Catholicism was another strike against the Irish poor, and only through conversion could they begin to approach salvation. The upper classes sought to ensure that the working classes understood the distance that existed between those at the top and those at the bottom, and philanthropy was another tool that reinforced an understanding of the impenetrable nature of class.[126]

NOTES

1. Mary Carpenter, "The Duty of Government to Aid the Education of Children of the Perishing and Neglected Classes," *Transactions of the National Association for the Promotion of Social Science* (1864), p. 437. Mary Carpenter (1807–1877), born in Exeter, England and the daughter of a Unitarian minister, was a child advocate and founder of a school for girls. She successfully lobbied for legislative improvements to educational provisions for children. See also Jo Manton, *Mary Carpenter and the Children of the Streets* (London: Heinemann, 1976).

2. Mary Carpenter, *On the Supplementary Measures Needed for Reformatories for the Diminution of Juvenile Crime* (London: Emily Faithfull and Co., 1861), p. 8.

3. See L. Perry Curtis, Jr., *Apes and Angels: The Irishman in Victorian Caricature* (Washington, D.C.: Smithsonian Institution Press, 1997); Kavita Philip, "Race, Class and Imperial Politics of Ethnography in India, Ireland and London, 1850–1910," *Irish Studies Review* 10, 3 (2002), pp. 289–302; Gertrude Himmelfarb, "Manners into Morals: What the Victorians Knew," *The American Scholar* 57 (Spring 1988), pp. 223–32; and Richard N. Lebow, *White Britain and Black Ireland: The Influence of Stereotypes on Colonial Policy* (Philadelphia: Institute for the Study of Human Issues, 1976).

4. Gertrude Himmelfarb proposes that nineteenth-century anthropologist Henry Mayhew's study of the London poor "contributed to an image of poverty that made the poor a race apart, uncivilized, unsocialized, less than human." Gertrude Himmelfarb, "Mayhew's Poor: A Problem of Identity," *Victorian Studies* (March 1971), p. 320. See also George Woodcock, "Henry Mayhew and the Undiscovered Country of the Poor," *The Sewanee Review* 92 (Fall 1984), pp. 556–57; and Richard Maxwell, "Henry Mayhew and the Life of the Streets," *Journal of British Studies* 17, 2 (Spring 1978), pp. 87–105.

5. The First Report of the Philanthropic Society (1788), pp. 13–14. As Stedman Jones notes, "Class [was] a life sentence, as final as any caste system." Gareth Stedman Jones, "Working-Class Culture and Working-Class Politics in London, 1870–1900: Notes on the Remaking of a Working Class," *Journal of Social History* 7 (1974), p. 493.

6. Nevertheless, as one charity suggested, upper-class persons could possibly adopt the "habits" of the poor. The Female Orphan House noted that by training a young, once wealthy girl to become a nanny or governess, she could be saved from adopting the "manners and ideas . . . of those of the lower classes." Report of the Female Orphan House (1875), p. 9.

7. L. Perry Curtis, Jr., *Anglo-Saxons and Celts: A Study of Anti-Irish Prejudice in Victorian England* (New York: New York University Press, 1968), p. 24; and Anne McClintock, *Imperial Leather: Race, Gender, and Sexuality in the Colonial Contest* (New York: Routledge, 1995), p. 61.

8. See Michel Foucault, *Power/Knowledge: Selected Interviews and Other Writings, 1972–1977*, ed. Colin Gordon (New York: Pantheon Books, 1980), p. 55. Foucault called it a *society of normalization* in which "the procedures of normalization came to be ever more constantly engaged in the colonization of those of law," p. 107.

9. Gramsci asserted that in order to maintain authority a measure of cooperation must be provided: "hegemony is primarily a strategy for the gaining of the active consent of the masses." Christine Buci-Glucksmann, "Hegemony and Consent," in *Approaches to Gramsci*, ed. Anne Showstack Sassoon (London: Writers and Readers Publishing Cooperative Society, Ltd., 1982), p. 119. See also Paul Johnson, "Class Law in Victorian England," *Past and Present* 141 (November 1993), pp. 147–69; and David Phillips, " 'A New Engine of Power and Authority': The Institutionalization of Law-Enforcement in England 1780–1830," in *Crime and Law: The Social History of Crime in Western Europe Since 1500*, ed. V. A. C. Gatrell, Bruce Lenman, and Geoffrey Parker (London: Europa, 1980), pp. 155–89.

10. Another way to ensure the distinction between the classes was through

diction, which the upper classes used as a device to enforce their authority. Language became a powerful tool in the nineteenth-century political and social spheres. "To speak the vulgar language demonstrated that one belonged to the vulgar class; that is, that one was morally and intellectually unfit to participate in the culture." Olivia Smith, *The Politics of Language, 1791–1819* (Oxford: Clarendon Press, 1984), p. 2. See also Pierre Bourdieu and John B. Thompson, *Language and Symbolic Power* (Cambridge: Harvard University Press, 1991), p. 21; Asa Briggs, "The Language of Class in Early Nineteenth-Century England," in *Essays in Social History,* ed. M. W. Flinn and T. C. Smout (Oxford: Clarendon Press, 1974), pp. 154–77; K. C. Phillipps, *Language and Class in Victorian England* (Oxford: Basil Blackwell, 1984); and Penelope J. Corfield, ed., *Language, History and Class* (Oxford: Basil Blackwell, 1991).

11. Abstinence workers, at times ignoring widespread alcoholism within the upper classes, focused their energies on ending what they saw as a perennial bad habit of the poor, in particularly the poor Irish. Elizabeth Malcolm, *"Ireland Sober, Ireland Free": Drink and Temperance in 19th Century Ireland* (Syracuse, N.Y.: Syracuse University Press, 1986).

12. Bourdieu titled this measure of "cooperation" between the two classes, "symbolic power," which suggested that there was a relationship between the two parties and that dominated groups are not passive but have an understanding of the power that others have over them. Bourdieu, *Language and Symbolic Power,* p. 23.

13. See in particular Gareth Stedman Jones, *Outcast London: A Study in the Relationship Between the Classes in Victorian Society* (Oxford: Oxford University Press, 1971; Harmondsworth, UK: Penguin Books, 1992).

14. Association for the Suppression of Mendacity in Dublin (1833), p. 25.

15. John R. Fowler, "Home Influences on the Children of the Dangerous Classes," *Transactions of the National Association for the Promotion of Social Science* 6 (1861), p. 457. J. R. Fowler was a member of the managing committee of the Prison Gate Mission (to be discussed in chapter 4).

16. Delia Gleeson, "A Girl Philanthropist," *New Ireland Review* 19 (August 1903), p. 376.

17. In *Heathcliff and the Great Hunger,* Terry Eagleton cites Gramsci when proposing that hegemony is " 'permanently organized consent' by which modern states exercise their authority." Britain, says Eagleton, failed to establish hegemony in Ireland because it never established this "permanently organized consent." While Britain may not have established hegemony throughout all of Ireland, as revealed in the Irish charitable records, Britain may have had some success establishing a measure of hegemony over Ireland's middle and upper classes. Terry Eagleton, *Heathcliff and the Great Hunger: Studies in Irish Culture* (London: Verso, 1995), p. 27; and Antonio Gramsci, *Selections from the Prison Notebooks,* ed. and trans. Quintin Hoare and Geoffrey Nowell Smith (New York: International Publishers, 1975).

18. Quoted in Curtis, *Anglo-Saxons and Celts,* p. 63. Curtis notes that while Sidney wrote most of the letter to Graham Wallas, Beatrice wrote these words. Late in the nineteenth century, under the leadership of Irish Member of Parliament Charles Stewart Parnell, many in Ireland began to agitate for Home Rule for the island nation.

19. As Friedrich Engels wrote, "whenever a district is distinguished for especial filth and especial ruinousness, the explorer may safely count upon meeting chiefly those Celtic faces which one recognizes at the first glance as different from the Saxon physiognomy of the native, and the singing, aspirate brogue which the true Irishman never loses." Friedrich Engels, *The Condition of the Working Class in England* (New York: Penguin, 1987), p. 124.

20. McClintock, *Imperial Leather*, pp. 38 and 56. See also Nancy Stepan, *The Idea of Race in Science: Great Britain 1800–1960* (Oxford: Oxford University Press, 1981); and Christine Bolt, *Victorian Attitudes to Race* (London: Routledge & Kegan Paul, 1971).

21. McClintock, *Imperial Leather*, p. 56. See also C. L. Innes, "Virgin Territories and Motherlands: Colonial and Nationalist Representations of Africa and Ireland," *Feminist Review* 47 (Summer 1994), pp. 1–14.

22. McClintock, *Imperial Leather*, p. 55.

23. Jennifer Davis records descriptions of poor Irish as "dirty, diseased, licentious, thriftless, criminal and politically volatile." Jennifer Davis, "Jennings' Buildings and the Royal Borough: The Construction of the Underclass in Mid-Victorian England," in *Metropolis: London Histories and Representations Since 1800*, ed. David Feldman and Gareth Stedman Jones (New York: Routledge, 1989), p. 11.

24. Curtis suggests that the Native Americans, were described with "darker skin and hair . . . and having more traits in common with their Celtic counter parts in Ireland." Curtis, *Anglo-Saxons and Celts*, p. 24.

25. McClintock, *Imperial Leather*, pp. 52–53. For example, the Greek geographer Strabo described the Irish as "more savage than the Britons, since they are maneaters, as well as heavy eaters, and since they count it an honourable thing when their fathers die to devour them." As quoted in Colin Adams, "Hibernia Romana? Ireland and the Roman Empire," *History Ireland* 4, 2 (Summer 1996), p. 21.

26. See "The Irish Frankenstein," *Punch* (4 November 1843); "The Tomahawk," *Punch* (18 December 1869); "The Irish Frankenstein" and "The Fenian Pest," *Punch* (3 March 1866); and "Two Forces," *Punch* (29 October 1881). Edmund Spenser in his *A View of the State of Ireland* (1633) advocated that the Brehon laws perpetuated Irish lawlessness and immorality and argued that the Irish were in "the most barbaric and loathy conditions of any people (I think) under Heaven . . . they are cruell and bloodie, full of revenge and delighting in deadly execution." As quoted in Richard N. Lebow, "British Historians and Irish History," *Eire-Ireland* 8, 4 (Winter 1973), pp. 16–17.

27. Lebow, *White Britain and Black Ireland*, p. 40.

28. *Punch* as cited in Thomas C. Holt, *The Problem of Freedom: Race, Labor, and Politics in Jamaica and Britain, 1832–1938* (Baltimore, Md.: The Johns Hopkins University Press, 1994), p. 319.

29. "I am haunted by the human chimpanzees I saw along that hundred miles of horrible country . . . to see white chimpanzees is dreadful; if they were black, one would not feel it so much, but their skins, except where tanned by exposure, are as white as ours." *Charles Kingsley, His Letters and Memories of His Life*, ed. Frances E. Kingsley (London: Macmillan & Co. Ltd., 1901), cited in Luke Gibbons, "Race Against Time: Racial Discourse and Irish History," *Oxford Literary Review* 13 (1991), p. 96.

30. Dublin Visiting Mission in Connection with the Society for Irish Church

(1883), p. 5. Historian William Lithgow wrote in 1632: "the Barbarian Moore, the Moorish Spaniard, the Turke, and the Irish-man, are the least industrious, and the most sluggish livers under the Sunne, for the vulgar Irish I protest, live more brutishly in their brutish fashion, than the undaunted, or untamed Arabian, the Devilish-idolatrous Turcoman, or the Moone-worshipping Caramines." Edward D. Snyder, "The Wild Irish: A Study of Some English Satires Against the Irish, Scots and Welsh," *Modern Philology* (April 1920), pp. 689–90.

31. Henry McCormack, *Moral-Sanitary Economy* (Belfast: n.p., 1853) as quoted in "The Garrett, the Cabin and the Gaol," *Irish Quarterly Review* (June 1853), p. 326.

32. Chief among those who settled the hinterlands of the thirteen colonies were the poor Irish who, among others, were referred to as "white Indians." Fintan O'Toole, "Going Native: The Irish as Blacks and Indians," *Etudes Irlandaises: L'Irlande Aujourd'hui* (Autumn 1994), pp. 123 and 125.

33. Gibbons, "Race Against Time," p. 98.

34. Ibid. In the American colonies, the Puritans were worried that they were surrounded by "savage papists and devilish savages." James Muldoon, "The Indian as Irishman," *Essex Institute of Historical Collections* (October 1975), p. 285.

35. *The Cure for Ireland by an English Connaught Ranger* (Dublin: Hodges and Smith, 1850), p. 6.

36. Frances M. Mannsaker, "East and West: Anglo Indian Racial Attitude As Reflected in Popular Fiction, 1880–1914," *Victorian Studies* 24 (Autumn 1980), p. 47. For other comparisons between India and Ireland see T. G. Fraser, "Ireland and India," in *An Irish Empire? Aspects of Ireland and the British Empire*, ed. Keith Jeffery (Manchester: Manchester University Press, 1996), pp. 77–93; Margaret Kelleher, *The Feminization of Famine* (Cork: Cork University Press, 1997); and Eamon de Valera, "India and Ireland," Address delivered at the India freedom dinner of the Friends of Freedom for India, on 28 February 1920, at the Central Opera House, New York City (Boston College, Burns Library).

37. As William Digby, a nineteenth-century social critic, noted, "In India Great Britain possesses a larger Ireland." S. B. Cook, *Imperial Affinities: Nineteenth-Century Analogies and Exchanges Between India and Ireland* (New Delhi: Sage Publishing, 1993), p. 30.

38. In 1813 Lord Hastings wrote: "The Hindoo appears at being nearly limited to mere animal functions and even in them indifferent. Their proficiency and skill in the several lines of occupation [to] which they are restricted are little more than the dexterity which any animal with similar conformation but with no higher intellect than a dog, an elephant or a monkey, might be supposed to be capable of attaining." As quoted in Liz Curtis, *Nothing But the Same Old Story: The Roots of Anti-Irish Racism* (London: Information on Ireland, 1984), p. 46.

39. Cited in Philip, "Race, Class and Imperial Politics of Ethnography," p. 297.

40. Joan Leopold, "British Applications of the Aryan Theory of Race to India, 1850–1870," *The English Historical Review* 83 (1974), p. 589. See also Douglas Larimer, "Nature, Racism and Late Victorian Science," *Canadian Journal of History* 25 (December 1990), pp. 369–85; Floya Anthias, "Race and Class Revisited—Conceptualizing Race and Racisms," *The Sociological Review* 38, 1 (February 1990), pp. 19–42; and Douglas Larimer, "Theoretical Racism in Late Victorian Anthropology," *Victorian Studies* (Spring 1988), pp. 405–30.

41. Leopold, "British Applications of the Aryan Theory," p. 602. The Church Missionary Society suggested that there was a glimmer of hope for Hinduism when it argued that it was "wholly degraded and without standing as the basis for a moral social system with a recognition that only a partnership of church and state could accomplish its regeneration." David W. Savage, "Evangelical Educational Policy in Britain and India, 1857–1860," *The Journal of Imperial and Commonwealth History* 3, 22 (September 1994), p. 437.

42. It is important to note that scholars do not always define race based simply on different physical characteristics. Vron Ware defines it as a "socially constructed category with absolutely no basis in biology; the term 'racism' encompasses all the various relations of power that have arisen from the domination of one racial group over another." Ware goes on to state that "what matters is that a person is either white or non-white, even though the implications of their particular kind of blackness, or non-whiteness, is fundamentally affected by their ethnic or cultural origin." Vron Ware, *Beyond the Pale: White Women, Racism and History* (London: Verso, 1992), xii.

43. Lebow, *White Britain and Black Ireland,* p. 27.

44. Bolt, *Victorian Attitudes,* p. 181. For discussion of British characterization of Indian males as effeminate, see Mrinalini Sinha, *Colonial Masculinity: The 'Manly Englishman' and the 'Effeminate Bengali' in the Late Nineteenth Century* (Manchester: Manchester University Press, 1995).

45. Bolt, *Victorian Attitudes,* p. 180. Bolt quotes writer H. B. Evans, who described Indians as "quick, apt and intelligent workmen, and make capital servants: the great success in the management of them is kindness and fair dealing, with tolerance of their harmless prejudices," pp. 178–79. As Said writes, "the Orient is seen as irrational, depraved (fallen), childlike, 'different'; thus the European is rational, virtuous, mature, 'normal.' " Edward Said, *Orientalism* (New York: Vintage Books, 1979), p. 40.

46. In 1890, Fabian Graham Wallas wrote of the native male during a visit to India: "these men are a different species of animals to ourselves—their physical and mental constitution are extraordinarily different . . . [these men are] feeble and weedy and often disgustingly sensual. Their character is fawning and groveling to superiors, bullying to inferiors, mean and deceptive to equals . . . ." Paul B. Rich, *Race and Empire in British Politics* (Cambridge: Cambridge University Press, 1986), p. 27.

47. Jane Elizabeth Dougherty, "Mr. and Mrs. England: The Act of Union as National Marriage," in *Act of Union: The Causes, Contexts and Consequences of the Act of Union*, ed. Dáire Keogh and Kevin Whelan (Dublin: Four Courts Press, 2001), pp. 202–15.

48. Curtis notes that descriptions of the Irish included such adjectives as "childish, emotionally unstable, ignorant, indolent, superstitious, primitive or semi-civilized, vengeful and violent." Curtis, *Anglo-Saxons and Celts,* pp. 52 and 54.

49. *Punch,* referring to the 1848 rebellion in Ireland. As quoted by Roy Foster, *Paddy and Mr. Punch: Connections in Irish and English History* (New York: Penguin, 1993), p. 180. Foster assesses the relationship between England and Ireland as portrayed in *Punch.* He argues that *Punch* was guilty of both stereotyping and being a harsh critic of the Irish. However, Foster asserts that on many issues concerning Ireland (for example, Home Rule) the Irish found support in *Punch.*

50. Passed in 1800, the United Kingdom of Britain and Ireland came into being in 1801. See Keogh and Whelan, *Act of Union*.

51. "Remedies for Ireland: Education, Industry, Prudence," *The Philanthropist, A Sanitary, Miscellaneous, and Popular Monthly Journal* (1 May 1847), p. 97 (their italics).

52. Morash emphasizes this conflation by noting: "Philological race theory depended upon physiological race theory, while at the same time physiology relied upon philology; each part used the other as an alibi. The net result was a system without a centre, in which the boundaries would stretch if pushed at any point. Chris Morash, "Celticism: Between Race and Nation," in *Ideology and Ireland in the Nineteenth Century*, ed. Tadgh Foley and Séan Ryder (Dublin: Four Courts Press, 1998), p. 213.

53. Miss Isabella Tod, "Boarding-out of Pauper Children," *Statistical and Social Inquiry Society of Ireland* 7, 5 (August 1878), p. 299.

54. The First Report of the Philanthropic Society (1788), pp. 13–14. It began by suggesting that children were "a tract of land, not indeed waste and barren, but as productive of noxious herbs and generating poisonous reptiles."

55. Philanthropists could save them from "the contamination too often springing from association with those older in years." *General and First Annual Report of St. Joseph's Reformatory School* (High Park: Drumcondra, 1862), n.p.

56. Carpenter, "The Duty of Government," p. 438.

57. Report [first] of the Committee of the Dublin Female Penitentiary (1813), p. 11. It hoped "to teach the unhappy and guilty female to remember what she was."

58. *House of Protection* (Dublin, n.d.) one page. One author argued that poor women were "insolent ungovernable subjects . . . [who display] untamable audacity and unconquerable obstinacy," and, like many charities, expressed the hope that penitents could become "gentle and docile [and] take instruction gratefully." "Begin at the Beginning," *Irish Quarterly Review* 8 (January 1859), p. 1188.

59. Dublin Female Penitentiary (1814), p. 10; and (1815), p. 9.

60. Kate Charlotte Maberly, The *Present State of Ireland* (London: James Ridgway, 1847), p. 28.

61. Caesar Lombroso, a late nineteenth-century criminal anthropologist, reinforced this attitude when he suggested that the poor British female's "moral sense is deficient; that they are revengeful, jealous, and inclined to vengeances of a refined cruelty." He further argued that criminal women were "big children; their evil tendencies are more numerous and more varied than men's but generally remain latent. When these are awakened and excited they produce results proportionally greater . . . [T]he criminal woman is consequently a monster." Caesar L. Lombroso, *The Female Offender* (London: T. Fisher Unwin, 1895), p. 151. According to J. J. Tobias, Caesar Lombroso was a leading criminologist during the nineteenth century. J. J. Tobias, *Crime and Industrial Society in the 19th Century* (London: B. T. Batsford Ltd., 1967), p. 93.

62. The median figure was 42.3 percent, but during the years 1870 to 1877 the percentage did not rise above 40. Beverly A. Smith, "The Female Prisoner in Ireland, 1855–1878," *Federal Probation* (December 1990), p. 71. See also Pauline M. Prior, "Mad, Not Bad: Crime, Mental Disorder and Gender in Nineteenth Century Ireland," *History of Psychiatry* 8, 32 (December 1997), pp. 501–16.

63. Maria Luddy, *Women and Philanthropy in Nineteenth Century Ireland* (New York: Cambridge University Press, 1995), p. 151. See also Maria Luddy, "Prostitution and Rescue Work in Nineteenth Century Ireland," in *Women Surviving: Studies in Irish Women's History in the 19th and 20th Centuries*, ed. Maria Luddy and Cliona Murphy(Dublin: Poolbeg Press, 1989), pp. 51–84.

64. Maria Luddy, " 'Abandoned Women and Bad Characters': Prostitution in Nineteenth Century Dublin," *Women's History Review* 6, 4 (1997), p. 486.

65. Luddy, *Women and Philanthropy*, p. 173.

66. See Barbara Welter, "The Cult of True Womanhood, 1820–1860," *American Quarterly* 18 (Summer 1966), p. 152; and Mrs. Kate Charlotte Maberly, "The Present State of Ireland" (n.p., 1847), p. 28.

67. Smith, "The Female Prisoner in Ireland," p. 72.

68. Dublin Discharged Female Roman Catholic Prisoners' Aid Society (1884), p. 11.

69. In 1897 the anonymous author of "The Magdalens of High Park" noted that once the Irish prostitute had taken up her occupation, "her downward progress is quick and short . . . [she becomes] a rock of scandal. She becomes a disgrace to her sex, a blot on society, one that must be avoided as the leper of old, because she is 'unclean.' " "The Magdalens of High Park," *The Irish Rosary* (April 1897), p. 178.

70. That is, ironing.

71. House of Refuge For Industrious and Distressed Females, of Good Character (Dublin, 1851), one page. Like many charities, it only accepted young women after they "produc[ed] unquestionable vouchers for the propriety of conduct." The charity also attempted to assist in their spiritual enlightenment and "to impress the duties of religion more deeply in their hearts."

72. Dublin Discharged Female Roman Catholic Prisoners' Aid Society, p. 11. See also Carolyn A. Conley, "No Pedestals: Woman and Violence in Late Nineteenth-Century Ireland," *Journal of Social History* (Summer 1995), pp. 801–18; and Beverly Smith, "The Irish General Prisons Board, 1877–1885: Efficient Deterrence or Bureaucratic Ineptitude?" *The Irish Jurist* 15 (1980), pp. 122–36.

73. It was more the case that young women were more easily "reformed" and thus reforming asylums could proclaim greater success, further enabling fundraising. Luddy, " 'Abandoned Women and Bad Characters,' " p. 497.

74. Report [first] of the Committee of the Dublin Female Penitentiary, p. 10. See also "Report of the British Ladies Society for Promoting the Reformation of Female Prisoners," *Irish Quarterly Review* 9 (1859–1860), pp. vi–viii.

75. Report [first] of the Committee of the Dublin Female Penitentiary, p. 7. Or for example, the Dublin Providence Home (1841) clearly noted that it was "designed for the advantage of poor *females of good character alone*," p. 5 (their emphasis). See also Niall Ó Ciosán, "Boccoughs and God's Poor: Deserving and Undeserving Poor in Irish Popular Culture," in Foley and Ryder, *Ideology and Ireland in the Nineteenth Century*, pp. 80–93.

76. Report [first] of the Committee of the Dublin Female Penitentiary, p. 7.

77. Dublin Discharged Female Roman Catholic Prisoners' Aid Society, p. 4. The Dublin Female Penitent Asylum stated that it saved young women "from being the disgrace and scourge of society" by training them in washing and mend-

ing of clothes so that they might come to be "ranked among [society's] useful and edifying members." Female Penitent Asylum (Dublin, n.d.), one page.

78. House of Refuge For Industrious and Distressed Females, of Good Character.

79. As Foucault wrote, "individuals are the vehicles of power, not its points of application." Foucault, *Power/Knowledge*, p. 98.

80. Association for the Suppression of Mendacity in Dublin, p. 24.

81. Ibid.

82. Ibid.

83. "The miseries of the outcasts, and the utter degradation of the destitute, in the slums and rookeries, have at length awakened such sympathy and aroused such interest, that a Royal Commission has been appointed to devise some plan, to diminish the appalling disgrace." Report of the Providence (Row) Night Refuge and Home (1884), p. 1.

84. This included cutting the prostitute's crowning glory, her hair. Not only did this change her appearance but, more importantly, it placed emphasis on rejecting the vanity that reformers felt prostitutes were prone to cultivate. Luddy, " 'Abandoned Women and Bad Characters,' " p. 496.

85. See Luddy, "Prostitution and Rescue Work in Nineteenth-Century Ireland," pp. 51–84. Luddy notes that the success rates of these asylums were questionable, a fact she attributes to their harsh regime and invasive tactics.

86. Foucault, *Power/Knowledge*, p. 105. See also Michel Foucault, *Discipline & Punish: The Birth of the Prison* (New York: Vintage Books, 1995), pp. 192–93 and 219.

87. Magdalen Asylum Guardians' Minute Books (November 1848) and Luddy, *Women and Philanthropy*, p. 114. See also Frances Finnegan, *Do Penance or Perish: A Study of Magdalen Asylums in Ireland* (Piltown, Ireland: Congrave Press, 2001).

88. Widdess argued that the Magdalen Asylum's use of numbers was to conceal the woman's identity. J. D. H. Widdess, *The Magdalen Asylum Dublin, 1766–1966* (n.p., 1966), pp. 5–6.

89. "The daily life of each penitent is made up of four things—prayer, silence, labour, and recreation." "The Magdalens of High Park," *The Irish Rosary* (April 1897), pp. 180–81.

90. Rosa M. Barrett, *Guide to Dublin Charities* (Dublin: Hodges, Figgis & Co., 1884), p. 78.

91. Helen Burke, *The People and the Poor Law in Nineteenth Century Ireland* (London: George Philip Services, 1987), p. 22.

92. The Cottage Home for Little Children (Dublin: 1889), p. 11.

93. Managing Committee of the Association for the Suppression of Mendacity in Dublin (1833), p. 10; (1834), p. 14; (1835), p. 11.

94. Included in the Second Annual Report of the Ladies Association of Charity of St. Vincent De Paul (1853), p. 27.

95. Strangers' Friend Society for Visiting and Relieving Distressed Strangers and the Resident Sick Poor (1832), p. 4.

96. First Report of the Philanthropic Society (1788), pp. 8–9.

97. Female Orphan House (1851), p. 3.

98. Francis White, Esq., *Report and Observations on the State of the Poor of Dublin*

(Dublin: J. Porter, 1833), p. 22. Another Dublin charity, the Association for the Suppression of Mendacity, called indiscriminate giving a mischievous practice from which those less deserving received more: "it may be fairly assumed that in many cases the street beggar receives more than the pauper in the Mendacity Institution." Association for the Suppression of Mendacity in Dublin (1834), p. 14.

99. Annual Report of the Strangers' Friend Society for Visiting and Relieving Distressed Strangers and the Resident Sick Poor, in Dublin and Its Vicinity (1836), p. 6. As Jeremiah Dowling wrote, "the demoralizing influence of out-door relief it would be impossible to estimate." Jeremiah Dowling, *The Irish Poor Laws and Poor-Houses* (Dublin: Hodges, Foster and Co., 1872), p. 26.

100. John Douglas, *Observations on the Necessity of a Legal Provision for the Irish Poor, As the Means of Improving the Condition of the Irish People, and Protecting the British Landlord, Farmer and Laborer* (London: Longman, Rees, Orme, Brown & Green, 1828), p. 20. Douglas noted that one contributing factor to the extensive poverty of the Irish, a people "almost below the human species, is the horrid practice of public begging."

101. Report of the Association for the Suppression of Mendacity in Dublin (1818), p. 2.

102. Female Penitent Asylum (Dublin, n.d.), one page.

103. Dublin Discharged Female Roman Catholic Prisoners' Aid Society (1884), p. 5. The Managing Committee of the Association for the Suppression of Mendacity in Dublin believed that the income from lace making would also teach poor females, "to consider themselves, as to a certain extent, *earning* the benefits conferred on them by the Institution." The Managing Committee of the Association for the Suppression of Mendacity in Dublin (1833), p. 24 (their italics).

104. Female Penitent Asylum (Dublin, n.d.), one page.

105. "As the Members entered the courts and alleys . . . the sick felt as if half their illness had left them; and the consideration of the persons above them in life, coming to them by the impulse of spontaneous charity." LAC (1852), p. 9.

106. LAC (1857), p. 7. Aylward was sure that through visits the poor "become relieved indeed, a light breaks upon their souls, joy beams in their countenances, and they forget for a time their miseries." LAC (1861), p. 6.

107. Daniel Foley, *A Missionary Tour of Ireland* (Dublin: Edward Bull, 1849), p. 7.

108. *General and First Annual Report of St. Joseph's Reformatory School for Catholic Girls* (Dublin: Browne and Nolan, 1862), n.p.

109. House of Protection for Distressed Young Women of Unblemished Character (Dublin, n.d.), one page. These women who had been "reduced to the last degree of danger and distress . . . by sickness [or] the wickedness of their superiors" could be found wandering the city streets seeking employment. The charity stated that because these poor women needed the House of Protection's help, they must have already "waded through the abominations which divided them from our Asylums; or, at least, had renounced their virtuous character and the world."

110. House of Protection, one page (their italics).

111. *Second Annual Report of the Committee of the Catholic Ragged Schools* (Dublin: J. F. Fowler, 1853), pp. 5–6.

112. Ibid.

113. See also Lebow, "British Historians," p. 3; and Mr. Ledyard's poem,

"Woman," as found in *A Lady, The Female Perceptor,* vol. 2 (London: B. R. Goakman, 1813), p. 25.

114. *Report of the Dingle and Ventry Mission Association, County Kerry, Ireland 1847* (Dublin: J. Dowling, 1848), p. 12.

115. Dublin Visiting Mission (1883), p. 3.

116. Report of the Ladies Irish Association for Promoting Religious Instruction of the Native Irish—Partly through the Medium of Their Own Language (1887), p. 7.

117. Dublin Visiting Mission (1855), p. 5.

118. Dublin City Mission (1833), p. 4 (their emphasis).

119. Sarah Davies, *Other Cities Also: The Story of Mission Work in Dublin* (Dublin: George Herbert, 1881), p. 10.

120. Miss Macpherson, "Little London Arabs," quoted in *Wanderers Brought Home,* ed. Sarah Davies (Dublin: George Herbert, 1871), p. 17. Here the conflation of race and religion appears clearly in the title.

121. Davies, *Wanderers Brought Home,* pp. 74–75.

122. Rev. Alexander R. C. Dallas, *The Story of the Irish Church Missions to the Roman Catholics Part I* (London: Society for the Irish Church Missions, 1867), p. 28.

123. Rev. J. N. Griffin, "An Occasional Paper to the Irish Church Missions to the Roman Catholics" (1856), p. 5.

124. Report of the Ladies Irish Association, p. 4. See also Irish Society for Promoting the Education of the Native Irish through the Medium of Their Own Language (1834), p. 15.

125. Desmond Bowen, *Souperism: Myth or Reality* (Cork: Mercier Press, 1970), p. 147.

126. Jones, "Working-Class Culture," p. 498.

CHAPTER 3

Conversion amidst Compassion: Saving the Souls of the Poor

"There is little communication between many of the charities and in a worst case scenario a pauper will go to a number of charities for relief so that the scheming hypocrite can reap a rich harvest," declared George Williams.[1] Williams, in 1902, followed an earlier example set by Rosa Barrett and published a catalogue listing the many charitable organizations in Dublin.[2] Both Barrett and Williams complained that the lack of cooperation among charities limited their effectiveness. Although both were circumspect regarding the cause for the uncooperative stance by Dublin's philanthropic organizations, historical evidence shows that many of the city's charities provided assistance based solely on religious denomination. The sectarian divisions that plagued Ireland's social and political life also characterized the island's charitable and social institutions. (See Table 3.1 for a breakdown of Dublin's denominations.)

Moreover, there was a small number of philanthropic organizations that sought to convert the poor, "especially [seeking] out Roman Catholics, teaching them from their own Bible the way of salvation through Jesus Christ."[3] In Dublin, while most charities sought to stay above the fray by limiting aid to those of their own denomination, there were, however, a few that were more than willing to openly confront conversion. Hence, in Dublin, two local philanthropists waged a very public battle over the souls of the city's poorest children. One was Ellen Smyly, a wealthy activist who founded homes to help the many abandoned children of Dublin's inner city, providing them with education and employment training.[4] Smyly stated in her records that she gave priority of admission to children of

Table 3.1
Denominational Breakdown of Dublin

Year	Anglican	Presbyterian/Methodist		Catholic
1861	19%	3% combined with Methodist		77%
1871	16.20%	1.83%	0.74%	79.24%
1881	15.84%	1.79%	0.77%	80.44%
1891	15.84%	1.43%	0.70%	82.21%

Source: Mary E. Daly, *Dublin: The Deposed Capital* (Cork: Cork University Press, 1984), p. 122, and Jacinta Prunty, *Dublin Slums: 1800–1925* (Dublin: Irish Academic Press, 1997), p. 235.

Catholic or interfaith marriage. While the Catholic Church in Dublin certainly sought to counter Smyly's efforts, it was Margaret Aylward and her Ladies Association of Charity that became the public face for the Catholic Church's anti-proselytizing campaign and Smyly's most public foe.[5] In 1859, Aylward contended that the Irish Church Missions, to which Smyly was closely affiliated, had divided Dublin into districts to send Ellen Smyly and her coworkers to visit the poor and bribe poor Catholic parents to send their children to Protestant schools.[6] Aylward claimed that the work of these organizations was "a gigantic conspiracy against the Church of God in Ireland, to rob her of her infants."[7]

In addition to understanding how the strained relationship between Smyly and Aylward mirrored broader interfaith tensions, the language within their records also disclosed their mutual belief in salvation through religious involvement. If they could get the poor to participate in their faith, either through church attendance or acceptance of the sacraments, then Smyly and Aylward believed that the poor's chance at redemption greatly improved. However, also within the language of these two charities can be found a divergence between how Smyly and Aylward suggested persons actually became poor. While Ellen Smyly's records reinforced the general stereotypes about how the sinful nature of the poor contributed to their impoverishment, Margaret Aylward, on the other hand, suggested that poverty was not the result of sin but the reverse. Thus, while most charities insinuated that a person sinned and then became impoverished, Margaret Aylward's writings indicated that she was proposing that sin came as a result of poverty. If this was the case, Aylward was challenging the most common paradigm, that each individual was responsible for his or her personal circumstances. Aylward's theory added complexity to the conversation and suggested that Victorian society needed to take greater responsibility for the poor's circumstances. Ultimately, however, regardless of how the poor became such, for both Aylward and Smyly, the key point was to get the poor to darken the church door as one step toward becoming contributing and moral members of society.

The records of Dublin's charitable organizations offer insight into how Ireland's sectarian battles marred the world of Irish charity. It is here that we can gain greater insight regarding how the religious tensions, simmering beneath the surface, at times boiled over into full-scale violence. By looking at the North Dublin Union workhouse records and then narrowing the focus to two of Dublin's private charities, the extent of Ireland's sectarian divisions becomes more evident.

Ireland's sectarian problems certainly date back to Britain's first efforts at ruling the island, which began serious advance during the reign of Queen Elizabeth I (1559–1603). Elizabeth, whose long reign helped to solidify Great Britain as a Protestant nation, would die only days before Hugh O'Neill, Earl of Tyrone and leader of the last determined effort to resist England's advance, surrendered to Elizabeth's representative in Ireland, Lord Mountjoy. Throughout the seventeenth century, the plantation of subjects from Scotland, Wales, and England into Ireland increased the Protestant population, particularly in the central and northeastern provinces.[8] At the end of the century, in order to give the Protestant minority political advantage and to punish Catholics for supporting James II's resistance to William of Orange, Ireland's Parliament, now dominated by a Protestant ascendancy, introduced a series of penal laws.

The penal laws divided Ireland and provided the Protestant minority with political, civic, and economic advantages over the Catholic majority. The laws restricted Catholics from working in the legal profession, holding a commission in the military, and retaining office in Parliament or other government agencies. Catholics could not buy land or hold leases for more than 31 years. While by the end of the eighteenth century Ireland's Parliament was no longer enforcing a majority of the penal laws, Roman Catholics, who made up approximately 80 percent of the population, now owned only 14 percent of the land.[9]

Although, throughout the eighteenth century, the British Parliament slowly turned back the laws that gave advantage to Anglicans over dissenters and Catholics, the damage was already done.[10] Ireland's Catholics received few of the economic benefits being experienced in the rest of the United Kingdom. Without investment in the industrial infrastructure, much of the populace, of which few owned the property they farmed, remained heavily dependent on the land. Not surprisingly, relationships between Catholics and Protestants were often less than congenial. Throughout the nineteenth century, sectarian hatred played an important role in Ireland's many episodes of agrarian violence, while religious discrimination characterized Ireland's social and political life.

During the early nineteenth century, Dublin, at the micro level, reflected the sectarian problems that plagued Irish politics. The administrative structure of early nineteenth-century Dublin was composed of a small group of Protestant men, some elected, although most were hereditary members of the city's guilds.[11] Called the Common Council, the membership then voted on representatives to be sheriffs, aldermen, and the city's mayor.[12] It was Dublin's business and professional leaders that made up this exclusive organization. Neither Catholics nor dissenters played a strong role on the Common Council until parliamentary reforms after 1832 further streamlined the governing of the island.[13] Gradually, as the historic restrictions of the penal laws were slowly worn away, the city's Catholic majority began to gain a measure of power in Dublin's local government. Over time, Dublin Corporation came to be dominated by small businessmen, of which, eventually, more were Catholic than Protestant.[14] While certainly not Dublin's sole problem, throughout the nineteenth century, sectarian tensions contributed to Dublin Corporation's inability to successfully resolve many of the city's structural problems.[15]

Sectarian strife could be found at many levels of Irish society, and this was certainly true regarding Ireland's philanthropic community. For example, when in 1867 the trustees of the Atkinson House (or the Home for Aged Females) found out that the "woman who is paid 2- a week for scouring etc. in the house is a R.C. It was resolved that her services be discontinued and a Protestant appointed in her place."[16] However, in the world of Irish charity, while such discrimination certainly hindered collaboration, it was accusations of religious conversion that roused sectarian furies. There remains a good deal of evidence on Protestant efforts to convert Catholics, and while Roman Catholics converted both for religious and pragmatic reasons, there is little documentation showing that considerable numbers actually left the Catholic Church.[17] Nevertheless, while the effort to convert was more prominent on the Protestant side (and obviously less necessary for the Catholic), it seems both groups feared that the other was seeking to steal members from their flock—particularly children. For example, in 1843 the Protestant Orphan Society stated that it was a powerful barrier against those who were "ever ready to take the children of poor Protestants and bring them up in the errors of the Church of Rome."[18]

For Dublin's social service institutions, one place where religious divisions were well documented is in the records from the local workhouses.[19] In Dublin, the guardians of the North Dublin Union workhouse regularly struggled with disputes that stemmed from religious animus. Evidence taken during the years of the famine revealed that, even though workhouse employees may have been overwhelmed by the unfolding tragedy around them, solving sectarian problems was a consistent part of the guardians' duties. At the simplest of levels, the guardians were often asking the poor law commissioners to settle disputes as to the religious status of children. For example, in 1845, when one young boy wanted to change his registered denomination from Protestant to Catholic, the guardians wrote to the commissioners that they were "desirous to know whether they can compel him to attend the Protestant worship? Or whether they can alter the registry and allow him to attend the Roman Catholic worship?"[20]

Most often it seems trouble arose between the clergy on staff. For example, in 1846 the NDU's Roman Catholic chaplain, Reverend Murphy, complained that the Protestant minister attempted to "forc[e] a boy named Wm. Murphy, to attend the Protestant place of worship."[21] The Protestant chaplain then responded in kind "that the Roman Catholic Chaplain had unwarrantably interfered with a member of his flock, named Keefe."[22] The Roman Catholic chaplain defended himself against the Protestant chaplain's accusations, stating that Keefe had "sent for him & requested him to administer to him the rights of the [Roman Catholic] Church."[23] The Board decided in favor of the Catholic chaplain because Keefe had made clear his desire to work with the Reverend Murphy.[24]

Throughout the crisis years of the famine, the NDU minute books contain a constant stream of questions on religious issues as the guardians attempted to maintain a superficial peace. In 1850, the Protestant chaplain grumbled that the Catholic chaplain was allowing his flock to pray the rosary in such a loud voice that he "could not, of course, fulfill the object of my visit at that time as the patient could not hear me, nor could I hear him."[25] The Protestant chaplain went on to remind the board "that no inmate of the house should be at liberty to conduct any service of the Roman Catholic religion in the wards and in such a tone in his own part and that of the patients belonging to his communion as to prevent anything or anyone else being read or heard."[26] He then threatened to turn up the volume on his own ministry.[27] At this the guardians reminded the employees of the workhouse that they should not permit events that would disturb residents.[28]

Problems also arose with other employees in the workhouse. In December of 1845, the Protestant chaplain registered a complaint against the Roman Catholic schoolmistress, Miss Power, because she would not allow a Protestant student to leave class to receive religious instruction. In reply, Power stated "that there was a difficulty as to the identification of the child [and] that she was writing for the advice of the Roman Catholic Chaplain in the matter."[29] Less than a year later, Power again retained a child in her classroom, refusing to have the youngster removed even though the child was registered in the house as a Protestant. The guardians reprimanded her for "gross break of the rules and regulations of this establishment" for disobeying their orders to return the child and apologize to the Protestant chaplain.[30]

While the local NDU guardians seemed well able to handle most of the spats that occurred between the Protestants and Catholics on staff, one serious disagreement occurred over the promotion of Miss Power, the Roman Catholic schoolmistress, to headmistress, instead of her Protestant colleague. It is here that a measure of prejudice on the part of some guardians may be visible. The poor law commissioners ruled that the headmistress, Miss Power, was to earn £25 annually, an increase from £15. This decision divided the guardians. It seemed that some of the guardians felt that the Catholic schoolmistress should not have been promoted over her Protestant counterpart, while others argued that, because she taught over 80 percent of the children and was competent, she should receive a promotion. The chairman eventually resigned his chair as accusations among the guardians increased. The assenting group accused the dissenters of religious prejudice, because they did not want to see a Catholic promoted ahead of a Protestant, and resolved, "that to overstep all the difficulties of this case simply to promote a Protestant subordinate appears to this board to have been a clear departure from the duties of the Guardians who [are] bound to consider the well being of the institution."[31] The guardians discussed the issue extensively and, while they promoted Miss Power, it appears to have been accompanied by lasting intense resentment by the members of the board.

In the end, Miss Power resolved the issue herself, by creating a predicament from which she could not be saved. The board discovered that she was pregnant and, although she had been secretly married, she had not adopted her married name, or as expected, resigned her position. The guardians agreed to her dismissal based on "the demoralizing tendency of her presenting herself in a state of pregnancy to the school children" while never having announced her marriage.[32] Power had reason to hide her betrothal because if she had revealed it, it is likely that she would have been relieved of her duties. For the most part, female employees who lived in the workhouse were expected to be single.

The records of the North Dublin Union provide insight into the hostilities that could be manifest between Catholics and Protestants. Such conflict was a disruptive force in the daily lives of nineteenth-century Dubliners, and neither Catholics nor Protestants were innocent in this war of words. In the records of Dublin's charitable institutions, whether they sought outright conversion or not, these organizations reflected the reality of Ireland's wider religious problems.[33]

Most charities sought to avoid sectarian controversy, and it seemed that the best way to dodge the stigma of souperism (offering soup for conversion) was to assist only those of their own denomination. Thus, for example, Mary Mercer founded Mercer's Endowed Boarding School for

Girls in 1735 for the education of "girls of respectable Protestant parents" while the Home for Aged Governesses and Other Unmarried Ladies (1838) supplied respectable Protestant women "a resting place for those who have passed a life of toil, and for others who, in youth, were tenderly brought up with a prospect of continued competency, but who have outlived resources or their friends."[34] The Magdalen Asylum (1766) on Lower Leeson St. aided "Protestant women after a first fall, and for those who were to become mothers."[35]

For Catholics, religious orders provided the bulk of charitable aid. There were, of course, lay Catholic organizations such as the Ladies Association of Charity, which will be discussed later. Others included the St. Joseph's Reformatory School for Catholic Girls, the Female Penitent Asylum, and the Dublin Discharged Female Roman Catholic Prisoners' Aid Society (1884), of which the latter two catered to incarcerated Roman Catholic females. The Association for Visiting Roman Catholics (1873) sent ladies to hospitals and workhouses to console, pray, and read to Roman Catholic patients, and the Catholic Rotunda Girls Aid Society (1880) aided unmarried mothers.[36]

The index of Barrett's *Guide to Dublin Charities* provides a listing of many local Dublin charities, and, generally, the religious affiliation of a charity was also a good indication of the religious denomination of the persons to whom that organization was willing to provide aid. A sample speaks to the religious divisions that characterized Dublin charity. (See Table 3.2.)

While Barrett provided such a catalog to prevent "wasteful overlapping of work," she did not seem to acknowledge the clear religious divisions that characterized the charities that she listed.[37] Barrett begged charities to work together in order to enhance the provision of aid. Clearly, however, she may have subconsciously recognized the intransigence that existed between Protestants and Catholics, because her own charity, the Cottage Home for Little Children, provided "a safe and happy shelter for the very young children of the industrious Protestant poor."[38] Ultimately, Barrett expressed hope that, by providing a list of charities, this information would help to overcome the charitable disorganization that existed among Dublin's philanthropies.[39]

Yet, sectarian tensions were only one part of a greater problem that also included a lack of cooperation between charities in general—regardless of denomination. This resulted in duplication in some areas while leaving gaps in others. Williams stated that he had published *Dublin Charities: A Handbook* in order to "overcome this state of disorganization, and it is hoped that it will be sort of a charity 'clearinghouse' and a source of help to societies and individual workers."[40] Williams argued that narrow eligibility requirements resulted in limited assistance. Despite the requests by Barrett and Williams, the philanthropic infrastructure of Dublin was characterized by organizational divisions as well as the same sectarian

Table 3.2
Denominational Divide: Local Dublin Charities

	Protestant	Roman Catholic
Homes for Fallen Women or Penitentiaries:	7	4
Societies for the Aid of Discharged Prisoners:	3	2
Asylums for the Aged and Homes for Workers:	20	3
Women Only:	14	2
Men Only:	3	0
No Religious Affiliation:	2	
Unclear:	3	
Orphanages and Schools (Includes training schools):		
Boys Only:	15	6
Girls Only:	20	14
Boys and Girls:	24	4
No Religious Affiliation:		
Infant Boys and Girls:	3	
Boys and Girls:	4	
Boys Only:	2	
Women and Girls Only:	6	

tensions that most of Ireland's Protestants and Catholics had probably experienced at some time during their lives. It was in the mid-nineteenth century that Ellen Smyly and Margaret Aylward joined the fray in order to battle for the souls of Dublin's poor children.

ELLEN SMYLY AND THE SMYLY HOMES

In 1850, Ellen Smyly opened her first outdoor school in Townsend Street to provide education for the children of the poorest districts in Dublin.[41] Smyly, from an upper middle-class background, married Josiah Smyly, a surgeon, with whom she had eleven children. All five of her daughters helped Smyly in her work, although Ellen, Anne, and Harriet were particularly involved with her in schools and orphanages.[42] Ellen and Anne worked in the Smyly homes for most of their lives and their names can be seen on the charity's committee lists; apparently, neither married.[43]

With the support of her family and many volunteers, Smyly effectively made running her homes a full-time career. In order to raise money, Smyly traveled throughout England and Ireland, where she spoke to various groups emphasizing the great need for accommodating Ireland's orphans. She appealed for support in local newspapers and the Smyly Home pamphlets, as well as other publications. The language of these publications reinforced the traditional Victorian attitudes toward the poor by suggesting that their sinful behavior contributed to their impoverished state. In addition, the charity sought to ensure that poor children avoided the sinful activity that it was sure the poor were inclined to commit.

In 1852, Smyly opened her first school, the Ragged Boys' School on Grand Canal Street. In 1853, she established a number of schools including the Girls and Infants' Ragged School at 18 Luke Street, and she built the Bird's Nest, a home for very young children, in Kingstown in 1859. That same year, Smyly founded homes in Dollymount for toddlers, and in Spiddal near the coast for children of delicate health. In 1861, she built another dormitory on Grand Canal Street to house young boys and opened a girls' dormitory on Luke Street. In 1872, Smyly founded the Elliott Home for Waifs and Strays, named in honor of Mr. William Henry Elliott, who donated a large sum of money towards the care of the Smyly children.[44] Smyly launched the Home for Big Lads on Townsend Street in 1883 and opened the "Helping Hand" Home on Hawkins Street in 1888.[45] Smyly provided all her children with housing, meals, clothing, and education. The Smyly Homes worked as a unit and, as the children aged, they were transferred between homes within the network. (See Table 3.3.)

Many of the youngest, whose cases were examined first at the Elliott Home, would then be sent on to either the Spiddal Home or Birds' Nest.[46] The Elliott Home cared for those who may have had a mother or other close relative in town. Boys admitted to the Elliott Home only remained until they were ten years old, when the charity moved them to the Boys' Home on Grand Canal Street. As the girls aged, Smyly placed them in service or sent the children on to the Girls' Home on Luke Street. The surviving charitable records suggest that the homes provided for significant numbers of children each year. For example, in 1882 "there [were] eighty at the Spiddal Home, and nineteen at lodging, waiting to get in; these, with the 230 in the Nest make up 329, and even this does not count all."[47]

While some children were placed in foster care, ladies who provided monetary contributions sponsored many of those that remained: "Eighty of our children are thus adopted; they call it, 'having ladies.' The ladies

Table 3.3
1888 Elliott Home Report

82 have been received
33 have gone out
9 to the Boys' Home in the Coombe and Grand Canal Street
6 elder girls to the Girls' Home
10 little boys to the Bird's Nest
7 to the Spiddal Home–"Nest by the Sea"
1 girl to service
1 little girl died

care very much for their children, and send them little presents, writing to enquire about them sometimes, and dearly caring about them."[48] The language here may give one pause to wonder how "dearly" these women, most of whom lived in a rarified world of luxury, could care for children who came from unimaginable poverty. There was no mention of visits by the ladies, and this may suggest that these women comforted themselves in knowing that they were helping to improve a child's circumstances without ever having to find out about the particulars.

Smyly's homes, similar to many nineteenth-century charities, worked to find employment for the most promising children and helped others to emigrate. In 1889, the Ragged Boys' Home, which stated that it could house up to 86, listed the numbers accommodated as well as to where many of the other boys ventured. (See Table 3.4.)

While some of the children may have found positions in Dublin as low-skilled laborers or shop clerks, the Homes were able, at times, to find better positions for others. As the Bird's Nest reported, "One girl, who had been with us for nearly six years . . . was recommended for a teacher . . . another . . . got a situation as a nursery governess [and] . . . two of our dear girls were placed in the Elliott Home, to help train and teach the little ones there."[49] Most, however, faced life in a factory or as a domestic servant.[50]

Smyly's Ragged Boys' Home rescued boys from the most terrible pov-

Table 3.4
1889 Ragged Boys' Home

The number of boys in the home on the first	
of January 1889	84
Number admitted during the year	33
Total Number benefited in 1889	117
Number passed out	37
Number in home in January 1890	80
Thirty-seven who left provided in this manner:	
Sent to service	7
Emigrated	4
Clerkships	3
Army	1
Trades	3
Taken by parents with consent of Smyly Home	7
Taken by parents without consent of Smyly Home	5
Transferred to other institutions	3
Sent to England	4

Source: Ragged Boys' Home (1889), p. 3.

erty and misery, and its report noted that of the boys admitted all were "badly in need of a home many of them in extreme poverty, and exposed to the many evils that surround such lads in a large city."[51] The evils to which the boys were exposed were also to be found in their own homes; as records asserted, the boys were raised in "so called" homes where they "saw or heard little else but what was evil."[52] The Ragged Boys' Home taught the boys skills that the charity hoped would make them independent and trained in "whatever they had a taste for; knitting, mat-making and leather-work."[53] However, such know-how would be unlikely to have taken the boys beyond their poverty. These handmade items were then sold to profit the Home. Industry was the order of the day, and the Ragged Boys' Home continually reminded its charges that salvation was earned through honest employment.[54] Along with education and job training, the Home noted that "great care is bestowed upon their moral and spiritual training; the discipline is firm, but not severe; every boy is taught to acquire habits of cleanliness and industry, and, as far as possible, little time is left for idleness."[55] Idleness, charitable records noted, led directly to sin. Many philanthropists believed that, if given the opportunity, the poor would return to what came innately, or, as Smyly colleague Sarah Davies stated, "their natural ferocity and wild wandering habits."[56]

What made the "Helping Hand" Home different from the other Smyly Homes was that it only accepted older boys who, "in their rough, untrained, and often ragged condition" needed assistance with both housing and employment training. Reiterating a theme common for Victorian charities, the "Helping Hand" Home suggested that without this assistance the boys would "increase the number of idlers who . . . wander aimlessly about the streets of our city, and fall into open sin."[57] When boys found employment and could then afford to pay something for their room and board, the Home moved them into separate rooms. This division reflected a general belief by philanthropists that those persons who paid their own way had proved themselves deserving and should be removed from all possible exposure to those who had yet to show themselves to be industrious and hardworking.

The above examples taken from the Smyly Home pamphlets paint a picture of the large operation that, according to the numbers, helped hundreds of children over the years. Training, though generally for unskilled employment, supplied the children future opportunity; emigration improved their chances in life and, for a select few, education provided them with the possibility of escaping the slums from which they came. The language within the records reinforced a general attitude that the children of the poor were inherently inferior and if not shown the right way to live could sink into the depravity of their parents. As the 1889 Girls&rsuqo; Home and Ragged School report noted, the surroundings of the children were awful "and the home influence is in most cases extremely bad."[58] The language also reiterated the philanthropists' desire of turning the poor into useful citizens, and the Ragged Boys' Home supplied this message when it stated that many of the boys "have been rescued from lives of crime, and are . . . being prepared for lives of Christian usefulness."[59] In spite of this, as well as Smyly's conversion agenda, there can be little doubt that her operation provided opportunities that many of Dublin's poorest children would have otherwise never been offered.

Nevertheless, Smyly's proselytizing was made clear throughout her records and overshadowed her benevolence. Unabashed, the records contain constant assertions regarding the saving of poor children from their Catholicism. For example, the "Helping Hand" Home stated that it admitted a young man who was "a bigoted Roman Catholic. But he found out the truth as it is in Jesus, and became truly converted to God."[60] The homes' blatant agenda facilitated tensions that could flare into violent disruptions that spilled into the streets of the city.[61] For example, Smyly supporter Sarah Davies described a series of incidents in 1857 including one during which "the female teachers were rolled in the mud and their bonnets torn from their heads."[62] According to Davies, that same year, another violent incident occurred during which a crowd chased a man they thought to be a souper out of a church, lost control, and began to assail local buildings: "the Ragged School-house was instantly attacked with stones. The Weavers' Hall was similarly assailed . . . and every person suspected of Protestantism was assailed. Luke's Schools were also assaulted; and a detachment of the mob broke the glass of Street Bride's Church, and wreaked their vengeance upon several private dwellings."[63] Some years later, the Bird's Nest Report of 1884 noted that the "Luther Commemoration stirred up afresh the enmity of the priests, and Cardinal McCabe looked about for some point of attack."[64] The report continued that the Bird's Nest was the target of the "Romish Papers," while the Nest was held "up to ridicule, sometimes describing it as the deadly enemy."[65] In 1885, local priests demanded that Catholic mothers claim their children from the Elliott Home and place them in the care of the Catholic Church. "In some cases these efforts were successful, and seven children in all were forcibly taken away."[66] The Bird's Nest pamphlet revealed that 1887 was quieter than 1886, during which "the tempest of antagonism which broke upon us in the winter of 1886/87 died away, leaving no great results."[67]

However, in 1890 problems reemerged when, at the Bird's Nest, visitors forcibly took a young girl from the home and, as they were leaving, "pushed [the matron] violently back" and before she could stop them, rushed away with the child.[68] The Bird's Nest gave no other explanation as to why the child was "stolen" and later reports did not reveal whether she was "given back." It is, however, easy to speculate that the youngster might have been the product of an interfaith marriage whose Catholic relatives believed she should be raised in the Roman Catholic tradition. The next year, the Bird's Nest Report recorded that more children were taken, "removed from light into darkness . . . and sent where its teaching is rejected."[69] While forcibly removing children from an orphanage does not appear to have been a frequent occurrence, it was not completely uncommon, as was noted earlier in the Ragged Boys' Home report of 1889.

As will be discussed later, Margaret Aylward was involved in a child snatching case. In Dublin's tense atmosphere, the fight for the souls of Irish children included kidnapping.

In addition to the Smyly pamphlets that provided readers with such updates, there were other publications affiliated with the homes that offered greater detail about the operation. Sarah Davies was editor of *Erin's Hope,* a juvenile magazine sponsored by the Irish Church Missions and published for over 20 years by women associated with the Smyly Homes. Davies also authored a number of books that discussed Smyly's work. Her writings generally maintained an anti-Catholic message.[70] For example, in Davies's *Them Also: The Story of the Dublin Mission,* she included short stories and poems such as one written by "a poor houseless Roman Catholic lad" who came to know the truth:

> I'm sure the Church of Rome is that foul abomination,
> So fully made known in the Divine revelation;
> She will tell you that she is founded on a rock,
> And with those pious slanders she has blinded all her flock.[71]

Davies's inclusion of such work, including the anonymous anti-Catholic poem below, could not have made her, Smyly, or the Irish Church Missions popular with Catholics as it implied that Catholics were enslaved by the Vatican.

> Dear Saviour, turn those erring hearts,
> Poor slaves of cruel Rome
> Oh, save the curses like the curst:
> Oh, bring them to Thy home![72]

While Davies may have hoped that her publications would somehow convince Catholics of the errors of their ways, it is unlikely that this was the end result. In fact, such works were only fodder for Catholics to argue that all Protestants were out to convert them.

Ultimately, Ellen Smyly's affiliation with the controversial figure, Reverend Alexander Dallas, and his Society for Irish Church Missions to the Roman Catholics solidified her reputation as a proselytizer.[73] Born in 1791, Dallas became the Rector of Wonston[74] in 1829, where he honed his skills as an evangelical preacher.[75] Dallas's interest in Ireland stemmed from his association with the millenarian movement that was popular with his evangelical colleagues. Among other things, the movement insisted that the Irish should be freed from Roman tyranny before the return of Christ.[76] In 1843, Dallas traveled to Ireland to begin his missionary work in the west. In 1847, he founded the Irish Church Missions, which hoped to communicate the gospel to Roman Catholics and offer them an alternative to the teachings of Rome.[77] With the help of a donation provided by a supporter, Dallas spread his good news by sending thousands of tracts to Irish Catholic traders and farmers.[78]

Soon after Dallas's arrival, the famine began. Within his writings, Dallas suggested that he believed that the blight was brought on by the Lord in order for Dallas to save the Irish from their Romanish delusions. Dallas, thinking that he was saving Catholics from themselves, did not see it as a sin to manipulate the populace in their weakened state.[79] Instead, for Dallas, the crisis was an opportunity that permitted him to "strike while the iron is hot."[80] Dallas believed that the famine exposed the Catholic Church as a fraud, because he found that in their desperate state, and often combined with offers of food or supplies, starving Catholics would convert.[81] While it cannot be proven that Dallas and his missionaries exchanged "soup" for conversion, the Irish Church Missions' records reinforce the view that converting the Catholics of Ireland was the primary agenda.

Although Dallas and his missionaries focused much of their work in the west of Ireland (building 21 churches and 30 schools), Dallas also saw great potential for his missionary efforts in Dublin's poorer districts.[82] Similar to famine victims, Dallas believed that the Catholic poor of the city's slums were in a weakened state, needing all the essentials of life and therefore ripe for conversion. As Dallas recorded, the slums of Dublin were "the stronghold of Papal darkness and intolerance. The appearance of the streets, once the abodes of splendour and opulence, now of squalor and wretchedness, indicated the fact; the same houses only sheltering now the famishing victimes [*sic*] of ignorance and vice."[83]

In relation to Ellen Smyly, Dallas placed himself in very a supportive role by donating money to and offering public encouragement of her homes, but in no way interfering with their administration.[84] After one visit to a Smyly Home where he met some of the young male graduates of one of her schools, Dallas wrote of encountering "a noble set of youths, rescued from vice and degradation, and from Romanish delusion, and all manifesting with Irish warmth their love and gratitude."[85] Ultimately, Dallas's financial support helped the Smyly Homes to broaden their work, but, at the same time, with the Roman Catholic Church in Dublin well aware of Smyly's affiliation with Dallas, Smyly's work only served to unashamedly fan the flames of controversy.[86]

While Smyly's intentions were noble, she purposely sought to convert children, knowing that as a result she would stir up a great deal of controversy. Yet, at the same time, these sectarian battles were a reflection of the greater problem throughout Irish society.[87] Ultimately, the Smyly Homes' agenda was unabashed in its mission. As coworker and supporter Sarah Davies wrote, "[o]ur Missionaries are not afraid of telling Roman-Catholics [*sic*] that this is darkness," and the Smyly Homes hoped to lead

Roman Catholics into the light of salvation.[88] So too, the language within the records of the Smyly Homes offered the traditional message that sin led to destitution and the path out of poverty was upon the road of religious practice, hard work, and moral living. When, in 1901, Ellen Smyly died, according to her granddaughter, "she left behind her seven Homes and four day schools free of debt and filled with children."[89]

MARGARET AYLWARD AND THE LADIES ASSOCIATION OF CHARITY

Not surprisingly, Smyly was not without her detractors. While Catholic religious orders administered much of the relief work done by and for the Catholics of Dublin, there were a number of lay Catholic organizations that worked to help the poor of the city. One such organization was the Ladies' Association of Charity of the Society of St. Vincent De Paul for the Spiritual and Temporal Relief of the Sick Poor. Local ladies established a Kingstown[90] branch in 1843 and a Metropolitan branch in 1852.[91] The Association had two types of affiliation, the active female visitors and honorary members. Honorary members included local clergy, businessmen, and the supportive husbands and brothers of active workers.[92] While women of the Ladies' Association of Charity went to the homes of the poor to provide succor, they also went to ensure that members of the flock were maintaining the faith and sought "to induce all to frequent the Sacraments, to hear Mass on Sundays and Holidays, to urge upon the parents the necessity of making their children attend catechism."[93] And, not unlike many visiting charities, the Ladies spread the message of sanitary practice, home economy, and moral behavior.[94] The Association asserted that, through hard work and faith in God, the poor could overcome their plight and become contributing members of society "by instilling into them high principles of morality, habits of industry and order."[95]

The Ladies Association's most famous member was Margaret Aylward. Born in Waterford in 1810, Aylward was the child of wealthy Catholic merchants. Her father, William, held property that included land, tenements, and ships, although his most lucrative work was in the export trades.[96] The Ursuline nuns of Thurles, County Tipperary, provided Aylward with her primary education, after which she returned to Waterford to work as a lay volunteer in the schools of the Presentation Sisters.

In 1834, Aylward followed her older sister, Catherine, into the Irish Sisters of Charity on Stanhope Street in Dublin, but she soon became unhappy with the goals that the convent set for her, and she left. Aylward's health, never robust, suffered under the trauma of leaving the convent and she traveled to France in order to recover. After a short stay, Aylward returned to Waterford and continued her work with the poor. She volunteered in the Presentation Sisters and Christian Brothers schools for needy children and the Mont de Piete pawn shop, which offered low interest rates to the poor.[97] In 1846, Aylward traveled to Dublin, and while staying with her brother in the suburb of Clontarf, she consulted a local doctor regarding her health.[98] While in the city, Aylward joined the Ladies' Association of Charity of the Society of St. Vincent De Paul in Kingstown.

In 1852, Aylward helped to establish—and became the secretary for—another branch of the charity in the Metropolitan Parish of Dublin. Aylward, who authored the Association's annual pamphlets, supplied impressive details regarding the work of the Ladies as well as the state of the poor. As she noted in many of their annual reports, the work was never ending. During the year 1852, for example, the records show that the Ladies made 3,591 visits to the sick and relieved over 200 families.[99] Of the many benefits of the organization, Aylward noted, "a great many blessings flow incidentally from the visitation of the sick. Parents who neglect their children are spoken to; children are sent to school; members of families absent from confession are induced to go; Mass is better attended; the designs of proselytisers detected and defeated."[100] Ironically, while there is no doubt that some Protestant charities were converting Catholics, it is also clear that the Ladies of the Association could be just as vigilant when trying to convince poor Catholics to remain active in their faith.

This coercion came in many forms. In trying to get the poor into the church, the Ladies made a very hard sales pitch, almost to the point of harassment. Aylward described that, when the Ladies discovered persons failing to attend to their religious duties, they "exerted all their influence to induce them to approach the sacraments; and, at the same time, spared no exertion to instruct such as needed it."[101] The tactics that the Ladies applied to those they visited were not dissimilar to strategies applied by Protestant Bible-readers, who persistently sought to introduce the Bible to poor Catholics. Thus, one member of the Ladies' Association spent seven months trying to return a poor man to "his Father's house [she] urged him, entreated him, exhorted him, to begin his confession, but all in vain."[102] Upon visiting another man, whom Aylward described as having lapsed from the faith, the records stated that the Ladies realized that "there was only one cure for the miseries of the whole family" and this was to ensure that the father attended confession.[103] Hence, the Ladies "visited him again and again" until he finally acquiesced.[104] In another episode, the mother of a young woman, who had not been to communion in many years, thanked the Ladies, stating that their "zealous perseverance" had encouraged her daughter to take the sacrament in order to be reconciled with God. While at first the young woman resisted, she had eventually acquiesced. Not long after the daughter died. As the mother indicated to the Ladies, she was sure that her daughter was at peace because of having returned to the Church.[105]

The Ladies also devised a set of inducements to ensure that parents sent their children to Catholic schools. While traveling through the alleyways and slums of Dublin looking for the sick, they also inquired as to which schools the children attended and sought to have parents send children to "approved Catholic schools," supplying "tickets for free admission, and premiums for regular attendance."[106] Once the children were enrolled in Catholic schools, the Ladies would then observe closely their whereabouts and progress.[107] In this way, the Ladies' Association monitored the poor in their own neighborhoods, entering into their homes and schools, exhorting them with sanitary advice, and attempting to ensure the practice of the faith. The Ladies, using similar tactics, showed that they were able to be just as aggressive as their proselytizing sisters in seeking to save the poor from both poverty and eternal damnation.

In particular, as the Ladies of Charity began to inquire into the work of other local charitable organizations, it was the proselytizing charities that most alarmed them.[108] As members of the Association delved further into the poor neighborhoods of Dublin, they soon discovered that there existed a number of government-funded orphanages whose agendas included conversion of Catholics. In her records, Aylward soon provided a report titled "Accessory or Accidental Works," which described what the Ladies did in order to combat proselytizing.[109] During their travels through the poor neighborhoods, as they visited parents and schools, the Ladies used a variety of methods to ensure that no Catholic was lost.

When discussing the work of proselytizing agencies, fear, intrigue, and suspicion laced Aylward's assertions and reflected her strong belief that Protestants were assaulting poor Catholics and working to convert them. More than once the language suggested her conviction that Catholics were in a great battle to save their own. "It appears that Parsons and their superintendents, and the wives and daughters of both, are the chief actors in this unholy war."[110] At times the descriptions took on a frenzied tone: "we have seen some of the legions of enemies against whom we fight—an enemy trained, vigilant, and possessing immense power over the legislation, executive, and institutions of the country."[111] The Ladies were prepared to do battle for their coreligionists and went so far as to go to these Protestant schools that, as Aylward noted, "cover *as the snares of the fowler,* the face of the city," hoping to confront the persons who administered these institutions.[112]

In one incident, the Ladies approached one headmistress who, in order to prevent the Ladies from talking to the "mostly Catholic" children, "seized [one child] by the waist, and carried [the child] away . . . another they dragged away by the arm."[113] During another visit when the schoolmistress permitted some of the children to talk to the Ladies, Aylward's account reads as if the children were on trial. It is heavy with the intimation of forced imprisonment. As the schoolmistress insisted that the students had come of their own free will, the children shouted denials.[114] In addition, as one encounter revealed, not only parents, but children also could come under the Ladies' resolute scrutiny. In one incident, Aylward described a situation that may have involved a Smyly school:

A Lady . . . recognised the dress given in the S__ Street Protestant school. . . . Stopping the child, she charged her with having been in the above school . . . the apparently innocent and artless denial of the child, deceived her for the moment. Again she repeated, whilst holding the garment, "This dress came out of the S__ School." Hereupon, a respectable-looking woman forced her way up to the lady: 'You are right, Ma'am, . . . that girl's mother lodges in my house and sent her to that school, and it was there she got it.' The child herself cast down her eyes, and then confessed the truth.[115]

Throughout the Ladies Association records, Aylward's language suggested that she was convinced that there was a great scheme to rob Ireland of her Catholics. In 1859, for example, Aylward listed all of the organizations that the Association believed were hunting down and coercing Roman Catholics to convert.[116]

While Aylward attacked those who sought to convert the poor, she nevertheless sympathized with desperate parents who accepted food, clothing, and cash as incentive to send their children to Protestant schools.[117] As Aylward noted, one man stated that "his children go to the Protestants because there is nothing else to keep them out of the Poor House."[118] Despite the fact that Aylward clearly understood parents' feelings of hopelessness and helplessness, she did characterize some as disloyal to God, and the Ladies' Association sought to undermine the "excuses, equivocations, and lies of the infatuated parents."[119] For example, during a visit when the Ladies met up with the Catholic neighbor of a young Catholic girl who was attending a Protestant school, Aylward noted that the neighbor was "all the while appearing to hold [the child's guardian] blameless: poverty, in the eyes of some is an apology for treason."[120] The records described that the Ladies "cheerfully," though with great zeal, pursued "poor children through the windings of the wretched lanes and courts," in order to uncover "this evil."[121]

Remarkably, the Ladies even showed a willingness to tempt legal trouble in their war to save the children. For example, the Ladies visited a school run by the Irish Church Missions. Both the superintendent of the school, as well as a Bible-reader for the Mission, called on the police to take down the Ladies' names. In Aylward's account, the school's superintendent indicated that he felt that the Ladies were harassing him—although Aylward's description leaves no doubt that she believed that the superintendent was the wrongdoer:

"These Ladies are about to persecute our people; they are organising a persecution against the Protestants."

> The Bible-reader, (who at this moment looked like an embodied fiend), the Superintendent or Minister, with the policeman and the crowd, advanced to the other Ladies. . . .
>
> "We want your names Ladies," said the policeman.
>
> "What authority have you to ask them?" was the rejoinder. "Take them to the station-house; make a clean job of it, man . . . ," said the Bible-reader.[122]

The Ladies would not cooperate and when the policeman called for further assistance, the women hailed a cab and left the scene. Later, the other members of the Ladies' Association indicated that they were sorry that their cohorts were not taken to the police station because it would have "give[n] an opportunity of unmasking more and more of this vile system of proselytising, and showing the base means used by its agents to attain their ends."[123]

In 1856, the Ladies actually assisted a young mother in her efforts to take her children from the Protestant orphanage in which she had placed them temporarily. The language in the records further reflects Aylward's belief that Catholics were doing battle with the legions of the devil. Aylward described the Protestant woman from whom the Ladies helped the Catholic mother take the children as having "been thirty three [sic] years in the trade, and had never suffered a defeat before; but she was determined to try another trick for old Beelzebub."[124] After snatching the children, one member of the Ladies Association welcomed the family into her home and, wrote Aylward, "thank God, the mother and her three children were rescued from the Nurse, the Devil, and the Swaddlers."[125] Aylward's language clearly showed her disdain and provided a sense of the seriousness with which she believed Catholics should take the work of such groups.

During her many days working in Dublin's poorest neighborhoods, Aylward's attention soon came to focus upon the plight of the children, and it is for them that Aylward discovered her calling.[126] In 1857, Aylward included in her Ladies' Association report a first description of Saint Brigid's Orphanage, which had saved some 43 children who "unless St. Brigid or some one for God's sake had taken them up, [would have] surely fallen into the snares of heresy."[127] While Aylward certainly cared about placing the children in a better environment where they received, at minimum, improved accommodation, the seriousness of her language suggested that her priority may have actually been with saving their souls. Aylward founded and administered Saint Brigid's, but she stated that she relied heavily on fellow collaborators including local priests and other members of the Ladies' Association.[128] Eventually, Aylward decided to devote herself full-time to the care and education of poor children, and while the work of the Metropolitan Branch of the Ladies' Association of Charity continued, Aylward eventually resigned her position as secretary.

Saint Brigid's primary goal was to find foster homes for children. Since

Aylward knew well the unhealthy atmosphere of Dublin's urban environment, she sought to send them to Catholic farmers in counties Dublin and Wicklow.[129] The orphanage required that a local priest recommend those who applied to be foster parents, and he was to provide detailed information about the family's economic and social circumstances.[130] St. Brigid's, which maintained strict rules regarding their responsibilities, paid foster families an annual stipend. Aylward desired that the parents would treat her orphans like members of the family and, she hoped, love them like their own and see that they "eat at the same table, play together, are clothed alike, call their nurses 'mother' and enjoy a mother's affection."[131] Nevertheless, like the other children of the family, the foster children were expected to contribute to the family farm. Aylward clearly stated, however, that "no person shall . . . attempt to put labour upon any child above its strength, or to treat it cruelly."[132] The fact that Aylward expected that children would be treated as members of the family suggested that she knew that many such orphans were not. Evidence shows that some foster parents regarded foster children as little better than slaves, and the system was open to great abuse. St. Brigid's enacted surprise visits, and these may have helped somewhat to ensure that the children were not being mistreated; unfortunately, it offered little guarantee.[133]

Foster parents were to see to the children's education and were expected to teach prayers and catechism. If a child failed to show evidence of learning during either of the two annual inspections or any of the surprise inspections, St. Brigid's did not pay the stipend until the child passed.[134] While certainly there is no surprise that the orphanage expected children to be trained in the practice of their faith, this expectation also reflected Aylward's belief that grounding in the church's teachings could prevent the temptation to sin. Aylward likely hoped that if in the future an orphan suffered financial hardship, he or she would have the religious training to keep them from misdeeds or conversion, and eventually, faith in the Lord would help lead such a child out of poverty.

While the work of Saint Brigid's progressed, Aylward again found herself faced with a crisis that was fostered by Dublin's intense sectarian atmosphere. In 1858, a little girl named Mary Mathews arrived at Saint Brigid's.[135] Her mother, Maria Mathews, a convert to Catholicism, had left young Mary with her Catholic father and, in 1857, moved to the Bahamas to work.[136] Just before her father, Henry Mathews, died, he entrusted his daughter to his employer, Mary Jordan, who then brought the girl to Saint Brigid's.[137] Maria Mathews returned from the Bahamas in 1858 and, not long after, began to make inquiries as to the whereabouts of Mary. When the mother learned that Mary had been placed with Saint Brigid's, she went to Aylward and demanded that the child be returned. Saint Brigid's had placed Mary with a nurse in Saggart, County Dublin, and, when

Aylward reluctantly asked that the child be brought in, Mary's foster mother informed Aylward that Mary was missing.

The court ordered Aylward to produce Mary and when she proved unable to do so, the authorities charged Aylward with kidnapping.[138] What is worth noting is that during the trial, Aylward indicated that she desired to separate the child from her mother. Aylward permitted her lawyer to adopt the unusual line of reasoning against the inalienable right of custody by the mother.[139] Aylward's extreme position may be a reflection of her feelings in two ways. First, Aylward's own maternal instincts were offended by the fact that Mary's mother had abandoned her child. Next, she may also have doubted the strength of Maria Mathews's conversion to Catholicism and, as Aylward's writings showed, she was willing to go to great lengths to avoid losing any member of the church. Aylward feared that Mary, upon returning to her mother, might become a Protestant. Ultimately, however, Aylward would not have knowingly broken the law and, if she could have, she would have returned the child. On November 7, 1860, Margaret Aylward was sentenced to six months in jail for contempt of court as a result of not having produced the child, although she was found not guilty of kidnapping.[140]

After her release from prison, Aylward was determined not only to strengthen the work of the orphanage, but also to open schools for poor children in the slum neighborhoods of Dublin.[141] Aylward opened schools throughout the city, including a number in some of its poorest neighborhoods. Aylward sought to reach those children in greatest need and, particularly, those that were the focus of the Irish Church Missions and the Smyly Homes.[142]

As Margaret Aylward expanded her work with children, she continued to write the records for St. Brigid's Orphanage and persevered in updating her readers on the activities of proselytizers, reminding them that "this gigantic system of corruption has gone on uninterruptedly since the great famine of 1847."[143] In her 1883 pamphlet, Aylward raged against these Protestant organizations. She summed up her argument by announcing that, while the Protestants had attempted to lower the number of Catholics in Ireland by conversion, they had failed even to bribe poor Catholics with food and clothing in order to take their souls.[144]

Eventually, Aylward and her coworkers formed themselves into a society called the Daughters of St. Brigid, though the women took no formal vows. Aylward, who had previously attempted to take vows, did not see herself equipped to establish a new order. Finally, under pressure from Dublin's Catholic Archbishop Paul Cullen, Aylward moved toward formally establishing a new order of religious women.[145] In 1867, the Sisters of the Holy Faith were canonically established as a religious congregation and Margaret Aylward became Sr. M. Agatha.

Margaret Aylward: A Different Voice

While Aylward's language offered insight into the fear and loathing that characterized the relationship between some of Ireland's Catholics and Protestants, Aylward's discussion of poverty as related to sin revealed an important difference between Margaret Aylward and many of her fellow philanthropists. As discussed in chapter two, most charities, both Catholic and Protestant, understood poverty to be the result of sin. Aylward suggested an alternative theory and proposed that poverty led to temptation and sin. For example, unlike many charities that argued that sin closed the heart and poverty resulted, Aylward implied a different cause and effect when she advocated that poverty infiltrated the heart and prevented good behavior. Aylward believed that, by opening the eyes of the poor to the knowledge of the Lord, the ladies would witness a "moment when [the] heart, which ringing poverty had almost sealed up, dilates with hope and gratitude and love."[146]

Aylward challenged Victorian middle-class norms by asserting that poverty led to ignorance and thus a failure to know moral behavior. When provided with knowledge and material means, the poor might avoid immoral action and pull themselves out of destitution. Of poverty Aylward wrote:

> The sorrows of the necessitous frequently paralyse their energy, and without it how can they escape the perils of destitution? and oh! how quickly are temptations strown upon the path of the very poor! The snares of the proselytiser are spread under their feet; and if the lover of the Divine truth still glows within their breasts, and preserves them for a while, the fatal spirit shop presents a stimulus to their cold, and weak, and scantily nourished frame.[147]

Here, Aylward urged that poverty saps the poor's energy and ability to function. She proposed that poverty advanced the desire to sin, and thus offers of food and money in return for conversion were more tempting. Poverty, Aylward implied, kept the Catholic poor ignorant of both intellectual and spiritual knowledge. Without these tools the poor were tempted to sin, slowly sinking further into indigence until eventually swept into the workhouse:

> We have observed that several poor children grow into maturity, and pass into manhood and womanhood, without having learned the mysteries of faith or their prayers. The consequence is that they are ashamed to go to confession, seldom hear Mass, and never a sermon. This is the very cancer of society, the feeder of the poor-house, the prison and the hospital.[148]

Aylward recognized that bodily needs outweighed all other considerations and the poor were willing to compromise their salvation in order to receive basic necessities; she suggested that "hunger drives them, the children, to seek help for the perishable body at the expense of the loss of the immortal soul in those proselytizing institutions which are avowedly established for the reception of Catholic children."[149]

Importantly, Aylward posed another nontraditional idea when she theorized that outside forces played a factor in the lives of the poor. She submitted that poverty was not an inherited state when she wrote that "some persons who had filled good situations were reduced, by the mysterious hand of providence, to the necessity of applying to our Association."[150] Aylward then argued that the poor's despondency over their poverty caused them to neglect themselves and their dwellings and that through visitation the Ladies could introduce order into their lives.[151] Aylward referred to the poor as "Elect of God," suggesting that poverty was not a punishment by God, and that the Lord saw the poor as special due to their difficult circumstances. Here Aylward challenged the argument for predestination, speculating that all God's children, rich and poor, could receive divine grace.

> To console, therefore, these children of affliction, to lift up their souls with resignation and hope, to Him "who chastiseth whom he loveth," to instruct them, and prepare them for the last ministrations of religion, in a word, to do for them all that human charity can accomplish to procure them a happy entrance into eternity.[152]

In doing so, Aylward was leveling the playing field, implying that class status did not necessarily suggest higher moral standing.

One key difference is that Aylward offered an alternative to the common theory that poverty resulted from sin. It shows that there were some in the charitable community who did not unquestioningly promote the Victorian middle-class message that the indigent's status was such due to sin. In this case, importantly, it was a charitable woman who was willing to advance an alternative, and possibly unpopular, theory regarding poverty. Aylward went so far as to imply that outside forces could have contributed to poverty, an implication that, if she had only taken one step further, would have led in the direction of, at minimum, Dublin Castle.[153]

Margaret Aylward died on October 11, 1889, but her work still continues as the Sisters of the Holy Faith have convents and schools throughout the world. Aylward was an excellent example of a woman from the upper classes who desired to put her talent and education to good use. Nevertheless, Aylward's language suggests her paranoia about the loss of Catholics and, at times, an unwillingness to see the larger picture that the physical needs of the poor trumped their spiritual ones. Aylward, like Smyly, was ahead of her times as she entered into the realm of the public sphere where she lectured to audiences, published, administered a charity, established an orphanage, and founded a religious congregation. She pushed the boundaries of woman's calling while remaining within the realm of woman's sphere. She was a forceful member of Dublin's community, bringing aid to hundreds of Dublin's poorest citizens.

Both Ellen Smyly and Margaret Aylward had more in common than they would have ever admitted. Like many founders of charities, both Smyly and Aylward promoted the theme that their volunteers were delivering the important directive that escape from poverty could only come through hard work, sanitary behavior, and a moral lifestyle. In addition, they encouraged the poor to actively practice their religion, the church being another edifice in the architecture of social control that the ruling classes used to their advantage. These two charities, like most, used religion as both carrot and stick, because they were confident that religious adherence would change the poor's behavior, improve their economic circumstances, and ultimately, save their souls.[154]

Nevertheless, Smyly's and Aylward's messages diverged on how they believed persons became poor. Aylward's language suggests that she suspected that poverty led to sin, and not, as Smyly's records implied, that sinful behavior resulted in poverty. If this indeed was Aylward's thinking, then she was one of a few voices deviating from the standard theme of personal responsibility. While Aylward deduced that poverty was a result of more complex circumstances, she nevertheless focused most of her energies on its consequences and not its causes.

While both these organizations were hindered by their religious manifestoes, their ultimate goal of saving children cannot be lost in the angry words and hostile agendas they established. Dublin's economic state fostered a deep poverty that could not be relieved by its few industries. These two women founded very successful charities that raised thousands of pounds and aided hundreds of poor children, providing them with otherwise unattainable opportunities.

Margaret Aylward and Ellen Smyly worked within the traditional roles of middle- and upper-class women by helping children and visiting the sick and poor. Both spoke on public platforms about their work and created full-time, unpaid careers through helping the poor. While many middle- and upper-class women made charity work an activity in which they were regularly involved, only a few turned it into a full-time career. Not only did the women of philanthropy manipulate the nineteenth-century social mores to create full- and part-time employment for themselves, they also enhanced social justice while achieving intellectual stimulation, personal challenge, and private fulfillment.

Finally, the evidence here has sought to show the deeply ingrained problem of Ireland's religious divisions. Sadly, religious discrimination could even be found in Ireland's charitable organizations, which sought to bring aid to those in greatest need. Thus, for example, the guardians of the workhouse were left to decide the religious denomination of children, and charities such as Smyly's believed that through conversion the poor would find salvation. Although Margaret Aylward stands out with a different message regarding the road to poverty, all of these people helped to weave the tangled web of historic, religious divisions that certainly held Ireland's poor tightly caught in the middle.

NOTES

1. George C. Williams, ed., *Dublin Charities: A Handbook* (Dublin: Association of Dublin Charities, 1902), p. 2.

2. Rosa M. Barrett, *Guide To Dublin Charities* (Dublin: Hodges, Figgis & Co., 1884).

3. Dublin Visiting Mission, henceforth DVM (1883), p. 3.

4. As the charitable pamphlets did, this chapter will apply the term orphan to the children that Smyly's and St. Brigid's aided. Technically, however, not all children were orphans. For example, due to financial crisis some parents chose to temporarily place a child in an orphanage.

5. Many of the extant pamphlets of the Smyly homes are at present held in the McCabe Papers of the Dublin Diocesan Archives. This attests to the watchful eye of the local Catholic hierarchy. Smyly records can also be found in the records of the Irish Church Missions.

6. Ladies Association of Charity, henceforth LAC (1859), p. 25. Smyly, according to Aylward, coerced Catholic parents "to whom they give a few shillings weekly, or put their names in the Protestant Registry Office, and thus they get their poor infants, and send them to some of the institutions."

7. LAC (1859), p. 27.

8. In the mid-seventeenth century, Cromwell and his army wreaked widespread destruction upon Ireland, after which he provided many of his troops with confiscated Irish land as reward for their service. See R. F. Foster, *Modern Ireland 1600–1972* (London: Allen Lane, 1988), pp. 101–16.

9. This low percentage may be somewhat deceiving because, as Whelan suggests, there was a percentage of Catholic sons who converted in name only in order to keep the land in the family. Kevin Whelan, *The Tree of Liberty: Radicalism, Catholicism and the Construction of Irish Identity 1730–1830* (Cork: Cork University Press, 1996), pp. 5–6.

10. The last, the legal right for Catholics to vote for members of Parliament, was not restored until 1829. See Alvin Jackson, *Ireland: 1798–1998* (London: Blackwell, 1998), p. 35.

11. Jacqueline Hill, "Religion, Trade and Politics in Dublin 1798–1848," in *Cities and Merchants: French and Irish Perspectives on Urban Development, 1500–1900,* ed. P. Butel and L. M. Cullen (Dublin: Tony Moreau, 1986), p. 247.

12. Mary E. Daly, *Dublin: The Deposed Capital* (Cork: Cork University Press, 1984), p. 203.

13. Thus, in 1823 Parliament united the English, Irish, and Scottish Boards of Revenue while it abolished Ireland's Board of Stamps in 1827. At about the same time, Parliament reestablished the Dublin Chamber of Commerce. Hill, "Religion,

Trade and Politics," p. 252. See also L. M. Cullen, "The Dublin Merchant Community," in Butel and Cullen, *Cities and Merchants*, p. 205.

14. By 1866 there were 43 Catholic members of the total 60. Religious tensions continued to hinder cooperation within the Corporation. In attempts to alleviate the situation, between 1850 and 1858 Dublin Corporation members mutually agreed to alternate annually the appointment of the city's lord mayor between Catholic and Protestant. However, between 1858 and 1869, as Catholics agitated for disestablishment of the Church of Ireland, the alternating lord mayor appointment became an annual battle. Daly, *Dublin: The Deposed Capital*, pp. 206, 211–12.

15. When in 1870 the Home Rule movement began, the divisions between the majority liberal Catholics and the minority conservative Protestants increased along religious lines. Daly, *Dublin: The Deposed Capital*, p. 213.

16. Minute Books, Atkinson House (Formerly Home for Aged Females), 21 June 1867.

17. Bowen argues that while the fear was real, and souperism, the offering of soup for conversion, did occur, there is little evidence that this practice was widespread. Desmond Bowen, *Souperism: Myth or Reality* (Cork: Mercier Press, 1970), p. 147. However, particularly during the Great Famine, Whelan argues that there were enough successful conversions to have strained greatly the relationship between Catholics and Protestants—especially in the west of Ireland. Irene Whelan, "The Stigma of Souperism," in *The Great Irish Famine*, ed. Cathal Póirtéir (Dublin: Mercier Press, 1995), pp. 135–54.

18. *Fourteenth Annual Report of the Monkstown Protestant Orphan Society* (Dublin: William Espy, 1843), p. 10. "The danger is great, that all the children, and the Protestant parents too, should become victims of that superstition." The Charitable Protestant Orphan Union or Orphan Refuge (1842), p. 14.

19. Robins describes the open hostility between Protestant and Catholic clergy: "to each the other represented the proselytizer waiting valpine-like to pounce on weakling members of the flock." Joseph Robins, *The Lost Children: A Study of Charity Children in Ireland 1700–1900* (Dublin: Institute of Public Administration, 1980), pp. 249–50. For Irish workhouses, unlike English ones, no clergy could act as a guardian due to sectarian divisions. John O'Connor, *The Workhouses of Ireland* (Dublin: Anvil Books, 1995), p. 67.

20. North Dublin Union, henceforth NDU (6 August 1845). There is no reference as to how this was resolved.

21. NDU (4 March 1846).

22. Ibid.

23. Ibid.

24. Ibid. As the NDU records then noted, "on motion of Mr. MacNevin, seconded by Dr. Geary that the Rev. Dr. Murphy acted only in discharge of his duty as a Christian Minister in attending to the pauper Keefe at his own expressed desire."

25. NDU (23 April 1850).

26. Ibid.

27. Ibid. The Protestant chaplain indicated that he would "claim a similar indulgence in that I may hold what I have long been anxious for a public and audible service for the sick and infirm of my own communion."

28. NDU (22 May 1850).

29. NDU (24 December 1845).
30. NDU (4 March 1846).
31. NDU (9 October 1844).
32. NDU (13 September 1848).
33. Of course there were charities that were nonsectarian in nature. In addition to the charities of the Religious Society of Friends, one of the best examples was the Sick and Indigent Roomkeepers Society, established in 1789, which offered help to all regardless of creed. Deirdre Lindsay, *Dublin's Oldest Charity: The Sick and Indigent Roomkeepers' Society* (Dublin: Trinity History Workshop, 1990).
34. Home for Aged Governesses and Other Unmarried Ladies (1877), p. 2. See also Williams, *Dublin Charities*, p. 114. Mary Mercer also gave the site for Mercer's Hospital.
35. Williams, *Dublin Charities*, p. 156.
36. Maria Luddy, *Women in Ireland: A Documentary History 1800–1918* (Cork: Cork University Press, 1995), p. 9.
37. Barrett, *Guide To Dublin Charities*, p. 78. Williams, however, noted that "little apparent bettering of the condition of the poor has resulted" from recent charitable efforts, and complained of the duplication of charities because of religious divisions. Williams, *Dublin Charities*, p. 12.
38. Cottage Home for Little Children (1888). Originally named the Kingstown Nursery, the charity, established in 1879, changed its name to Cottage Home for Little Children in 1882.
39. Barrett, *Guide To Dublin Charities*, p. 10.
40. Williams, *Dublin Charities*, p. 10. See also L. McKenna, S. J., "Co-Ordination of Charity—A Need and an Example," *The Irish Monthly* 45 (1917), pp. 279–91.
41. Jacinta Prunty, *Dublin Slums 1800–1925* (Dublin: Irish Academic Press, 1997), p. 250. Smyly, née Franks, was born November 14, 1814.
42. Vivianne Smyly, "The Early History of Mrs. Smyly's Homes and Schools," Speech given 29 May 1976, Dublin Smyly Home Reunion, n.p. (Author was Smyly's granddaughter).
43. Smyly, "The Early History," n.p. Another daughter, Louisa, married a Rev. Robert Stuart and went with him as a missionary to China where they established missionary schools in the Province of Fukien.
44. Ibid.
45. For a complete listing of Smyly and Irish Church Missions schools and homes, see Prunty, *Dublin Slums*, p. 248.
46. Bird's Nest Report, henceforth BNR (1882). The charity trained the children to serve but "especial care is taken to give them a sound knowledge of the Word of God. The girls learn knitting, sewing and housework, and even little ones take their share in the work of the Home."
47. Ibid.
48. BNR (1882), p. 4.
49. BNR (1888), pp. 3–4.
50. BNR (1888), p. 4. "Another is in a family where the place of house maid has, for the last fourteen years, been filled by Birds' Nest girls. Seven others, sent to service during the year, are reported as doing well."
51. Ragged Boys Home, henceforth RBH (1885), p. 3.
52. RBH (1889), p. 4.

53. RBH (1883), p. 4. "Admission to the wood-carving class is an honour only to be obtained by boys of very good conduct, and who are able to present for inspection a pair of well knitted socks, their own unaided work."

54. RBH (1883), p. 4. Ragged Boys Home's records stated that such discipline then resulted in the Home "never hav[ing] any difficulty in providing places for those that are ready to leave."

55. RBH (1885), p. 5.

56. Sarah Davies, *Them Also: The Story of the Dublin Mission* (London: George Herbert, 1864), p. 97.

57. "Helping Hand" Home, henceforth HHH (1892), pp. 3–4.

58. Girls Home and Ragged School (1889), p. 3.

59. RBH (1889), p. 4.

60. HHH (1892), p. 6. The records of the Ragged Boys Home suggested that there was a clear change in the appearance of a child who converted and that Roman Catholics are "much influenced by the sudden, visible change in the appearance and conduct of the boys." RBH (1889), p. 4.

61. See Prunty, *Dublin Slums*, pp. 256–58.

62. Davies, *Them Also*, p. 62. "The people were roused up to a pitch of intense excitement by the frequent harangues of the priests, and they only waited the match to set all on fire." See *Freeman's Journal*, May 25, 1857.

63. Davies, *Them Also*, p. 62. "A mob gathered from every lane and byway in the Liberties, joined with those who had been in the chapel, and proceeded en masse to the Coombe." See *Freeman's Journal*, May 14, 1857.

64. BNR (1884), p. 5.

65. Ibid.

66. Elliot Home Report, henceforth EHR (1885), p. 4.

67. BNR (1887), p. 4. The following year the Bird's Nest brushed aside problems and only made a brief mention, as it assured its readers that "friends will be anxious to know about the attacks made in the *Catholic Times*. They did us no harm." BNR (1888), p. 6.

68. BNR (1890), p. 3.

69. BNR (1891), p. 5.

70. Davies was also the author of *Holy and Ivy: The Story of a Winter Bird's Nest* (Dublin: George Herbert, 1871), *Saint Patrick's Armour: The Story of The Coombe Ragged School* (Dublin, 1880), *Wanderers Brought Home: The Story of the Ragged Boys' Home* (London, 1871), and *Other Cities Also: The Story of Mission Work in Dublin* (Dublin: George Herbert, 1881).

71. Davies, *Them Also*, p. 143.

72. Davies, *Them Also*, p. 158.

73. Desmond Bowen, *The Protestant Crusade in Ireland, 1800–70: A Study of Protestant-Catholic Relations Between the Act of Union and Disestablishment* (Dublin: Gill & MacMillan, 1978), p. 218. Much of Dallas's work was focused upon Connaught, where Dallas said that the "people were in the 'darkest state of ignorance with the least amount of education,' " p. 219.

74. Village not far from Winchester, near the southern coast of England.

75. Bowen, *The Protestant Crusade*, p. 210.

76. Bowen, *The Protestant Crusade*, p. 213. Bowen characterizes Dallas as an extremely intelligent man; however he also asserts that "Dallas possessed a

strange, fanatical mind . . . to him Catholic worship was idolatry—gross superstition used by the priests to keep the people subject to themselves and the hierarchy." Bowen, *Souperism,* p. 138.

77. Jacinta Prunty, *Lady of Charity, Sister of Faith: Margaret Aylward, 1810–1889* (Dublin: Irish Academic Press, 1999), p. 41.

78. Bowen, *The Protestant Crusade,* p. 215.

79. Bowen, *The Protestant Crusade,* p. 222.

80. Bowen, *Souperism,* p. 115.

81. Alexander R. C. Dallas, *The Story of the Irish Church Missions to the Roman Catholics Part I* (London: J. Nesbit, 1867), pp. 82–83. "Nothing is comparable to famine. It seems as though the whole man, the requirements of his body, the thoughts of his mind, the feelings of his heart, were all placed together in a crucible, and melted down by the fiery trial of famine into a mad craving for food, with strong yearnings, powerless through weakness."

82. Prunty, *Dublin Slums,* p. 250.

83. Prunty, *Dublin Slums,* p. 255, as quoted from Dallas, *The Story of the Irish Church Missions,* p. 178.

84. Maria Luddy, *Women and Philanthropy in Nineteenth Century Ireland* (New York: Cambridge University Press, 1995), p. 97; and Prunty, *Dublin Slums,* p. 250. According to Prunty, donations paid for the upkeep of the homes and care of the children. Prunty, *Lady of Charity,* p. 42.

85. Alexander R. C. Dallas, *Continuation of the Story of the Irish Church Missions to the Roman Catholics* (London: J. Nesbit, 1869), p. 297.

86. In her biography of her husband's life, Dallas's wife wrote of her husband's visit to Dublin to lay the cornerstone of the Bird's Nest Orphanage. She also wrote that Dallas said that the Smyly's Homes "were a continual source of interest and encouragement." Mrs. Alexander Dallas, *Incidents in the Life and Ministry of the Reverend Alexander R.C. Dallas A.M.* (London: J. Nesbit, 1871), p. 466.

87. Prunty argues that there "can be no doubting" the animosity between Dublin's Catholics and Protestants. Prunty, *Dublin Slums,* p. 256.

88. Davies, *Other Cities Also,* p. 10 (her emphasis).

89. Smyly, "The Early History."

90. Kingstown was the Dublin suburb now called Dun Laoghaire.

91. Jacinta Prunty, "Margaret Louisa Aylward," in *Women, Power and Consciousness in Nineteenth-Century Ireland,* ed. Mary Cullen and Maria Luddy (Dublin: Attic Press, 1995), p. 60. St. Vincent De Paul established the Association of Ladies Charity in 1617 in rural France, intended for ladies to visit the sick poor.

92. Prunty, *Lady of Charity,* pp. 22–23.

93. LAC (1854), pp. 7–8.

94. Ibid. Members were encouraged "to insist, as far as they can, upon cleanliness, order, industry, and regularity being perceptible in their homes."

95. LAC (1855), p. 5.

96. Assisi Sr. Tatten, "A Brief Account of the Life and Work of Margaret Aylward Foundress of Sisters of the Holy Faith" (unpublished article), pp. 1–2; and Prunty, "Margaret Louisa Aylward," p. 56. Notes Prunty, Aylward was born into "one of the most prominent of" Catholic merchant families in Waterford. Prunty, *Lady of Charity,* p. 13.

97. Prunty, "Margaret Louisa Aylward," p. 57.

98. Aylward had entered an Ursuline convent in 1846 but only remained two months. This experience again exacerbated Aylward's poor health. Prunty, *Lady of Charity*, pp. 17–18.

99. LAC (1852), p. 13.

100. LAC (1859), p. 25.

101. LAC (1856), p. 8.

102. LAC (1853), p. 10. "She then had the happy thought of the Confraternity of the Precious Blood of our Divine Lord. One month after she had executed this pious design, God's all-powerful grace seemed to have touched his heart: he promised he would go to confession. He did so."

103. LAC (1856), p. 6.

104. Ibid.

105. LAC (1852), p. 18.

106. LAC (1853), p. 13.

107. "We, moreover, kept a register of these names, with notes of the [Catholic] schools to which they were sent. We occasionally visited the schools, in order to see the attendance of the children, and sought to secure permanent attendance, by promises of clothes, which were distributed at Christmas and Easter." LAC (1852), p. 21.

108. "Our endeavours in this department realised discoveries of a fearfully extended and active organisation for the perversion of the children of the Catholic poor." LAC (1852), pp. 20–21.

109. The importance of the Ladies' "accessory or accidental works" was reflected by the fact that there was an antiproselytising fund separate from the main account.

110. "For this purpose, every place of offence has been seized, the School, the Regimental School, the Hospital, the Charitable Foundation, the Orphan House, the Government Grant, the Court of Justice, the Legislature, and all this while we were dreaming that we were emancipated." LAC (1859), p. 27.

111. LAC (1858), p. 25.

112. LAC (1852), p. 21 (her emphasis).

113. Ibid.

114. "You come of your own free will, [the mistress] said. We deny it, we deny it, rejoined the juvenile crowd. Murmurs and whispers of bribes, and of 'being forced' to the school, ran through the crowd." LAC (1852), p. 22.

115. LAC (1853), p. 14.

116. LAC (1859), pp. 24–26.

117. "Some of the members [of the Association] attended at the Sunday-schools, where crowds of unhappy Catholics, men and women were to be found, lured by the offer of a small cut of bread, and then obliged in return to listen to blasphemous language, and a sermon from the minister." LAC (1856), p. 9.

118. LAC (1852), p. 23. "Parents who sacrifice souls for food, raiment, and employment." LAC (1852), p. 22.

119. LAC (1856), p. 9.

120. LAC (1855), p. 8. The pamphlet noted that the Ladies were able to get the young girl away from the Protestant school and into a Catholic school.

121. LAC (1856), p. 9.

122. LAC (1856), pp. 9–11.

123. Ibid.

124. LAC (1856), p. 12.

125. LAC (1856), p. 13.

126. Tatten, "A Brief Account," p. 6.

127. St. Brigid's Orphanage, henceforth SBO (1857), p. 14.

128. Prunty, *Lady of Charity,* pp. 56–58.

129. Prunty, *Lady of Charity,* p. 67. The children were either orphans or given over by parents unable to care for them.

130. Placing children with other families was not a new practice. The Protestant Orphan Society, established in 1828, noted that it sent orphans to homes of hard-working Protestant families "of certified religious and moral character" that their minister recommended. Protestant Orphan Society (1832), pp. 23 and 34.

131. SBO (1857), p. 14.

132. Prunty, *Lady of Charity,* p. 70.

133. Recent research reveals that well into the twentieth century widespread abuse of foster children and youngsters in industrial schools was perpetrated by the persons who ran such programs. See Mary Rafter and Eoin O'Sullivan, *Suffer the Little Children: The Inside Story of Ireland's Industrial Schools* (Dublin: New Island Books, 1999).

134. If the children continued to fail, these tests then St. Brigid's would remove the children from the homes. SBO (1858), p. 18; and Prunty, "Margaret Louisa Aylward," p. 69. First, "a premium of 10 shillings for each child that is able to recite fairly the ordinary Catholic prayers. [Second,] a premium of ten shillings when the nurse presents a certificate of the child's confirmation. [Third,] a premium of ten shillings when the child can read and write fairly." SBO (1858), p. 19.

135. See Prunty, "Margaret Louisa Aylward"; and Mary Peckham Magray, "The Strange Case of Mary Mathews: Religion, Gender & the Construction of Irish Catholic Identity," paper presented at the American Conference for Irish Studies, Albany, N.Y., April 1997.

136. *Freeman's Journal* (29 May 1858).

137. Prunty, "Margaret Louisa Aylward," p. 72; and Mary Peckham Magray, *The Transforming Power of Nuns: Women, Religion and Cultural Change in Ireland: 1790–1900* (New York: Oxford University Press, 1998), p. 84.

138. Prunty questions the impartiality of the court because the judge was the brother of a member of the Irish Church Missions—the organization often under attack in the records of the Ladies' Association of Charity. Prunty, "Margaret Louisa Aylward," p. 80.

139. Magray, *The Transforming Power of Nuns,* p. 85.

140. Prunty, "Margaret Louisa Aylward," p. 73. It would later be discovered that the child had been taken by a man to live in Belgium. Prunty, "Margaret Louisa Aylward," p. 72. Interestingly enough, it appears that Mary Matthews herself may have eventually taken religious vows and entered a convent. Magray, *The Transforming Power of Nuns,* p. 85.

141. Prunty, "Margaret Louisa Aylward," p. 75.

142. SBO (1863), p. 15. By 1869 the Holy Faith Sisters had opened 37 schools in Ireland.

143. "The yearly income of the 'Irish Church Missions Society' used to be, in

former years, over forty thousand pounds. But this large sum did not represent the total raised for Irish Proselytism." SBO (1883), p. 4.

144. For all her intense hostility, Aylward hoped that not all Protestants, particularly not Irish ones, were proselytizers and wrote, ". . . it would appear from all this that respectable Protestants will not in the future degrade themselves by contact with this vile system of Proselytism, that the fanatics of England will, and perhaps soon, see they have been duped." SBO (1883), p. 5.

145. Prunty, "Margaret Louisa Aylward," pp. 76–77.

146. LAC (1856), pp. 7–8.

147. LAC (1855), p. 4.

148. LAC (1858), p. 9.

149. Save the Child Organization (1884), p. 3 (provided within the 1884 SBO Twenty-Seventh Annual Report).

150. LAC (1857), p. 4.

151. LAC (1858), p. 6.

152. LAC (1852), p. 5.

153. Dublin Castle was the central location for the British administration in Ireland.

154. "[Ladies] may instruct them, bring them back to the practice of important duties which they have neglected, instill into them habits of industry and order, look to the instruction and education of the little ones of the fold, prepare them for the Sacraments, and dispose them for death." LAC (1854), p. 4.

CHAPTER 4

An Inner Light: The Charitable Work of Dublin's Quakers

As the Quaker's ragged school records stated: "We have to praise and thank God for their willingness to come to the various meetings, and although many of them are sunk deep in sin, we believe that as they listen to the story of the Saviour's love, week by week, it will sometime take root and bring forth much fruit."[1] The ragged school sent a lady visitor to the homes of the poor. After being welcomed by the "roughest of the people," she recruited adults to come to the school's regular scripture meetings. Although their records noted that many were "sunk deep in sin," Irish Quakers hoped that through a message of Christian redemption they could reform these people. Here, the Religious Society of Friends expressed a common theme for philanthropists: sinful behavior was characteristic of the poor, but if they were willing to be schooled by those above them, their circumstances could be improved. Thus, the Religious Society of Friends, whose founding tenets called for the equality of all and which was known for its innovative and progressive ideas, by the nineteenth century advocated some of the same class prejudices as their fellow philanthropists. As the society's accounts reflected, while Friends never sought religious conversion, particularly of Ireland's Catholic poor, it had succumbed to the temptation to promote Victorian stereotypes of them.

By the eighteenth century, the engine of industrialization had transformed British society, and Friends had not remained unaffected. The Religious Society of Friends was one of the dissenting sects who, barred from Westminster, found their power through industrial activity. Already well established in Ireland, many members created successful businesses and grew wealthy in the developing market economy. Such success altered the nature of the Society, a sect that originally had sought to separate itself from the mainstream. Nevertheless, as their businesses flourished, Friends increasingly participated in it. For example, in 1868, Jonathan Pim, a prominent activist during the famine, would be the first Irish Quaker to enter Parliament, where he would remain until 1874.[2] Hence, the changing nature of Irish Friends can be found throughout the records of their charitable endeavors.

George Fox founded the Religious Society of Friends during England's civil war of the mid-seventeenth century. One of the more unique post-reformation religious denominations, the Society came to be known as Quakers because Fox called on the members to "quake" before the Lord.[3] Fox expected members to reject political, social, and gender hierarchy as well as the many trappings of the emerging consumer society. Friends disavowed an established church, refused to swear oaths of loyalty, derided social rank, spurned priests and sacraments, and declined to recognize the authority of the government. The Society expected its members to live simply and address each other as "thee" or "thou," leaving social rank undistinguished.[4] With a centralized leadership that governed over democratic structures that included monthly, quarterly, and yearly meetings, the Society became highly organized.[5] Despite Fox's call for Friends to live an unadorned lifestyle, he did not feel that this precluded them from seeking to achieve financial success, which, argued Fox, was a gift from God that should be returned to the community.[6]

One essential tenet for the Society was its belief that God was present in everyone—rich and poor, Protestant and Catholic, male and female; each person had the "Inner Light."[7] "The Society of Friends has always borne its testimony to the claim of women to an equal share with men in an unpaid ministry, which must be exercised by those who are led to it by 'the Inner Light,' in their everyday walk."[8] This understanding of human equality resulted in the society encouraging its women members to assert greater autonomy. Women Friends held leadership positions and played important roles in the daily functions of the society, and if they showed affinity and talent, Friends encouraged them to preach to a public audience.[9] Like the men, women Friends ran their own monthly meetings and organized into subcommittees that were expected to accomplish assigned tasks. Women were in charge of the funds they raised, although the Society generally anticipated that they would use the money for charitable activities.[10] While women were very active and visible in the society, they were nonetheless expected to choose the traditional roles of marriage and motherhood while taking care of hearth and home.

Although today Friends are associated with pacifism and quietism, during the Society's early years they gained a reputation for charismatic leaders whose revolutionary ideas fostered a willingness to disagree with the political and religious authority of the day. Thus, while Friends supported Oliver Cromwell in his efforts, they were more than willing to criticize him for his failure to pursue legal reforms.[11] Records show that at times, Friends even insinuated violence, for example, when Friends told seventeenth-century political leaders that if they did not provide justice to the masses, "they would be overturned like others before them."[12] Ultimately, however, the society proved to be much more interested in sharing their message of social justice rather than forcing it upon others. Nevertheless, their frank talk did place Friends at odds with Britain's political administration and, during the seventeenth century, authorities arrested Quakers as enemies of the state.[13] Later, in the eighteenth century, Friends experienced the same restrictions that Westminster imposed upon all dissenters.

The Society was a traveling ministry and from its beginning, both men and women Friends made their way to Ireland to preach as well as create a community. Although early on most Friends settled down to farm, a variety of factors, including war at the end of the seventeenth century and sporadic agricultural crisis, encouraged Quakers, especially those in the southern part of Ireland, to shift from agriculture to industry and gravitate toward towns, particularly Dublin.[14] By the eighteenth century, Friends could be found throughout the island playing an ever more prominent role in local industries as various as farming, shipping, printing, milling, and banking.[15] For example, Bewley's Cafes and Jacob's Biscuits, which remain popular in Ireland today, were two of a number of very successful Quaker businesses. In Dublin, where the majority of Irish Friends resided, Richard Webb was a successful printer, the Pims made their mark in shipping, draping, and the Irish railway system, the Shackletons ran a flour milling business, and the Roberts had cafes on the popular Grafton and Dame Streets.[16] The Hoggs were coffee and tea merchants and the Hallidays were grocers.[17] As long as members acted in good faith and paid all debt in a timely manner, it was acceptable for them to be in business. If, however, a Friend failed on either count, the Society might investigate and aid him if found deserving or disown if not.[18]

Thus, by the late eighteenth century, as Friends throughout Britain increasingly profited from the rapid advances in industrialization, they were now interacting more closely with political authorities both locally and nationally. In addition, while Friends still sought to separate themselves from mainstream society, they were decreasingly at odds with it; still social activists but no longer radical actors. In particular, for Irish Friends, events at the end of the eighteenth century may have furthered their acceptance of British authority.

As Ireland watched the political developments both in North America and later in France, a small group of well-educated Protestants, who had schooled themselves in the ideals of the Enlightenment, soon recognized both the injustices that Britain had imposed on Irish Catholics as well as the political and economic inequities between the two islands. The United Irishmen, an organization formed in 1791 by Presbyterian dissenters, demanded both political rights for Catholics as well as greater independence for Ireland from Westminster. Emboldened both by the American victory as well as hoped-for French support, the United Irishmen became increasingly vocal.[19]

The Religious Society of Friends, despite its pacifist stance, found its members increasingly caught up in this revolutionary agitation. Fox had established the Society as a radical response to the chaos of revolution, and Friends' daily lives were dedicated to the creation of an equitable society. Naturally, as revolutionaries in France, North America, and now Ireland were espousing similar ideals, Friends found themselves with an ideological family much larger than they could have ever hoped for.

The Society's stand against violence had been established in its early days and it expected Friends to renounce "fightings with outward weapons" as stated in the Quaker Peace Testimony presented to Charles II in 1660.[20] As the summer of 1798 approached and tensions as well as acts of violence increased, the Society's most common problem appeared to have been the possession of firearms by Friends who were unwilling to relinquish them because they too were targets.[21] However, there is also evidence that some Friends may have been actively sympathetic to the ideals of the revolutionaries. One of the best examples can be found in the diary of Mary Leadbeater, who revealed that the Friends of Ballitore, a village in County Kildare, not only had ties to revolutionary France, but also actively sympathized with the cause of the United Irishmen.[22] Indeed, it appears that Mary and her husband William had plans to relocate to France where they would participate in the establishment of a technical school that would provide both free and fee-paying education to children, thereby furthering the ideals of the Enlightenment. Due to the outbreak of war in 1793, in the end, neither Mary nor her husband went to France.[23] Ultimately, however, her sympathetic activity did not equate to espousal of violence and Leadbeater never faltered from her dedication to change through peaceful means.

When violence broke out, revolutionaries demanded that all take sides, and Friends were soon caught in the middle as they refused to declare allegiances. This quickly put members in danger. Leadbeater and the Friends of Ballitore were clearly caught.[24] Ballitore found itself in the midst of rebellion forces when on May 24, 1798, local men and women took up arms against the state's soldiers. Three days later the military burned the village and executed United Irish sympathizers.[25] Leadbeater and her family would survive the experience and rebuild, but such an encounter must have shaken everyone who witnessed the widespread bloody violence of the summer of 1798.

While evidence shows that by the late eighteenth century, Friend's earlier radicalism was already softening, for Irish Quakers, the events of 1798 may have furthered this progression. In other words, as their financial success required Friends to work with the mainstream, the violent end to the ideals of the Enlightenment may have also helped Friends to further reconsider their relationship with the establishment. Nevertheless, the Society did not completely leave its roots behind. In order to continue to express their desire for social and political change, the Religious Society of Friends shifted away from verbal support of radical politics toward social transformation through philanthropic activism.

IRISH FRIENDS AND THE GREAT FAMINE

The Rebellion of 1798 had revealed Ireland to be a possible back door to the invasion of England, and Prime Minster William Pitt, who also saw the economic potential of uniting the two countries, now eagerly pushed for the demise of Ireland's Parliament. The Union of 1800 brought an end to Ireland's political independence for over a hundred years, and this increasingly placed Ireland in a subservient position to the workshop of the world. Nineteenth-century Britain continued its impressive expansion, and soon enough the sun would never set on its empire. Ireland, as a result of changes in tariff laws, became Britain's breadbasket and was feeding the hungry workers of England's growing industrial towns. However, when the economic prosperity that the Napoleonic Wars fostered came to an end, Ireland found itself in an increasingly precarious position. While the price of grain dropped, tenants' rents remained high. Ireland's rising population, of which most were ultimately renting land from otherwise absentee landlords, was becoming almost solely dependent upon the potato.[26] Yet, by the 1840s the root crop had already proven to be unreliable, having failed sporadically during the early years of the nineteenth century.[27] Thus, when in the mid-nineteenth century the total failure of the potato occurred, the population of the island was decimated.

The famine of the 1840s was not the first time that Friends had organized to provide aid during times of agricultural crisis in Ireland, but it would be their greatest test.[28] In 1845, the blight appeared sporadically, but, with complete failure in 1846, Friends recognized that the hardship would be extensive and were among the first to organize relief efforts. Soon enough, members of the society were traveling through the nation sending back letters that discussed the growing calamity. Such letters were vital to the Friends' efforts to generate donations.[29] Correspondence sent by James Hack Tuke, a York Quaker who traveled throughout Ireland, clearly spelled out an essential part of the problem. Tuke wrote that most small farmers were "rack-rented tenants at will, and have no confidence in the justice or mercy of those who have the land."[30] In other words, small farmers were living with tenuous leases, being overcharged for the land they rented, and having little legal recourse to rectify the situation.

In 1846, under the direction of Jonathan Pim and Joseph Bewley, the society established the Central Relief Committee (CRC) of the Religious Society of Friends, which attempted to organize and direct aid to those in need. Friends worked to raise money and collect food, clothing, and other essentials.[31] Friends perceived the economic domino effect that would occur with the failure of the potato and recognized that the expected increase in the price of food would make it unaffordable for the poor, particularly because "wages given on public works were barely sufficient to support life . . . families, could not afford to spend any money except on food. The small shopkeepers consequently lost their trade."[32] This message was echoed by a letter from a Friend, forwarded to James Grogran, M.P., which described that many smallholders were totally reliant upon the potato. As a result, the poor were now completely dependent upon public works, whose payment "for want of cheap food, can barely supply the cravings of nature in a family of ordinary size."[33] Despite the natural rise in food prices, the British government neither increased the wages for public works nor sought to limit the price of food.[34] As one witness complained:

> Oatmeal which had up to a very late period been selling here at 14s. per cwt (112lbs), has within the last two weekly markets here risen to the exorbitant price of 18s. 6d. per cwt, placing it almost beyond the reach of the great bulk of the population . . . Flour and meal of every other description have risen proportionately in price and this too at a time when all employment, either upon public works or from farming operations, has ceased.[35]

Friends argued that many of Ireland's troubles resulted from Parliament's economic mismanagement and political malfeasance.[36] However, unlike the Society's early writings that called for the fundamental change of governmental structures, the CRC's criticism in its publication of the events of the famine, titled *Transactions of the Central Relief Committee of the Society of Friends During the Famine in Ireland 1846–7*, revealed Friends' moderating radicalism.[37] As recorded in *Transactions,* when the authors criticized the Corn Laws for keeping the price of grain high, they wrote using the passive voice and suggested that if the trade in corn had been unrestricted, "the price of food being allowed to sink to its natural level, would have placed bread and other cereal products within the reach of a larger class of people."[38] When chastising policies that sanctioned landlord absenteeism, Friends obliquely stabbed at the government for permitting landlords to have "availed themselves to a great extent of this fatal privilege."[39] Friends implied that if the government had not tolerated landlords' amassing great debts and had forced them to improve the land, the state of Irish tenants would have been less tenuous when agricultural disaster struck.[40]

When discussing the poor laws, *Transactions* correctly noted that "the law itself . . . was insufficient for relief of such distress."[41] To be fair, the creators of the poor laws had envisioned the workhouse as a place of refuge for elderly, orphans, and the ill and never imagined a catastrophe as great as the famine. Yet, Friends' language revealed the society's clear perception of the larger role that the government played in Ireland's endemic poverty. They were willing to criticize both the government's failure to invest in industry as well as solve the historic inequitable distribution of Irish land.[42] As the cosecretary of the CRC, Jonathan Pim, wrote: "The people lived on potatoes because they were poor; and they were poor because they could not obtain regular employment. This want of employment seems in great measure to have arisen from the state of the law, and the practice respecting the occupation and ownership of land."[43] While Pim's point shows his effort to assess clearly the roots of the problem, in truth, the want of regular employment was also the result of the minimal industrial development in Ireland, which aggravated the inequitable land distribution.[44]

While *Transactions* sought to criticize Britain's economic policies, the Friends' reproach of the British government was milder than that of their forebears. The Friends' unwillingness to clearly characterize the British government as an actor in the drama of the famine reflected the Society's steady integration into mainstream society. The Society of Friends, many of whose members ran profitable businesses, had certainly benefited from the government's economic adherence to laissez-faire policies, and explicit criticism could certainly have brought accusations of hypocrisy. Additionally, as will be shown later, the Friends' increasing acceptance if not advancement of Victorian social theories can be found elsewhere in the language of their records.

Throughout the early years of the crisis, the CRC established a variety of innovative programs. Most famously, in 1847, Friends established a soup shop in Dublin that offered soup twice a day. Instead of giving the broth away, Friends sold tickets for a penny to all comers so that persons could buy tickets and then donate them to the poor.[45] Other CRC activity included the provision of loans and seed to farmers and assistance to fishermen regarding the cost to repair equipment, and a clothing fund that was so successful they needed a large warehouse to receive, sort, and distribute garments.[46] In 1847, two ships with £10,000 worth of food sailed from Liverpool to western Irish ports.[47] Friends also donated money toward the establishment of training facilities in hopes of providing young people with alternative vocations.[48] Finally, the Committee eventually went so far as to buy a farm of over 400 acres in Colmanstown, County Galway, in hopes of soon turning a profit.[49] Although the famine raged on until 1851, by 1849 the CRC had concluded most of its relief efforts. One reason behind the early summation is that in 1847, the British government shifted away from public relief works and was increasingly unwilling to facilitate the Friends in their efforts to supply aid.[50] By 1849, CRC funds were depleted and the only project that remained for the long term was the model farm at Colmanstown.[51]

Surprisingly, Friends, who gave so much toward famine relief, felt that their efforts had been insufficient. The authors of *Transactions* inaccurately suggested that "we see but too clearly that we have failed in several undertakings in which we at first entertained sanguine hopes of success."[52] Helen Hatton argues that the Friends viewed their efforts toward famine relief as a business investment. If reviewed only for the overall effect that the Society had in Ireland, then the Religious Society of Friends did fail.[53] However, with hindsight, history shows that despite their small numbers the Religious Society of Friends offered one of the more important and well-known programs of famine relief. When writing *Transactions*, it seems likely that events were still too fresh for Friends to be able to clearly discuss their work during the famine. Impressively, the less than 3,000 members of the Religious Society of Friends in Ireland, with donations from the United States and England, raised over £200,000 in cash, food, and equipment toward famine relief.

Ultimately, the hard work done by the Society demonstrated that Friends rejected the providential arguments that God sent the crisis to punish the people of Ireland for their Roman Catholicism and feckless ways. In addition, Friends came out of the famine untainted; they had never participated in the proselytism that did occur.[54] Friends' innovative work to aid the suffering during the famine was an indication of their feeling of duty to all God's children, in whom they believed the Inner Light was reflected. Nevertheless, by the nineteenth century, many Friends had become successful within Britain's laissez-faire economic system, and *Transactions* revealed a softening of the Friends' tone when it came to criticizing the mainstream political authority. Despite their changing tone, *Transactions* showed that Friends clearly understood the injustices that the British political and economic system fostered.[55]

IRISH FRIENDS AND DUBLIN CHARITY

Throughout Ireland, membership in the society never reached more than a few thousand. Their largest contingent was in Dublin, where census figures show that the city's population between 1861 and 1881 dropped from 254,808 to 249,602, while Friends' numbers increased from 812 in 1863 to 915 by 1880.[56] Hence they consisted of less than one percent of the city's population. As mentioned above, by the nineteenth century, Dublin Friends had established many successful businesses. Nevertheless, the fruits of their labor had increasingly tempted some Friends away from the simple lifestyle to which Fox had called Quakers to live.[57] As an American Friend who visited Ireland in the nineteenth century noted, "she was greatly surprised by the lavish style and dress of Irish Friends and the abundant entertainment."[58]

Importantly, however, one place where Friends sought to remain above the fray was in relation to the nation's religious divisions. While sectarian tensions characterized much of Ireland's charitable infrastructure, there were those who sought to avoid such battles and offer aid without religious qualification. Most prominent of these was the Religious Society of Friends. This is not to say that Friends did not seek to bring the Christian message to those they helped, but conversion was not part of the society's agenda.[59]

Throughout the nineteenth century Friends' names can be found among many of Dublin's charities as well as on the committees of other organizations that offered social support, including hospitals and workhouses. Dublin Friends had long been in the charity business, as exemplified by the Meath Place Mission, which Friends founded in 1686. The mission's records reveal that it offered the poor a variety of activities including a Day School, Mothers' Meetings, and a Friends Adult School. The Friends' Ragged School, the records noted with regret, was only open one day per week. As the ragged school minutes suggested, this was a great disadvantage because during the rest of the week, the children were "surrounded by the worst forms of evil."[60] This evil, as the records go on to suggest, was the local adults who did not amend their sinful habits. Here, Friends, like so many local philanthropists, insinuated that it was sin that brought the poor to, and maintained them in, poverty.[61]

Meath Place also housed the Sick Poor Institute, a medical dispensary established in 1794, for the relief of the poor neighborhoods in Dublin where "there was enough disease and poverty to call into action the sympathies of the benevolent."[62] To complement the work of the Sick Poor Institute, in 1816 Meath Place's Women's Committee opened the Dorset Nourishment Dispensary, which supplied medical and surgical assistance and facilities in which food and comfort insured recovery.[63] This dispensary was part of a larger network of similar medical facilities that dotted the nation. While by the early nineteenth century Ireland had a well-established network of hospitals, there were also smaller facilities and country infirmaries that sought to serve the sick.[64] The Dorset Nourishment Dispensary eventually became part of a network of voluntary dispensaries throughout Ireland that depended on private funds to survive.[65] The mission's medical staff assisted patients on-site, or visited those who could not make their way to the institute from their own "miserable dwellings."[66] Daily, local medical officers recommended more than one hundred persons who needed medical attention.[67]

While it was for the poor that Friends established the Sick Poor Institute and to whom the dispensary gave aid, it is noteworthy that in 1850 the records stated that this work acted as a "break-water to stem the tide of epidemics which, but for such a defense, might have poured a destructive torrent upon the wealthier and more favoured districts of the city."[68] Here Friends indicated that while the primary role for the institute was the provision of aid to the poor, it also worked as a barrier that could save the wealthy not only from the suffering but also from the stigma of the diseases of poverty such as dysentery, typhus, or cholera. Disease did not recognize class boundaries, and Friends were not immune from the desire to maintain the neighborhood barriers that divided rich and poor. Many Friends, although certainly not all, had settled in wealthier regions where they increasingly enjoyed the pleasures afforded by financial success.[69]

Another innovative service of Meath Place was the Liberty Crèche, opened in 1824. The crèche provided a stable and safe environment for children and permitted parents to work without fear for their children's safety.[70] Women Friends recognized that it was essential for poor women to work outside the home and acknowledged that many had no one with whom they could leave their youngsters.[71] For a penny per day, the Liberty Crèche accepted children from "respectable women" who, nevertheless, needed to earn an income.[72] Yet, their innovation went only so far, as Quakers defined "respectable" as women who were either married or widowed. Revealingly, the crèche did not actually accept children of unmarried mothers until 1953.[73] Surprisingly, while Friends promoted many unconventional social opinions including that of women's equality, Friends limited the crèche to "respectable" women. It is here we see Friends adopting a more conservative social agenda, one that would please Ireland's middle class—persons with whom Dublin Friends now more closely associated.[74]

In 1860 Friends established the Strand Street Institute, which housed a variety of programs including Sunday schools, sewing circles, young men and women's meetings, Bible classes, and industrial employment training. Strand Street sought to generate income through subscriptions, fundraisers, and the sale of finished goods. Friends established this lifeline for their community by supplying the poor with everything from shelter and a hot meal to literacy classes. The Strand Street Institute, located at 66 and 67 Great Strand Street in Dublin, held a diversity of programs on a variety of days:

Ragged School Free Breakfast	Sunday 8 to 9:30 A.M.
Sabbath School for Boys, Girls & Infants	Sunday 8:30 to 9:40 A.M.
Bible Classes for Young Men	Sunday 8:30 to 9:40 A.M.
Bible Classes for Young Women	Sunday 8:30 to 9:40 A.M.
Flower Mission	Sunday 9:40 A.M.

Men's Conversational Bible Class	Sunday 3:30 P.M.
Meeting for Boys and Girls	Sunday 5 P.M.
Gospel Meeting	Tuesday 8 P.M.
Mothers' Meeting	Tuesday & Wed 3 to 5 P.M.
Young Women's Association	Wednesday 8 P.M.
Girls' Sewing Class	Tuesday 4 P.M.
Youth Christian Association	Thursday 8 P.M.

Total Abstinence Association, each alternate Monday evening. Library for adults, open on Sunday 5 P.M. and Thursday 9:30 P.M.[75]

Of the many activities housed under Strand Street's roof, the Mothers' Meeting Association, which was a common event for many nineteenth-century charities, supplied a space for poor women to comfortably gather.[76] The Association provided food, drink, and often Scripture readings. Here, Friends desired to instill diligence into their "poorer sisters" to improve their habits of economy and "better [home] management—the simple tales of a wife's sacrifice or a mother's love."[77] By improving the fiscal habits of mothers, Friends believed that they would then pass on these lessons to their husbands and children. In addition to on-site activities, the Mothers' Meeting Committee raised money in order to send women into the neighborhoods to read the Bible to the poor. Through encouraging "temperance, truth or honesty," women Friends reinforced the call for poor women to be sober, industrious, and moral.[78]

The Strand Street Institute, like most charities, continually advocated that the poor spend their money wisely. The Mothers' Meetings encouraged the women to put away small amounts in a savings bank so that if an emergency arose they would have the funds upon which to rely. Yet, at the same time, the institute did not give cash payment for the women's sewing work. For example, the records of 1896 noted, "when the class is over they receive payment in orders for coal, for clothing, or for provisions. Some of them allow the money to stand to their credit for future use."[79] Friends likely hoped their fiscal advice would instill a sense of moderation, frugality, and industry into these poor women. However, while Friends encouraged the poor to save their money, they did not trust the poor to actually do so. Friends' records expressed that they did not believe that the women could refuse the temptations offered by "the public houses which surround us."[80] Quakers may have accepted contemporary theories that the poor were inclined to waste what little they earned and thus needed to be shown how to save.[81] However, Friends' own records suggested that this assumption may have been presumptuous. On Friday afternoons among the group of women sewing and reading, only "occasionally one is partially drunk and abusive," while the rest appeared to behave with decorum.[82]

In 1883, Strand Street established a ragged school on its premises. During the school's first year, prior to the morning classes, Friends supplied bread to the children, but within a year, the charity offered them a free breakfast.[83] The breakfast may have been the most nutritious meal of the children's day, as so many of the parents could only provide their children with little more than bread and cheese. Like most charities, Strand Street sought to train the children in some useful occupation. Girls learned to sew their own clothing, but, as another way of encouraging industry and discouraging total reliance upon the largesse of others, they were expected to pay for their own materials. Naturally, the school taught boys light carpentry, making "picture frames, cane mats and baskets, illuminating texts, etc."[84] While offering the children more skilled activities may have been beyond the charity's financial ability, it was also true that the training that the ragged school provided maintained the children in the station to which they had been born. Hence, given the Friends' call to reject social hierarchy, employing such traditional charitable activities also communicated their willingness to preserve the class divisions that Victorian society had increasingly hardened. Of course, the ragged school included prayer and Scripture readings in the cycle of the school day, hoping to impart the lessons of moral and ethical behavior.[85]

Friends also saw the need to assist young adults, many of whom faced difficulties during this awkward stage of their lives. In 1883, Friends founded the Young Women's Association for those employed in shops or as domestics. The fact that Friends limited aid to the employed may have reflected traditional Victorian notions regarding the poor: they were unemployed because they were lazy and sinful and, thus, employed young women were such due to their hard work and moral superiority. On the other hand, given Dublin's few employment options, not to limit membership may have resulted in an overwhelming flood of applications for assistance.[86] The Association held meetings every Wednesday evening and included Bible readings, lessons on sewing, or "work for some charitable object."[87] While Friends hoped that the classes would provide the young women with an education and thus broaden their opportunities, most important, Friends hoped the young women would mimic their Quaker mentors, who were offering themselves as moral role models.

Young men were not to be left out, and in 1885 Friends purchased a dormitory to provide shelter for males. The young men were not merely given residence in the home, but instead a bed and meal came at the cost of two pennies. Not unlike their fellow philanthropists, Friends hoped to make young lads industrious so that they would "feel more dependent on their own efforts for support."[88] Strand Street hoped to provide teenagers with a sense of pride in their independence that could inspire them to respect their own community and thus become self-supporting members of it.

Strand Street continued its important work into the twentieth century, giving relief to the desperately poor residents of Dublin's slums.[89] The numbers that Friends reached, the diversity of activities they offered, and the funds raised all furnish evidence that Strand Street was highly successful in helping many of Dublin's poor. For example, and not unlike many local charities, women Friends also visited the Dublin poor in their own homes in hopes of bringing aid, providing advice, and teaching sanitary and economic techniques. In 1875 the committee noted that the number of visits had dropped from the previous year to 888, "which we regret, for we consider this . . . work of great importance."[90] While Friends may have seen this drop as a reflection of a need to redouble their efforts, nevertheless, this was evidence of the extensive time and energy these volunteers donated to those in need.

Women Friends spearheaded many innovative programs to help the poor, particularly poor women of the community.[91] In 1876, Friend Mary Edmundson helped to establish and was honorary secretary for Dublin's Prison Gate Mission, which worked to aid women recently released from prison.[92] The committee that ran the mission met every two weeks and included men and women Friends as well non-Friends. Surviving committee minutes detailed the mission's activities from the very mundane, such as complaining about the price of bread, to the more pragmatic task of procuring washing contracts from the Meath and Adelaide Hospitals.[93] The records provided little detail about the members of the Prison Gate Mission's governing body. Nevertheless, similar to the majority of lay charities in Dublin, it was run by a group of upper-class persons who attempted both to alleviate suffering as well as to change the habits of the poor. The women volunteers went to the gates of Dublin's Grangegorman Street Prison during the morning and offered recently released women a free breakfast and encouraged them to come to the mission. Volunteers also involved themselves in training classes, led scripture readings, and oversaw the hiring of the matrons and other women who worked for the mission.

The mission offered some women housing and gave daily meals to all who worked for it. Prison Gate trained women in laundering and sewing, while it attempted to find employment for some, or help others to emigrate.[94] While the Prison Gate Mission offered religious service during its daily schedule, like all Quaker charities, it did not restrict aid on the basis of religious denomination. George Williams described in his *Dublin Charities: A Handbook* that volunteers from the Prison Gate Mission met women "as they leave prison, in order to try and reclaim them from their evil life and companions . . . also to afford a shelter to young women who come up from the country, have been unable to find employment, and wish to be saved from falling into evil ways."[95] The Prison Gate Mission did limit itself to women who had served very brief prison terms, thereby reflecting a general theme by social activists that women who had a history of criminal activity or prostitution were irredeemable.[96] The mission desired to reform the women: "if willing to work, they are put into the sewing class, disciplined if possible, and made industrious, and then sent home or to service or into the laundry."[97] It did have some successes and sent some girls out to local employers.[98]

The Prison Gate Mission sought to provide activity for the women that might eventually gain them employment but, like most charities, the training was generally in low-skilled occupations, as the Prison Gate's laundry emphasized. Not only did the laundry provide income, it also played the dual role of encouraging the theme of cleanliness that was part of the nineteenth-century sanitary mission. Charities consistently trained women as laundresses, focusing on the cleansing of sullied material. While laundering was certainly a trade in which women could find employment, having these women, whom charity workers believed were "soiled," spend their days washing may be considered a metaphor for spiritual and bodily cleanliness. Philanthropists may have subconsciously thought that by training these women in the hard work of washing away stains they were also teaching them to avoid the dirt of sin.

Regardless, the economic lifeline for the charity was the laundry. This was shown when in 1883 the charity sought to procure a horse and cart in order to improve the quantity and promptness of laundry deliveries. A few months later, the board discussed improvements and agreed to increase the heating power of one of the drying closets at a cost of £7.[99] Unfortunately, neither income from the laundry, subscriptions, nor donations covered the cost of providing for dormitory, breakfast, and other essentials; but the mission remained ever vigilant for the procurement of other laundry contracts.[100] Consistently, the committee sought out other opportunities to raise money.[101] Other efforts included exhibiting the women's work in festivals such as the Edinburgh Industrial Exhibitions in 1886 or the Exhibitions of Women's Industry in Glasgow in 1888.[102] Interestingly, in 1887, the mission provided women with the opportunity to learn carpet weaving and glove making.[103] Here, the Prison Gate Mission sought to provide women with a skill that held the potential of being more financially rewarding.[104]

In another effort to raise cash, the mission attempted to secure the patronage of a titled person to be associated with the mission's work in hopes of generating more donations. The secretary read a letter that stated that, "owing to the number of engagements which the Countess of Aberdeen had at present she could not name a day for visiting the missions but that later on she hoped to do so."[105] Extant charity pamphlets reveal the varieties of dignitaries who sponsored Irish charities, including a selection of aristocratic peers. For example, in 1813 the Dublin Female Penitentiary listed the Viscountess Lorton as patroness; in 1843 the Magdalen Asylum's Vice Patroness was the Dowager Lady Powerscourt; in 1863 the Protestant Orphan Society included the Marquis of Downshire and the Lord Bishop of Meath as patrons; and in 1900 St. Patrick's Nurses Home named the Lady Ardilaun and the Countess of Meath as supporters. The higher the dignitary's profile, charities believed, the more likely a charity was to secure generous donations. Nevertheless, even with the various fundraising-activities, the Prison Gate Mission's accounts were often overdrawn and, like many charities, the mission's finances grew tighter as early enthusiasm for the charity waned.[106]

From 1883–1885 the minutes noted that the Prison Gate Mission was in search of another building that it could convert into a dormitory for some of the women at the mission.[107] Similar to other philanthropic organizations that sought to assist fallen women, the Prison Gate Mission's desire to supply housing not only served a very important practical need for the women but also provided the mission with a captive audience. Prison Gate proposed that the upper rooms of the dormitory be used by younger women, in hopes of keeping them from wandering the streets in the evening and meeting up with unsavory characters.[108] They wanted to keep these younger women away from older or more "experienced" women because, as philanthropist Mary Carpenter suggested, reformatories should not expose young girls to those with sexual experience because "the presence of a girl who has mysterious and forbidden knowledge is a most dangerous stimulant to evil."[109] In keeping with this effort the Prison Gate sent some of its younger attendees to the Girls Training Home on Lower Baggot St. The home was intended for girls "in danger from bad companions or bad homes," and it sought to help girls "of any religion, and those in danger from their surroundings of growing up to recruit the ranks of the fallen."[110] Friends' assumption of their particular duty to restrain young women in order to save them from bad companions reflected acceptance of the Victorian middle-class belief that younger women were both more easily saved as well as more easily seduced and therefore more in need of protection.

While charities believed the young to be more easily reformed, the language of charity reflected their overall understanding that the poor needed to be guided by those above them in social rank. While women Friends hoped that they were role models for penitents, they also often discussed the mission's inmates as children and, like children, they were rewarded if good and punished if bad. For example, during a meeting in December of 1885, Miss Foot, the Prison Gate Mission's matron, brought notice that nine of the women had been disorderly at Christmas and should be brought before the committee at the next meeting.[111] On January

14, 1886, when the next meeting occurred, inexplicably only four of the nine women appeared before the committee to be reprimanded. The charity then resolved that "Miss Foot should kindly draft a code of rules for the better keeping of order in the institution to be submitted at next meeting."[112] The fact that the charity wanted to impose further restrictions emphasizes that it not only thought of the women as lacking in self-control, it treated them as such.[113]

The Prison Gate Mission's work was typical of many of the charities that dealt with reformed prisoners or ex-prostitutes. While the Prison Gate Mission could not confine the women, it sought to control their behavior through the implementation of strict rules upon those who partook of its services.[114] Ultimately, whether the women emigrated or found a job in Ireland, the Prison Gate Mission attempted to aid some of the most vulnerable in Irish society.[115]

A CHANGING SOCIETY

The nineteenth century was a time of great change for the Religious Society of Friends in Ireland. The society moved to direct intervention via philanthropy, leaving behind their earlier radicalism. During the nineteenth century, Friends' businesses became increasingly successful and Friends involved themselves in local politics. As some Friends enjoyed the fruits of their labor, they drifted farther from the radical tenets upon which Fox had founded the society. While Friends acknowledged that economics and governmental mismanagement contributed to poverty, their records included some of the same rhetoric as their middle-class brothers and sisters by suggesting that the poor contributed to their fate due to personal sin.

Yet, the Society continued to cling to some of its nontraditional ideas, and it never failed to encourage women to have a visible role in Quaker activities as well as authority within the Society.[116] This is not to say that women Friends had equal opportunity, nor were women permitted to hold any of the Society's top offices.[117] Such limitations did not deter them, however, and throughout the century women Friends were not only activists for the poor of the city, but at the same time, they sought to break down the barriers that society had placed before all women.

As a result of such encouragement, Quaker women were among the more prominent activists for international causes, including antislavery and women's suffrage.[118] In Ireland, one of the most well known Quaker women was Anna Haslam.[119] Haslam began her public life by working for improved opportunities for women's education but eventually moved into political activism when she founded the Dublin Women's Suffrage Association in 1876.[120] For this, Dublin's first suffrage organization, Anna served first as secretary and eventually as president for life, organizing the association's public meetings, writing campaigns, publications, and speaking engagements.[121] By the century's end, women could vote for poor law guardians, while Haslam herself lived to vote in the 1918 general elections.[122] The Religious Society of Friends, from its foundation, expected its members to be active in ending injustice, and it is this work for which the Society believed women's contribution to be particularly critical. Women such as the Prison Gate's Mary Edmundson or Anna Haslam were the type of social activists whom the Society of Friends encouraged and facilitated.

In Dublin's tense atmosphere, where sectarian hostilities could at times flare, the Religious Society of Friends offered aid to all in need regardless of creed. The tensions and hostilities among Dublin's charities and poor assistance organizations (workhouses, etc.) should not be underestimated. While scripture readings and Bible school were part of their mission to the poor, Friends were not proselytizers. The poor of Dublin benefited immeasurably from the work of the Religious Society of Friends, who offered them a safe environment in which to find succor. While the poor may have appreciated the unencumbered aid, it seems that the nonsectarian attitude taken by Friends had little influence upon the behavior of their fellow philanthropists, and late in the nineteenth century, Dublin's charities continued to be organized along denominational lines.

By the nineteenth century, in Dublin, where many Friends had found financial success, some had also adopted a comfortable lifestyle. The laissez-faire economic policies of the British government helped their businesses to profit, and Dublin Friends were involved in local politics as well as the administration of local relief agencies. Yet, for Friends to have harshly criticized the government would not only have risked accusations of hypocrisy, but possibly brought criticism that could have threatened their financial and social successes. The nineteenth century may have tested the Religious Society of Friends' original tenets, and it is within their charities that we may find their radical nature slowly adapting to the weighty responsibilities and painful trials that came with financial and social success. In the final assessment, however, it must be remembered that Ireland benefited from the efforts of the members of the Religious Society of Friends, and their charitable innovations were the models that other agencies, including the British government, sought to emulate.

NOTES

1. Friends' Ragged School, henceforth FRS (1905), p. 7. These records are contained in the Friends library in Dublin, Swanbrook House.

2. Maurice J. Wigham, *The Irish Quakers: A Short History of the Religious Society of Friends in Ireland* (Dublin: Historical Committee of the Religious Society of Friends in Ireland, 1992), p. 91.

3. See Phil Kilroy, "Quaker Women in Ireland, 1660–1740," *Irish Journal of Feminist Studies* 2, 2 (Winter 1997), p. 1. The term Quaker will be used sparingly, and, in general, members and the Society will be referred to as Friends.

4. See Wigham, *The Irish Quakers,* pp. 60–61. Those who chose to marry a non-Quaker could be disowned.

5. Alan Cole, "The Quakers and the English Revolution," *Past and Present* 10 (November 1956), p. 48.

6. Helen Hatton, *The Largest Amount of Good: Quaker Relief in Ireland, 1654–1921* (Montreal: McGill-Queens University Press, 1993), p. 24. Apparently, Fox was a shrewd businessman. See Michael Mullett, "George Fox and the Origins of Quakerism," *History Today* 41 (1991), p. 30.

7. "A Quaker must act on the direction of God's presence within every person, the Inner Light, a spirit moving without a theoretical superstructure." Hatton, *The Largest Amount of Good,* p. 27. See also Richard S. Harrison, "Spiritual Perception and the Evolution of the Irish Quakers," in *The Religion of Irish Dissent 1650–1800,* ed. Kevin Herlihy (Dublin: Four Courts Press, 1996), p. 69.

8. Emily Janes, "On the Association Work of Women in Religion and Philanthropy," in *Woman's Mission: A Series of Congress Papers on the Philanthropic Work of Women,* ed. Baroness Angela Burdett-Coutts (London: Sampson, Low, Marson & Co., 1893), p. 140.

9. See Sheila Wright, "Quakerism and Its Implications for Quaker Women: The Women Itinerant Ministers of York Meeting, 1780–1840," in *Women in the Church,* ed. W. J. Sheils and Diana Wood (London: Basil Blackwell, 1990), pp. 403–14; and Jean R. Soderlund, "Women's Authority in Pennsylvania and New Jersey Quaker Meetings, 1680–1760," *William and Mary Quarterly* 44, 4 (October 1987), pp. 722–49.

10. See Margaret Morris Haviland, "Beyond Women's Sphere: Young Quaker Women and the Veil of Charity in Philadelphia, 1790–1810," *The William and Mary Quarterly* 51, 3 (July 1994), pp. 419–46.

11. Cole, "The Quakers and the English Revolution," p. 44.

12. Cole, "The Quakers and the English Revolution," p. 41.

13. Wigham, *The Irish Quakers,* p. 23. Both Hatton and Wigham suggest that Friends' charitable work and its highly ordered style may have originated out of the Society's early days and their "Meetings for Suffering," in which Friends worked to help members who had been arrested by the British authorities. Hatton, *The Largest Amount of Good,* pp. 18–19; Wigham, *The Irish Quakers,* pp. 24, 28, 63–67. See also James Walvin, *The Quakers: Money and Morals* (London: John Murray Publishing, 1997), pp. 81–90.

14. Wigham, *The Irish Quakers,* p. 44.

15. Wigham, *The Irish Quakers,* pp. 32, 36, 44. See also Arthur P. Williamson, "Enterprise, Industrial Development and Social Planning: Quakers and the Emergence of the Textile Industry in Ireland," *Planning Perspectives* 7 (1992), pp. 303–28.

16. Vicky Cremin, *The Liberty Crèche 1893–1993* (Dublin: n.p., 1993), p. 6.

17. Wigham, *The Irish Quakers,* pp. 90–91; Hatton, *The Largest Amount of Good,* p. 259.

18. Wigham, *The Irish Quakers,* p. 59.

19. 1798 has received a good deal of attention. Of the many sources, see David Dickson, Dáire Keogh, and Kevin Whelan, *The United Irishmen: Republicanism, Rad-*

icalism and Rebellion (Dublin: Lilliput Press, 1993); and Jim Smyth, *Men of No Property: Irish Radicals and Popular Politics in the Late Eighteenth Century* (New York: St. Martin's Press, 1998).

20. Glynn Douglass, *Friends and 1798: Quaker Witness to Non-Violence in 18th Century Ireland* (Dublin: Historical Committee of the Religious Society of Friends in Ireland, 1998), p. 3.

21. Douglass, *Friends and 1798*, pp. 21–22.

22. Kevin O'Neill suggests that despite Leadbeater's commitment to nonviolence, "her sympathies and hopes were in close alignment with radical republicanism during the years of upheaval." Kevin O'Neill, "Mary Shackleton Leadbeater: Peaceful Rebel," in *The Women of 1798*, ed. Dáire Keogh and Nicholas Furlong (Dublin: Four Courts Press, 1998), p. 140. See also Kevin O'Neill, " 'Almost a Gentlewoman': Gender and Adolescence in the Diary of Mary Shackleton," in *Chattel, Servant or Citizen: Women's Status in Church, State and Society*, ed. Mary O'Dowd and Sabine Wichert (Belfast: Institute of Irish Studies, 1995), pp. 91–102.

23. O'Neill, "Mary Shackleton Leadbeater," p. 153. Leadbeater also offered moral support to Malachi Delany, an organizer for the United Irishmen. John D. Beatty, ed., *Protestant Women's Narratives of the Irish Rebellion of 1798* (Dublin: Four Courts Press, 2001), p. 196.

24. O'Neill, "Mary Shackleton Leadbeater," pp. 144–46.

25. O'Neill, "Mary Shackleton Leadbeater" p. 161.

26. Cormac Ó Gráda, *The Great Irish Famine* (London: MacMillan Press, 1989), p. 25. By the 1840s, evidence suggests that at least half of the population of eight million relied heavily upon the potato as their only source of sustenance.

27. Ó Gráda, *The Great Irish Famine*, pp. 20–21.

28. Irish and English Friends sought to provide aid during the agrarian problems that visited Ireland in the early part of the century. See Hatton, *The Largest Amount of Good*, pp. 58–59.

29. William Forster and James Hack Tuke, among others, traveled throughout Ireland describing the miserable state of the people—particularly of the west. Hatton, *The Largest Amount of Good*, pp. 86–91. See also Rob Goodbody, *A Suitable Channel: Quaker Relief in the Great Famine* (Bray: Pale Publishing, 1995), pp. 25–27.

30. James H. Tuke, *A Visit to Connaught in the Autumn of 1847* (A letter addressed to the Central Relief Committee of the Society of Friends, Dublin), p. 14.

31. The individual members of the CRC not only donated money but also a great deal of their time. Goodbody, *A Suitable Channel*, p. 13. Friends sometimes gathered as many as three days a week to survey applications for aid.

32. Religious Society of Friends, *Transactions of the Central Relief Committee of the Society of Friends during the Famine in Ireland 1846–7*, henceforth *Transactions* (Dublin: Hodges & Smith, 1852), pp. 52–53.

33. Letter to Edward Grogran, Esq., M.P., for Presentation to the House of Commons, Dublin 13th of Eleventh Month, 1846.

34. Mary E. Daly,"The Operations of Famine Relief," in *The Great Irish Famine*, ed. Cathal Póitéir (Dublin: Mercier Press, 1995), pp. 130–31.

35. "Letter to T. N. Redington from James Conry," cited in Liam Swords, *In Their Own Words: The Famine in North Connacht 1845–49* (Dublin: The Columba Press, 1999), p. 71.

36. Hatton, *The Largest Amount of Good*, p. 64. Quakers knew that since the late

eighteenth century exports from the country had risen dramatically while the state of the peasantry remained unchanged.

37. Mullett, "George Fox," p. 28; Hugh Barbour and J. William Frost, *The Quakers* (Westport, Conn.: Greenwood Press, 1988).

38. Religious Society of Friends, *Transactions*, p. 19. The Corn Laws triggered the application of tariffs on foreign corn if domestic prices fell below a certain price. The Corn Laws were ended in 1846.

39. Ibid.

40. Religious Society of Friends, *Transactions*, p. 10.

41. Religious Society of Friends, *Transactions*, p. 13.

42. Hatton, *The Largest Amount of Good*, p. 64.

43. Religious Society of Friends, *Transactions*, p. 9.

44. British legislation had worked to hinder Irish competition and severely undermined Ireland's cotton, silk, and wool industries, which then steadily suffered economic retraction. In 1699 Parliament forbade the export of Irish woolens, and the silk trade was devastated when Parliament reduced the tariffs on Italian silks in 1824. "By 1832, fewer than 150 looms remained." Joseph V. O'Brien, *"Dear Dirty Dublin": A City in Distress, 1899–1916* (Berkeley: University of California Press, 1982), p. 10.

45. The British government later established soup shops based on the Quaker model. Goodbody, *A Suitable Channel*, p. 29; Religious Society of Friends, *Transactions*, p. 53. Hatton records that a Friend made a donation of fifty soup boilers, which were so large that "after the Famine they were used as watering troughs for cattle, which occasionally drowned in them." Hatton, *The Largest Amount of Good*, p. 105.

46. Religious Society of Friends, *Transactions*, p. 70.

47. Wigham, *The Irish Quakers*, p. 86; Hatton, *The Largest Amount of Good*, p. 156; Goodbody, *A Suitable Channel*, p. 34.

48. Religious Society of Friends, *Transactions*, p. 77.

49. Wigham, *The Irish Quakers*, p. 87; Religious Society of Friends, *Transactions*, p. 95.

50. This early assistance included free shipping and storage of food. Wigham, *The Irish Quakers*, p. 86.

51. Wigham, *The Irish Quakers*, p. 87. When agrarian crisis occurred again in 1863, Friends sold the farm and gave away the money.

52. Religious Society of Friends, *Transactions*, pp. 5, 445. "In reviewing our proceedings for the two years and a half which have elapsed since the formation of this association, and in contemplating the present unhappy condition of our county, the conviction is painfully forced on us, that the public bounty distributed through us . . . whatever may have been their value in affording temporary alleviation of wide-spread misery, have produced scarcely any permanently useful results."

53. Hatton, *The Largest Amount of Good*, p. 267. See also Thomas P. O'Neill, "The Society of Friends and the Great Famine," *Studies* 39 (1950), pp. 203–13.

54. See Irene Whelan, "The Stigma of Souperism," in Cathal, *The Great Irish Famine*, pp. 135–54; and Hazel Waters, "The Great Famine and the Rise of Anti-Irish Racism," *Race & Class* 37, 1 (1995), pp. 95–108.

55. It must be noted that blame for increasing the suffering of many can also

be placed upon Irish farmers who, during the famine, hoarded food in order to profit from price increases. See Cormac Ó Gráda, *Black '47 and Beyond: The Great Irish Famine in History, Economy and Memory* (Princeton, N.J.: Princeton University Press, 1999), p. 135.

56. However, during this time, the population of Dublin's suburbs rose from 70,323 to 95,454. Daly, *Dublin: The Deposed Capital* (Cork: Cork University Press, 1984), p. 3; Prunty, *Dublin Slums 1800–1925* (Dublin: Irish Academic Press, 1997), p. 14; Swanbrook House Library, Religious Society of Friends Record of Statistics (1863; 1880).

57. In the early nineteenth century the society experienced a split and there appeared a more puritan form of Quakers known as the "White Quakers." It seems that some Quakers were increasingly unhappy with "the hypocrisy of preaching simplicity and otherworldliness from a position of more than comfortable affluence." Wigham, *The Irish Quakers*, p. 80. See also Charles Dellheim, "The Creation of a Company Culture: Cadburys, 1861–1931," *The American Historical Review* 92, 1 (February 1987): p. 15.

58. Wigham, *Quakers in Ireland*, p. 58; Walvin, *The Quakers*, pp. 58–59.

59. This may stem from Fox's desire for discipline of his followers and fear that overly enthusiastic converts could "lead to excesses and false doctrine." Hatton, *The Largest Amount of Good*, p. 18.

60. Meath Place offered children a ragged school that supplied a free breakfast to students. FRS (1905), p. 7.

61. Ibid.

62. The Sick Poor Institute employed six physicians, two surgeons, and an apothecary to help the local poor. Sick Poor Institute, henceforth SPI (1848), p. 3.

63. Cremin, *The Liberty Crèche*, p. 4.

64. Ronald D. Cassall, *Medical Charities, Medical Politics: The Irish Dispensary System and the Poor Law, 1836–1872* (Suffolk: Royal Historical Society, 1997), p. 1.

65. The Medical Charities (Ireland) Act, 1851, placed the dispensary system under the administration of the Irish Poor Law Commission, which became the equivalent of a national board of health. Cassall, *Medical Charities, Medical Politics*, p. 78. See also Helen Burke, *The People and the Poor Law in Nineteenth Century Ireland* (London: George Philip Services, 1987), pp. 153–55.

66. Cremin, *The Liberty Crèche*, p. 4.

67. Ibid.

68. SPI (1850), p. 5.

69. The Dorset Street Dispensary persevered into the twentieth century, eventually hiring nurses to work with the poor throughout the slums of Dublin.

70. See Cremin, *The Liberty Crèche*, pp. 8–10.

71. It was not uncommon for poor women to leave their children alone or in the care of older siblings because they knew of no person or place to turn to for help. However, this was not always the case. Neighbors often helped neighbors in the care and discipline of children. See Ellen Ross, *Love and Toil: Motherhood in Outcast London, 1870–1918* (New York: Oxford University Press, 1993); and Sonya Rose, *Limited Livelihoods: Gender and Class in Nineteenth-Century England* (Berkeley: University of California Press, 1993).

72. Cremin, *The Liberty Crèche*, p. 1. The Liberty Crèche was one of the first

institutions in Dublin to offer day care to working mothers, and between 1893 and 1896 the crèche took in on average 61 children each day.

73. Cremin, *The Liberty Crèche,* p. 1; Luddy, *Women and Philanthropy in Nineteenth Century Ireland* (New York: Cambridge University Press, 1995), p. 89. Interestingly, in 1943 the Liberty Crèche committee expressed concern about this policy, but the matron blamed the other mothers, stating that they would not send their children to the school if an unmarried mother's child was accepted. Cremin, *The Liberty Crèche,* p. 1.

74. The Liberty Crèche was not alone. Rosa Barrett's Cottage Home for Little Children required proof of parents' marriage for any children it accepted. Cottage Home for Little Children (1882).

75. Strand Street Institute, henceforth SSI (1884), p. 2. Regarding Irish Friends and alcohol, see Elizabeth Malcolm, *"Ireland Sober, Ireland Free": Drink and Temperance in Nineteenth-Century Ireland* (Dublin: Gill & MacMillan, 1986), pp. 66–67; Wigham, *The Irish Quakers,* pp. 75, 90; and Goodbody, *A Suitable Channel,* p. 74.

76. See F. K. Prochaska, "A Mother's Country: Mothers' Meetings and Family Welfare in Britain, 1850–1950," *History* 74 (October 1989), p. 394.

77. SSI (1871), p. 16.

78. Ibid. If accurate, the numbers that appeared at these events must have been overwhelming, as well as a reflection on Dublin's impoverished population, as the Mothers' Meeting recorded that during 1869, three hundred to four hundred women attended and provided "their cheerful faces and pleased attention throughout." SSI (1869), p. 20.

79. SSI (1896), p. 19.

80. Ibid.

81. See Paul Johnson, "Class Law in Victorian England," *Past and Present* 141 (November 1993), pp. 147–69; and David Phillips, " 'A New Engine of Power and Authority': Institutionalization of Law-Enforcement in England 1780–1830," in *Crime and Law: The Social History of Crime in Western Europe Since 1500,* ed. V. A. C. Gatrell, Bruce Lenman, and Geoffrey Parker (London: Europa, 1980), pp. 155–89.

82. SSI (1896), p. 19. The Quakers had already addressed the importance of abstinence years earlier in 1878 when they sought to establish a "Total Abstinence Union," which, Friends hoped, would be "productive of good, not to the Mothers only but to their families." SSI (1878), p. 12.

83. SSI (1883), p. 10. In 1883, the funds raised for the children's breakfast-fund was approximately £44.

84. SSI (1896), p. 20.

85. In 1896 the records show that the ragged school added marching to the children's daily regimen, likely both to give them exercise but to also teach them the art of following instruction and establishing order. Friends noted that the exertion was "sometimes noisy but, nevertheless, they do learn, and can be quiet and orderly if they choose." Drilling also instilled the idea of working as a team and obeying instructions; Friends saw both of these qualities as valuable to any civil society. SSI (1896), p. 20.

86. See also Anne Jellicoe, "The Condition of Young Women Employed in Manufactories in Dublin," *Transactions of the National Association for the Promotion of Social Science* 6 (1861), pp. 640–44. Jellicoe provides interesting discussion of the variety of employment options for women who needed to work but also reveals

that a very small percentage of Dublin's female population was employed. See also Bernadette Whelan, *Women and Paid Work in Ireland 1500–1930* (Dublin: Four Courts Press, 2000); Mona Hearn, *Below Stairs: Domestic Service Remembered in Dublin and Beyond 1880–1922* (Dublin: Lilliput Press, 1993); and Mary E. Daly, "Women in the Irish Workforce from Pre-Industrial to Modern Times," *Soathar* 7 (1981), pp. 74–82.

87. SSI (1884), p. 19; SSI (1886), pp. 22–23.

88. SSI (1885), p. 19.

89. Strand Street's average annual income from 1870 to 1900 was £152.

90. SSI (1875), p. 13.

91. One innovative example was Bloomfield Hospital, founded by Friends in 1807; it was one of Dublin's earliest psychiatric facilities.

92. Mary Edmundson, who by the time she was 30 was a widow with five children, was a very active member of Dublin's Quaker community. Richard S. Harrison, *A Biographical Dictionary of Irish Quakers* (Dublin: Four Courts Press, 1997), p. 42. As Theodore R. Webb noted, "the workers at our Ragged School are fellow labourers of the ladies of the Prison Gate Mission." *Glimpses of Ragged School Workers* (Dublin: n.p., 1869), n.p.

93. "Mrs. Sibthrope handed over £146, "realized by the sale of work held on the 16th and 17th week. There was also the sum of £14 handed in realized by Plain work sold which was made at this mission." Prison Gate Mission, henceforth PGM (31 May 1883).

94. PGM (28 September 1883). The minutes of May 3, 1883 recorded that "it was approved to assist two of the girls who are anxious to emigrate." Assistance came in the form of cash, a ticket, or possibly clothing. Or, for example, the mission agreed to furnish "Fanny Murray the loan of £10 to enable her to travel to Manchester to a situation."

95. George C. Williams, ed., *Dublin Charities: A Handbook* (Dublin: Association of Dublin Charities, 1902), p. 158.

96. See Luddy, *Women and Philanthropy*, p. 173.

97. Rosa M. Barrett, *Guide to Dublin Charities* (Dublin: Hodges, Figgis & Co., 1884), pp. 9–10.

98. PGM (5 April 1883). The Committee noted that "three more girls were sent to situations at Mr. Richardson's Mills . . . [from whom] the Superintendent . . . received favourable reports."

99. PGM (3 May 1883; 28 September 1883).

100. PGM (31 May 1883). The Secretary reported that "according to instructions he has signed [an] agreement with the Royal Hospital respecting the laundry contract."

101. PGM (4 October 1883). In October of 1883, the committee resolved to "ask Mrs. Eustace to draw up an appeal to be inserted in the daily paper as regards to funds."

102. The exhibit in Edinburgh took place, but apparently sales did not go as well as hoped. The mission responded to a request that the pieces from the Edinburgh exhibit be sold at a reduction of 25 percent by stating that the Prison Gate committee could not allow a greater reduction than 10 percent. PGM (25 March 1886; 22 September 1887).

103. Luddy, *Women and Philanthropy*, p. 171.

104. Then, on March 31, the minutes record that Mrs. Eustace stated that the Committee of the Molyneux Asylum (a school for the young and a home for the aged blind located on Leeson Park in Dublin and established in 1815) was very anxious that the Prison Gate Mission might allow them to use the model loom for the carpet weaving. The Asylum also requested that it send one of its pupils to learn the craft, enabling her to return to teach it to the mission's other inhabitants. "Mrs. Eustace was of the opinion that if such permission was granted certain conditions should be insisted upon by this committee." PGM (31 March 1887).

105. PGM (25 March 1886). The Countess of Aberdeen (Ishbel Marjoribanks, 1857–1939) was the wife of the Irish Viceroy. Aberdeen established the Irish Home Industries Association and would later found the Women's National Health Association, which fought against the spread of tuberculosis. Luddy, *Women and Philanthropy,* pp. 189–90. See also Nellie Ó Cléirigh, *Hardship & High Living: Irish Women's Lives 1808–1923* (Dublin: Portobello Press, 2003), pp. 147–67.

106. Maria Luddy, "Prostitution and Rescue Work in Nineteenth-Century Ireland," in *Women Surviving: Studies in Irish Women's History in the 19th and 20th Centuries,* ed. Maria Luddy and Cliona Murphy (Dublin: Poolbeg, 1989), p. 68.

107. On October 9, 1884, Mr. Jones related: "the House 31 Quin St. which he stated . . . was in a very dilapidated condition and would cost from £80 to £100 to put in order. It was accordingly decided not to take further steps in the matter." PGM (9 October 1884). Eventually, the mission purchased the land upon which it would build the dormitories. See PGM (13 August 1885; 8 October 1884; 23 October 1884; 13 August 1885).

108. PGM (1 November 1883).

109. Mary Carpenter, *On the Supplementary Measures Needed for Reformatories for the Diminution of Juvenile Crime* (London: Emily Faithfull and Co., 1861), pp. 4–5.

110. Barrett, *Guide to Dublin Charities,* p. 9. The Girls Training Home, reopened in 1883, had previously been the House of Refuge, established in 1802. PGM (14 June 1883). See also Williams, *Handbook of Dublin Philanthropic Organizations,* p. 222.

111. PGM (31 December 1885).

112. PGM (14 January 1886). Unfortunately, although the minutes reveal that the regulations were instituted, they supply no details. Two years later on December 28, 1888, Miss Rice, the matron, reported that "the Xmas Dinner to the women had passed off most satisfactorily. One-hundred women enjoyed good things provided and the conduct during this festive season was all that could be desired." PGM (28 December 1888).

113. On June 29, 1888 the board reported that two Quakers generously sent 104 of the women in the mission on an excursion to Howth: "Through the kindness of Mr. William Fry and Miss Friend who had generously contributed all the expenses." Here again, the minutes recorded the behavior of the women at the outing who, the records suggested in a manner not unlike how one would describe children, behaved "most exemplary and left a pleasing impression on the visitors." PGM (29 June 1888).

114. Many asylums had rather imposing restrictions. The Magdalen Asylum in 1843 noted that "no visitor be admitted without permission of the Vice Patroness or one of the governesses." Magdalen Asylum Guardians' Minute Books (24 November 1843).

115. The weekly average for women helped by the mission from 1883 to 1889

was 99, with the weekly average for the number of women in the dorms from 1886 to 1889 being 49.

116. "Their sense of individual responsibility was highly developed and Quaker women received a great deal of support from their own families within their own communities from their activities." Luddy, *Women and Philanthropy,* p. 197.

117. Dorren McMahon, " The Irish Quaker Community 1870–1925" (M.A. thesis, University College Dublin, 1985), p. 70. See also Kilroy, "Quaker Women in Ireland," pp. 8–9.

118. For example, Mary Edmundson set up a branch of the Friends Total Abstinence Association in addition to the previously mentioned Prison Gate Mission. Harrison, *A Biographical Dictionary of Irish Quakers,* p. 42. Women Friends also eventually became active in politics. See Maria Luddy, "Women and Politics in Nineteenth-Century Ireland," *Women & Irish History,* ed. Maryann Gialanella Valiulis and Mary O'Dowd (Dublin: Wolfhound Press, 1997), pp. 89–108; Margaret Ward, "'Suffrage First—Above All Else!' An Account of the Irish Suffrage Movement," *Irish Women's Studies Reader,* ed. Ailbhe Smith (Dublin: Attic Press, 1993), pp. 20–44; and Cliona Murphy, *The Women's Suffrage Movement and Irish Society in the Early Twentieth Century* (Philadelphia: Temple University Press, 1989).

119. The fact that Haslam (1829–1922) has always been affiliated with the Quakers is ironic given the fact that she was disunited from membership at the age of 25 when she married Thomas Haslam, a lapsed Quaker. Harrison, *A Biographical Dictionary of Irish Quakers,* p. 60. See also Carmel Quinlan, *Genteel Revolutionaries: Anna and Thomas Haslam and the Irish Women's Movement* (Cork: Cork University Press, 2002).

120. Mary Cullen, "Anna Maria Haslam," *Women, Power and Consciousness in Nineteenth-Century Ireland,* ed. Mary Cullen and Maria Luddy (Dublin: Attic Press, 1995), p. 174.

121. Cullen, "Anna Maria Haslam," p. 169–71, 174. This work also led to her support for the growing trade union activism both in Ireland and Britain.

122. Cullen, "Anna Maria Haslam," p. 188. Ironically, however, for a woman whose ideals were so liberal in relation to social issues, Haslam maintained a conservative political stance. Anna Haslam was a Unionist who was certain that England governed Ireland well. Anna lived to vote for a Unionist candidate in the 1918 general elections. For discussion of Quaker women as socially conservative, see Nancy A. Hewitt, "The Fragmentation of Friends: The Consequences for Quaker Women in Antebellum America," in *Witnesses for Change: Quaker Women over Three Centuries,* ed. Elisabeth Potts Brown and Susan Mosher Stuard (New Brunswick: Rutgers University Press, 1989), p. 104.

CHAPTER 5

The Good Nurse: Women Philanthropists and the Creation of a Career

> Every women, or at least almost every woman, in England has, at one time or another of her life, charge of the personal health of somebody, whether child or invalid,—in other words, every woman is a nurse.
>
> —Florence Nightingale

Involvement by the women of philanthropy in the evolution of nursing has not been extensively examined in the context of professional lives in Ireland. Like their sisters in Europe and the United States, upper-class Irish women were integrally engaged in improving nursing as a vocation, as well as helping to fashion a career into which not only working-class but also eventually middle- and upper-class women would enter.[1] Women philanthropists had long integrated nursing work into their charities, the agendas of which often included some form of visiting and relieving the sick poor. Such experience made their participation in the reform of professional nursing, as well as the improvement of nursing education, a logical next step.

While this book has sought to chronicle the language of charity and its promotion of control of the poor, this chapter shows social control in action as nursing reformers sought to create a nurse in their image. Whether it was the nursing school, the nurse in the hospital, or the visiting nurse, reformers impressed upon their nurses the same ideals that charities advocated for the poor: moral behavior, sanitary practices, and an emphasis upon the importance of hard work. This chapter shows that in the records of hospitals, nursing schools, and visiting nurse organizations, what charitable women, hospital boards, and nurse reformers promoted was the creation of nurses who would be models for those in the working classes to whom they brought aid.

In the mid-nineteenth century, British and Irish society called for improvement of nurse training for a variety of reasons. These included an expansion in the number of hospitals and medical facilities established to cater to the poor, Florence Nightingale's well-publicized trip to the Crimea, the increase in middle-class women's involvement in philanthropy, and the sanitary reform movement that was part of the philanthropic agenda.[2] Using these four factors as a guide, this chapter will follow the evolution of hospital nursing in nineteenth-century Dublin. Most ladies did not feel that they could respectably enter a salaried position; instead they helped to reform nursing and, in so doing, furthered one of philanthropy's most fundamental tenets: the shaping of a respectable and honest working class. Through an examination of the records from a selection of Dublin's hospitals, nursing schools, and visiting nurse programs, the evidence reveals how middle- and upper-class Irish women put into action the ideology behind middle-class Victorian charity and helped to begin the process of making nursing a respected career for women.

As upper-class women made their way into Britain's hospitals, they were generally willing to work in two capacities. First, many volunteered their time as members of hospitals' ladies' committees. In many cases, hospitals appointed these women to be responsible for seeing to the day-to-day running of the hospital and maintenance of supplies. Commonly, the ladies' committee reported on hospital needs to the board of directors who then voted on whether to implement their suggestions. Until the position of lady superintendent was established, ladies' committees might also have been in charge of hiring nurses and ensuring their good behavior. Some among these women also established charities and nursing schools that trained women to nurse in hospitals or in private homes. In addition, and a common task for the women of philanthropy, the ladies' committee found innovative ways to raise funds for the hospital.[3]

The second capacity in which upper-class women participated in nursing reform was as lady superintendent of nurses.[4] As the title denotes, a lady superintendent was a woman from a middle- or upper-class background, almost always unmarried, with a measure of formal education and medical training.[5] Such a woman was able to respectably fill this position because she acted as an administrator who guided, molded, and directed nurses, just as her upper-class sisters managed servants.[6] As St. John's House, an early nurse training facility located in England, suggested, "it was later found best that the Lady Superintendant [*sic*] should be responsible for many of the details which had first been undertaken by the master, but which lay more in the province of the lady of the house."[7] The lady superintendent hired and fired, as well as ensured that nurses were properly trained, performed their duties, had the right supplies, and received adequate room and board.

Both of these roles reflected Victorian society's presumption that upper-class women, as members of the ruling class, were to direct the activities of those perceived to be their social inferiors. Victorian society's class-consciousness made it deferential in nature. Thus, hospital administrators and doctors alike, then, desired a lady to take the position of lady superintendent, because, not unlike in society in general, she could be a moral role model who commanded the respect and obedience of her working-class nurses.[8] Nevertheless, while often welcomed for their efforts, the entrance by ladies into the hospitals was not without complications. Among these included the class frictions that arose because the lady superintendent or members of the ladies committee were of the same or possibly higher-class stature than the doctors or administrators from whom they might be expected to take orders. Another problem was that many upper-class women feared the loss of respectability if they accepted a salary or were extensively involved in physically demanding labor. Hence, into the twentieth century, few upper-class British and Irish women were willing either to train as nurses or to enter into a career as a lady superintendent. Nevertheless, the minority of middle- and upper-class women who made their way into hospital administration soon began to make greater demands for improvements for themselves as well as their nurses.

In the hospital, ladies confronted a medical administration whose hierarchical nature was analogous with Victorian society. Doctors represented a medical middle class that would eventually win the battle to gain the respect of, as well as authority over, hospital administrators. Nurses and other staff epitomized the relatively oppressed lower-middle and working classes. Moreover, the records reveal that hospitals sought to achieve tight restraint over the least powerful of their employees. Thus, nurses, most of whom were being housed on hospital premises, were expected to abide by a strict curfew while following a regimented daily schedule. Failure to comply could result in reprimand. However, the records also show that as the century progressed and hospitals sought to hire nurses with medical training, rigorous routines were gradually loosened to allow for coursework and clinicals. The expansion in the number of medical institutions, as well as the dynamic within them, reflected the class conflict within British and Irish society. The hospital, another edifice in the growing architecture of control, became one more structure in the increasing institutionalization of society.

The increasing involvement of women in the reform of nursing coincided with the beginning of the movement for women's emancipation. Women's fight for access to education and employment was all part of the greater movement by women for civil rights. This is most evident in the suffrage movement.[9] Nursing reform allowed middle- and upper-class women to attain positions of power over both the reforms and the nurses. Working with the upper administration of hospitals afforded another opportunity for philanthropists and lady superintendents to respectably find themselves in a public position for which they could wield relative influence.[10]

Susan Beresford was a good example of this early struggle by women to gain a measure of control within the hospital. First hired by Dublin's Baggot Street Hospital in 1884, Beresford disagreed with some of the limitations imposed upon her authority as the hospital's lady superintendent. In a letter just two months after she was hired, Beresford announced her resignation and explained, "No Lady who has had any experience of the very great difficulties of a training school would work under such rules."[11] Although they were impressed that she would resign as a result of these hospital regulations, the board of governors nevertheless accepted her letter of resignation. While Beresford lost this battle, she eventually won the war. Baggot Street rehired her and gradually provided her with the extensive authority she sought. Susan Beresford, as lady superintendent, stood fast to her demands for autonomy and implemented important reforms in the nursing programs in several of Dublin's leading hospitals.

Prior to the twentieth century, most medical assistance was provided in the home, and it was expected that the females would nurse the sick. While society had argued that women's gentle nature made them naturally adept at nursing, caring for the ill was hard, physically demanding work that required long hours of constant attention. Outside the home, most ladies could neither respectably accept nor engage in such demanding labor. Mrs. J. N. Higgins argued for a lady "or at least an educated person" to lead nurses, yet the nurses themselves should be taken from the laboring poor, "both because they are most numerous and also because amongst them there exists no prejudice against girls leaving their homes."[12] Thus, because reformers were generally unable to recruit nurses from the middle and upper classes, they worked instead to mold working-class women into the respectable nurses they desired. As hospital care expanded and the Victorian era of moral reform was ushered in, efforts to improve the reputation and behavior of nurses were inevitable, and it was upper-class philanthropists who sought to lead the way.

Dublin was Ireland's center for medical and nurse training. The city hosted an extensive range of hospitals, universities, and medical training facilities. In 1667, Trinity College, which Queen Elizabeth I founded in 1592, established the College of Physicians, which was eventually associated with Sir Patrick Dun's Hospital, located close to Dublin's city center. At this time, physician and surgeon were differing professions, and in 1784, the Royal College of Surgeons of Ireland was established and eventually affiliated with Mercer's Hospital, both of which were situated near Dublin's central park, St. Stephen's Green.[13]

In 1684, Charles II chartered the Royal Hospital, Kilmainham for military veterans.[14] With a design similar to the Hôtel des Invalides in Paris, Kilmainham could house up to 300 men.[15] Nevertheless, as the hospital could not accommodate all of those who needed medical assistance, it divided them into outpatients and inpatients. Kilmainham also housed the children and widows of military men on the premises and, at times, acted as a charity.[16] The Royal Hospital, which today is the Irish Museum of Modern Art, was constantly in financial straits, and although the British government proposed shutting it a number of times during the nineteenth century, Kilmainham did not close until after World War I.

In 1774, the Irish government named Cork, Dublin, Limerick, and Waterford as the four cities where they would build institutions to house poor, helpless persons along with vagabonds and "sturdy beggars."[17] Called houses of industry, these establishments put the healthier inmates to work, provided medical facilities (which in Dublin eventually became the Whitworth Medical Hospital), hired physicians to care for the inmates, and enlisted unpaid female inmates as nurses.[18] In the early part of the nineteenth century, an outbreak of fever put a strain on the Whitworth Hospital, and the governors asked the government for financial assistance to pay for the building of a fever hospital. In 1803 the Hardwicke Fever Hospital was completed, and in 1807 an outpatient dispensary opened, followed by the opening of the Richmond Surgical Hospital in 1811. In 1838, Westminster passed the Poor Law of Ireland Act, and the house of industry in Dublin became the North Dublin Union Workhouse. The hospitals, which had garnered a reputation as teaching hospitals, became independent.[19] In 1733, the will of Dr. Richard Steevens, a successful Dublin physician and twice president of the Royal College of Physicians, established Dr. Steevens' Hospital.[20] At the time of its establishment, the hospital could hold 40 patients and catered to "sick and wounded persons whose distempers and wounds are curable."[21]

In 1745, Bartholomew Mosse opened in Dublin the first lying-in/maternity-teaching hospital in Britain or Ireland.[22] Midwifery was one area of medicine in which women historically dominated. Midwives were usually older women, married or widowed with their own children, who passed their knowledge down through generations. However, by the eighteenth and nineteenth centuries, more men were becoming midwives, although not without the criticism that it was improper and morally dangerous for a man to assist a woman in childbirth.[23] Known as the Rotunda (because of its beautiful rotunda entrance), the hospital offered training to both midwives and surgeons in hopes of sending them to aid women in the more rural parts of the country. The Rotunda trained many of Ireland's Jubilee and Dudley district nurses and to the present day operates as a maternity hospital, located not far from the top of one of Dublin's main thoroughfares, O'Connell Street.[24]

At the close of the eighteenth century Sir Patrick Dun's Hospital, named after a president and fellow of the Royal College of Physicians, was established as a training hospital.[25] Dun's physicians trained medical students from Trinity, Oxford, and Cambridge and offered both nursing and midwifery training.[26] Throughout the nineteenth century, Dun's worked to improve facilities and quality of staff in order to refine the medical assistance provided to the poor of Dublin. In 1831, six doctors purchased a house on Upper Baggot Street and opened the City of Dublin Hospital, also known as the Baggot Street Hospital. The hospital was able to care for 50 patients and sought to aid all but mental illness; it accepted patients regardless of religious affiliation.[27]

As has already been shown, in addition to its monumental poverty, nineteenth-century Dublin was also a city that suffered greatly due to religious strife. Predictably, hospitals reflected the city's religious divisions. For example, in 1839 Albert Walsh founded the Adelaide Institution and Protestant Hospital, which catered exclusively to Protestants. In 1861, the hospital also established one of the first nursing schools in Dublin, which naturally only accepted Protestants as nurses, providing them a year of training.[28] While the Adelaide was the most explicit about its agenda, many of Dublin's hospitals only hired persons of a specific religious denomination. Dublin's medical establishment was another stage upon which Ireland's sectarian battles were waged, as both Catholics and Protestants sought to ensure that their coreligionists received medical care.

To this end, Roman Catholic nuns were more than willing to enter into the fray in order to save the souls of Catholics, and in so doing, they performed a leading role in the establishment and operation of Irish hospitals. The nineteenth century was a time of dramatic change for the Roman Catholic Church in Ireland, and women took religious vows in ever increasing numbers.[29] By 1900, 22.4 percent of Irish convents were attached to hospitals.[30] Religious women were able to make a considerable impact upon nursing, because society perceived that their vows provided them with a calling to help the poor. Furthermore, nuns' vows allowed them to push the boundaries of Victorian women's roles without loss of respectability.

Many of Ireland's more prominent nuns were women who came from its small but growing Catholic middle class. A contingent of Catholic families had held on to their land and fortunes in spite of eighteenth-century penal laws, while, by early in the nineteenth century, there were others who had reaped financial benefits through trade. In Dublin, two prominent Catholic women made a wide-ranging impact on the city's medical scene. The first was Mary Aikenhead, a physician's daughter, who was born in 1787 and grew up in Cork. In 1808 Aikenhead relocated to Dublin, where she laid the foundations for the Sisters of Charity, which Rome canonically recognized in 1833.

It was at this same time that Aikenhead and her companions watched as cholera spread rapidly through the narrow, dirty, crowded streets of Dublin. Seeing how this crisis sorely tested Dublin's medical facilities, Aikenhead decided to use £3,000 she had received as a dowry from a young novice to establish a hospital. Aikenhead recruited Dr. Joseph O'Farrell, a Catholic, to be her medical advisor and sent three of her nuns to Paris to learn hospital administration.[31] In 1834, the Sisters of Charity opened St. Vincent De Paul Hospital in a house near the city's center on St. Stephen's Green. While the hospital eventually moved to Dublin's fashionable outer suburbs, St. Stephen's Green was then, as it is now, one of Dublin's more exclusive Georgian Squares. By establishing her hospital in so privileged an area of the city, Aikenhead was not only making herself accessible to the city's poor who would have lived within walking distance, but was also placing a Catholic hospital on a site that could not help but be noticed by the city's Catholic and Protestant elite.

When William Callaghan died in the early part of the nineteenth century, he left his adopted daughter, Catherine McAuley, with £28,000. With her inheritance, in 1827, Catherine McAuley purchased a house on Baggot Street that she opened to educate poor girls.[32] McAuley recruited other single middle- and upper-class women to live and work in her home. Problems arose with local community opposition to the arrival of poor girls into the wealthy neighborhood and to women living together without religious vows and under no male authority. Although it was never McAuley's original intention, she succumbed to the local Catholic Archbishop's pressure and established the Sisters of Mercy, today the largest congregation of nuns in the world. In 1851, McAuley bought land on Eccles Street in Dublin in order to establish a hospital. The Sisters of Mercy completed their hospital, the Mater Misericordiae, in sections and accepted the first patients in 1861.[33]

Both St. Vincent's and the Mater Misericordiae gave Catholics access to the medical profession, while the women who worked in either hospital were expected to be members of, or enter, the community. Not only did the two hospitals serve Catholic patients, but they opened the door for Catholic doctors and nurses who would have the opportunity to practice their profession. The Mater and St. Vincent's were part of the growing effort by Dublin's middle- and upper-class Catholics to strengthen their position in Irish society. Nevertheless, the dynamic within Dublin's Catholic hospitals would not have been greatly different from the city's other medical establishments, and the nuns would have strictly maintained a clear social hierarchy and rigid rules for all hospital staff.[34] While neither hospital trained lay women as nurses until late in the century, nevertheless, nuns were at the forefront of nineteenth-century nursing reform, and not only must they be credited with helping to pave the way for other women to follow, but they also helped to eliminate the boundaries that hindered Dublin's Catholics from participation in the local work force.[35]

Dublin's well-developed medical infrastructure was an excellent setting in which nuns, nurses, and the women of philanthropy could all work toward the reform of nursing. Certainly, the city needed these organizations—and more, as throughout the nineteenth century, Dublin was challenged by famine and epidemic disease alike. While the numbers in Table 5.1 appear impressive, it must be kept in mind that most of these hospitals were quite small in size.[36]

NURSING IN THE NINETEENTH CENTURY

> It is charity to nurse sick bodies well; it is greater charity to nurse well and patiently sick minds and tiresome sufferers.
>
> —Florence Nightingale

In general, Florence Nightingale, born in 1820, remains the mother of nursing, and it is she who has garnered extensive scholarship. Historians regard her as the key proponent for the evolution of professional nurse training, changes in sanitary practices, reform of military medical services, and hospital reform in the late nineteenth and early twentieth centuries.[37] Nevertheless, recent scholarship has shown that Nightingale was neither the first nor the most successful at nursing reform, and the myth created by the Lady with the Lamp has slowly begun to tarnish.[38]

During Nightingale's Crimean campaign, the British newspapers championed her work.[39] Money along with offers of help poured in from the public. A national appeal was created that eventually became the financial basis for the Nightingale fund as well as a school for nurse training, for which Nightingale accepted an administrative role. Nevertheless, Nightingale was very much convinced that amongst other things, "disease arose from particular states of moral and social order," and the rules of the Nightingale School placed more emphasis on discipline than medical knowledge.[40] Nightingale established a very strict daily regimen for her nurses, as she presumed that, through restraint and moral behavior, nurses could be made an example to their patients.

Nurses were not necessarily trained to do anything more than provide comfort to a patient and keep the hospital or home in clean, working order. Hence, for many hospitals, any woman could be appointed to nurse.[41] For example, in Dublin, the records of the Baggot Street, Kilmainham, Dr. Steevens', and Sir Patrick Dun's hospitals all noted that they promoted ward maids to assistant nurses. Dr. Steevens' records showed in 1879 that the hospital's ward maids were "supposed to do double duty as assistant nurses and scrubbers."[42] The Baggot Street's records indicated

Table 5.1
Selection of Dublin Hospitals, Medical Schools and Nursing Schools

	Year Established
College of Physicians	1667
Dr. Steevens Hospital	1733
Mercer's Hospital	1734
St. Patrick's Hospital	1745
The Rotunda Lying-In Hospital	1745
Royal College of Surgeons	1784
Royal Hospital for Incurables	1792
Hardwicke Fever Hospital	1803
Cork St. Fever Hospital	1804
Richmond Surgical Hospital	1811
Coombe Hospital	1823
Royal Victoria Eye and Ear Hospital	1814
National Children's Hospital	1821
City of Dublin Hospital (Baggot Street)	1831
St Vincent De Paul Hospital	1834
Adelaide Institution and Protestant Hospital	1839
Mater Misericordiae	1854
Dr. Steevens Hospital Medical School	1857
Adelaide Hospital Nursing School	1861
Dublin Nurses Training Institution	1866
The National Maternity Hospital	1884
Red-Cross Nursing Sisters-House and Training School	1884
City of Dublin Nursing Institution	1884
Mater Misericordiae School of Nursing	1891
Dublin Metropolitan Technical School for Nurses	1893

Source: Irish Medical Directory (Dublin: Sealy Bryers and Walsh, 1890).

Note: In 1881 Dr. Steevens Hospital accepted probationers from a local nurse training school run by Mrs. Eliza Browne that "train[ed] women for private nursing and for nursing the poor in their own homes." Doctor Steevens Hospital, 15 September 1881.

that the ladies' committee decided that probationer nurses could not alone complete their tasks and "assistant nurses be selected from the ward maids."[43] Hospitals often hired temporary nurses who were unlikely to have much medical training. In addition, for the night shift, many hospitals continued to employ women with little or no formal instruction, even when the day nurses were increasingly required to have some medical schooling.

Before Florence Nightingale burst onto the scene, the image of the for-hire private nurse was not universally positive. Charles Dickens immortalized the nurse in his novel *Martin Chuzzlewit,* in which "Sarah Gamp" was the elderly, unpleasant, drunk, unhelpful nurse who more often stole from her patients than nursed them.[44] "She may be lazy, dirty, drunken, profligate, or herself infirm, but has come upon the parish, so she is sent out to nurse her helpless brethren and sisters."[45] Historians have validated the existence of Dickens's "Sarah Gamp" by finding examples of nurses who were drunk, disorderly, sexually promiscuous, or charged with criminal acts while on the job.

Dublin's hospitals had their share of Sarah Gamps. For example, in 1835, Sir Patrick Dun's board resolved that the nurse Finnamore be dismissed for accepting a gratuity of spirits and noted that the matron should have more fully investigated the "finding of three bottles of spirits in said Nurse's trunks."[46] Dun's early minutes recorded that the matron requested the dismissal of nurses for insolence, irregularity, neglect of duty, and misconduct. In 1837, two nurses were dismissed, one for drunkenness and the other for violence of temper.[47] Throughout 1851 and 1852, the hospital accused one nurse of insubordination and another of impropriety and reprimanded a third because her neglect may have caused the death of a patient.[48] Baggot Street Hospital also had problems, and their lady superintendent, S. Helena Bewley, quickly solved them. In 1884, Bewley eliminated a number of nurses who continued to defy the authority of the doctors and hospital administration. Bewley reported: "one of the nurses of the male surgical ward was discharged for negligence and impertinence to one of the members of the surgical staff and shortly afterwards the nurse in the female surgical and gynecological wards had to be dismissed on account of gross impropriety of conduct."[49]

For Dublin's Royal Hospital Kilmainham, many of its nursing problems can be traced to the fact that the hospital frequently hired the untrained wives of men who either worked in or were patients of the hospital. For example, in 1871, Kilmainham learned that nurse Catherine Mullins gave birth to a child instead of, as she told administrators, going on holidays in the country. Mullins explained to staff surgeon Dr. Carte that she had married one of the patients, Ian Walsh.[50] Four years later in 1875, the staff surgeon complained that nurse Mary Lowry was frequently intoxicated while on duty and then requested that she be dismissed.[51] In 1876, the deputy master wrote a letter to the secretary of Kilmainham and complained that head nurse Hall was drunk and abusive to nurse Gilmore. Hall, whom the minutes mentioned again for "want of steadiness," was then permanently demoted and, in 1878, was dismissed for repeatedly being inebriated while on the job.[52] While the hospital had clearly installed rules regarding the behavior of the nurses, evidence shows that some of Kilmainham's nurses resisted if not altogether ignored the regulations.

Yet the nurses were not the only ones guilty of indiscretions. In 1874, the character of a Kilmainham matron, Anne Boileau, came under question when the hospital accused an inmate of raping a young girl in Boileau's employ. The accused, George Turner, who was frequently seen leaving Boileau's apartment, was alleged to have attacked the girl more than once. The mother of the child, Mary Ann Kirnan, testified that when she complained, Boileau, in an attempt to have Kirnan drop the charge, offered her a bribe.[53] Although hospitals sought to have matrons whose upstanding character could be inspiration for the nurses, Boileau's involvement with less than savory individuals revealed that this was not always so easily accomplished.[54]

Hospitals' ladies' committees also dealt with nurses who behaved inappropriately. In 1871, a letter to the board from Mrs. F. M. Trench, a lady visitor with the Sir Patrick Dun's Hospital, stated that the lady superintendent had informed her of having twice caught four nurses dancing in the room of a resident doctor.[55] The consequence of this apparently shocking behavior resulted in Dun's firing the resident and fining two of the nurses who had attended the festivities both times.[56] In 1874, Sir Patrick Dun's fired both a midwife and a medical student when, together, they inexplicably left the hospital from 10 P.M. to 2 A.M. Trinity College went on to suspend the student for six months after finding evidence for the "charge of immoral conduct."[57]

On the other hand, when, in 1880, nurse Norreys went to Dun's board and announced that a resident doctor, Mr. Johnston, had seduced her and she was now pregnant, the board decided that Norreys's accusations were without merit.[58] The board's failure to believe Norreys while accepting the word of Johnston, who denied the allegations, likely reflected both gender and class bias. Presumably, Norreys was a woman of lower-class status. Thus, the upper-class members of the hospital's board may have believed that, due to her social status, if a relationship had developed, she was the seductress. In addition, the board may have been inclined to believe Dr. Johnston in the first instance because he was a man, and secondly because he was well educated and quite possibly from the same social background as the men who judged him. While hospitals supplied their nurses with training, housing, and a salary, the administration did not believe that this made these women equal. Not unlike local charitable organizations, the upper-class persons who worked for the hospital would have believed that the working classes were morally and intellectually inferior and in need of guidance from their social superiors. Thus, those of higher class status such as the ladies' committee, the lady superintendent, and even student doctors were trustworthy, while apparently, other staff members were often not. In the end, however, the nurses did not always believe that they were bound by upper-class rules of etiquette and, at times, they rebelled against the hospital's constraints, pushing back against the controls being imposed from above and provoking response from the hospital's administration.

It should be noted, however, that while historians cite the many entertaining incidents regarding the bad behavior of nurses, these must be countered by illustrations of the hard-working, honest, caring nurses who desired a career in health care. There are countless names that did not make it into the record books simply because their actions gave no cause for reproach. Like other professions in which women dominated, the road to legitimacy was often blocked by Victorian society's limited expectations of the female's capabilities. Scholars are now seeking to revise the poor image of the nineteenth-century nurse.

In order to improve the image of the nurse, some sought to install upper-class women who, they argued, with their breeding, education, and moral character, would make gentle nurses. Others, however, wanted working-class women who, with their physical strength and work experience (meaning familiarity with taking direction), would make more deferential nurses, less likely to question doctors' authority and more easily controlled. More nurses came from the latter group, and thus reformers took up the mantle of improving the character of the working-class nurse.[59] Nursing reformers assumed that the "true nurse" would have the qualities very much attributed to women of the upper classes. Thus, they described that she needed to be "gifted with a peculiar talent for business . . . [with a] healthy, cheerful continence, with sound teeth . . . not too lusty . . . [have a] mild and amiable disposition . . . attentive to cleanliness; a neat appearance . . . a cheerful gentle manner, with an encouraging tone of voice, . . . of an obliging temper . . . who may be implicitly relied upon [and] above all things observing the orders of the medical attendant with punctuality, as the smallest deception is an unpardonable fault."[60] The anonymous author of *A Manual for Midwives and Monthly Nurses* added to the above list that the good nurse was to be "of irreproachable moral character, but she ought to have a deep sense of religion . . . and tender sympathy for the sufferings of others."[61] Some went so far as to argue that "a good nurse must be a good cook" and "be a light sleeper and an earlier riser."[62]

If she was a good nurse, as portrayed by Mrs. Rooke in Jane Austen's *Persuasion*, she might attain the unusual position of being somewhere above a servant yet below an equal.[63] "And she," said Mrs. Smith, "besides nursing me most admirably, has really proved an invaluable acquaintance . . . [she] thoroughly understands when to speak. She is a shrewd, intelligent, sensible woman."[64] Not only would the good nurse know when to speak, but reformers also cautioned the good nurse against having a loose tongue. "A nursetender is necessarily a confidential person, above a servant and trusted with many things as a friend."[65]

Philanthropists and nurse reformers alike wanted the good nurse to be a model of cleanliness, maintain a healthy lifestyle, and be an example to the poor of self-control, honesty, and moral behavior. The key requirement for all nurse-reformers was that a good nurse unquestioningly obeyed the medical man. She was to follow his orders without hesitation: "your position as to the medical attendant is quite secondary; you are to receive and implicitly obey his orders."[66] As Florence Nightingale advised her nurses, "let no woman suppose that obedience of the doctor is not absolutely necessary."[67] *The Lancet* cautioned that nurses should "strictly confine themselves to their proper sphere, and not trespass upon the duties either of medical officer or chaplain."[68] Thus, not unlike wife to husband or nun to priest, it was not the nurse's place to question the doctor, only to provide his prescribed care. Nevertheless, while this was the simple hierarchy reformers envisioned, evidence suggests that in reality these relationships between doctors and nurses were often much more complex.

As the century progressed, hospitals and reformers desired to train nurses not only to be obedient, hardworking, gentle, and vigilant; but they were also trying to change the image of the nurse from the sexually deviant Gamp to the asexual, moral, and attentive young woman. Reformers wanted the "good nurse" to be immune to the sexual desires of her male patients, and they believed that by limiting nursing to unmarried women, they could further constrain sexual misconduct. Thus, reformers wanted to place restrictions on nursing recruits as another function of social control by the upper classes over the lower. Nightingale herself established "vigilant patrolling and supervision of patients and workers into many of her hospitals and nursing reforms," because she had a great mistrust of the ability of both nurses and patients to have restraint over their sexual desires.[69]

Nineteenth-century reformers urged the nurse to be of formidable character. She was to be an advisor to the poor as to how they could improve their lives. Reformers also expected that the nurse would "conduce to make the life of the working man a more successful affair."[70] She was to be a font of information regarding friendly societies, pawnshops, and lending libraries, and ultimately the nurse was expected to have some knowledge of the law, including the questions of marriage and recovery from debt.[71] The women of philanthropy hoped that a nurse would become a lady but if not, she was to act like one and be a model to her peers. However, as research on nineteenth-century nursing shows, most of the women that entered nursing were not the hoped-for women of virtue. Thus, while reformers worked hard to construct the good nurse, evidence shows that many times nurses resisted the discipline reformers attempted to impose.

REMUNERATION, RETIREMENT, AND RESTRICTION

How much to pay a "good nurse" was integral to the debate for nursing reformers. Some reformers argued that nurses should make less in order to emphasize the vocational aspect of nursing, while others argued that a good nurse could not be recruited unless given a reasonable salary. Records show that throughout the nineteenth century, Dublin hospitals did not compensate their nurses well.

T. Percy Kirkpatrick, historian of Dublin's Dr. Steevens Hospital, shows that while in the eighteenth century Dr. Steevens's provided nurses with a room and paid them £12 a year, "it is not easy to see how the nurses were able to provide themselves with food and clothes on such a wage."[72] Kirkpatrick argues that if the price of food went up, nurses must have felt "actual want" and speculates that nurses may have obtained some food by stealing from the meals of their patients.[73] In Dublin's Royal Hospital, Kilmainham during the nineteenth century, the income of nurses can be tracked and compared with the salaries of other employees (see Table 5.2). Like the Kilmainham, in addition to salary, most hospitals provided accommodation and possibly board.

Table 5.3 shows an 1857 list of salaries of the hospital's administration and other male employees. Their income was considerably higher than that of the nurses.[74] Certainly it is not surprising that these men, who were well educated and had more training, were paid a better salary. What is more interesting is that by later in the century the Royal Hospital, many of whose nurses were not well trained, was actually paying almost the same annual income as the better trained nurses of Dun's or Baggot Street Hospitals. In this case, it seems that gender and class status may have had more to do with income than education or training.

In 1866, the Dublin' Nurses Training Institution, which had also contracted its services to Dr. Steevens Hospital, guaranteed nurses to Dun's "at a cost not exceeding £30 per nurse and £25 per assistant nurse."[75] Twenty years later things were little better and, by the early 1880s, Baggot Street paid nurses somewhere below £25 per year. In 1884 S. Helena Bewley, the lady superintendent for Dublin's Baggot Street Hospital, argued for raises for her nurses because, "from my personal experience I do not think that really competent persons can be procured [for] under £25 a year."[76] By 1895 Dun's lady superintendent, Margaret Huxley, sought a £5 raise for nurses to £30 per annum.[77]

Table 5.2
Royal Hospital Kilmainham Nurses/Matron Salaries

Name	Title	Date	Salary	Comments
Ann Boileau	Matron	1856	£60	widow
Ann Hoggan	Nurse	1857	£28	
Ann Green	Nurse	1857	£23	
Jane Galavin	Nurse	1857	£19	
Ellen Hall	Nurse	1873	£28	
Eliza Peters	Nurse	1873	£23	
Isabella Carter	Nurse	1873	£19	widow of officer
Matilda Hurford	Matron	1874	£60	widow of officer
Margaret O'Regan	Nurse	1882	£28	widow of officer; promoted to Head Nurse in 1883 when Hurford retires & paid £36
Anne Dolan	Nurse	1882	£23	
Catherine O'Brien	Nurse	1882	£19	
Catherine Truewith	Nurse	1884	£23	widow of officer
Isabella Carter	Nurse	1882	£28	widow of officer

Note: The difference in salary between women hired during the same year is not explained but may be the difference between an infirmary nurse and an upper house nurse.

As the evidence shows, however, hospitals paid matrons and lady superintendents a considerably higher salary than their nurses. For example, in the 1860s Sir Patrick Dun's paid its lady superintendent £60 per annum and supplied her with residence, coal, gas, and laundry facilities.[78] By the 1880s, Dun's paid lady superintendent Margaret Huxley £100 per annum plus room, board, and extras. Comparatively, Dun's head midwife made £40 annually plus room and board.[79] In 1884, when Baggot Street Hospital created the position of lady superintendent, it supplied her with a furnished residence in the hospital, paid her £100 per annum, and gave her six weeks of vacation.[80]

Table 5.3
1857: Royal Hospital Kilmainham Administrative Salaries

Name	Title	Salary
Lord Seaton	Master	£100
Revd George Hare	Chaplain	£250
Mr. George Fredd Dunn	Secretary and Treasurer	£260
Doctor J.W. Macauley	Physician and Surgeon	£300
Captain John Chadwick	Adj. & Act Quarter Master	£150
Mr. Charles Smith	Clerck to Secretary	£90
Revd. Edw. Kennedy	R.C. Clergyman	£50
Captain Thomas Gibbons	Resident Captain	£56
William Saunderson	Quartermaster Sergeant	£55

The lady superintendent's salary did not only acknowledge her social status; hospitals also compensated the lady superintendent for her administrative responsibilities. Baggot Street's lady superintendent was to hire and fire all nurses and probationers and to ensure that the nurses, probationers, and wardmaids had everything they needed from bedding to food. Additionally, she was to take "all money due for the services of the Nurses which shall be paid to her, or received by the Matron or Nurses, and shall account with the Secretary once a week for the same."[81] As her duties clearly indicated, the lady superintendent was an important member of the hospital's administration. Nevertheless, Baggot Street clearly defined that the lady superintendent "shall conform to whatever rules may hereafter be made by the Governors."[82]

While comparative statistics on wages are difficult to obtain, it is valuable to note that in 1867, Britain's skilled laborers earned between £50 and £73 annually, poorly skilled between £35 and £52, and unskilled between £10 and £36.[83] In Dublin for that same year, laborers' wages increased from approximately £23 to £31.[84] Less than twenty years later in 1883, Dublin's skilled laborers were making about £88, while the unskilled made only £36 per year.[85] In 1905, family incomes showed steady but slow improvement. For example, skilled laborers in Belfast made over £90 annually, similar to what Dublin's skilled laborers were making.[86] Yet, by the early twentieth century, while nurses were making anywhere from £30 to £50 per year working 16 hour days, "Irish working men were striking for a

44 hour week and a typist or clerk earned £200 per annum."[87] Unlike most laborers, most hospitals did supply nurses with room, board, uniforms, and other essentials, yet even into the twentieth century it appears that nurses failed to make a salary commensurate with their training.[88]

In addition to salary, one benefit that most hospitals gave to nurses was housing. Early in the century, because hospitals granted accommodation to nurses, some also permitted their families to reside with a nurse. Prior to the mid-nineteenth century nursing reforms, there appears to have been no universal prohibition against housing married nurses with their children.[89] It seems that in Dr. Steevens Hospital it was not unusual for nurses to have family members living with them on the premises, and the hospital even hired a nurse's adult daughter to substitute when her mother was absent, "and sometimes a daughter was appointed at a reduced salary to assist her mother."[90] Kilmainham's infirmary nurse, Jane Jeffcott, had succeeded her mother, while Baggot Street granted Mrs. Finlay, the matron, her usual leave for vacation, gave her £10, and appointed her daughter Mrs. Brereton to represent her during her absence.[91]

Nevertheless, while housing was certainly a benefit, it was also a way to further control the activity and behavior of nurses, and evidence showed that hospital administrations implemented prohibitive measures upon nurses. Kilmainham required that the matron, to whom the hospital provided regulatory authority over nurses, would supply a written report on "any case of neglect of duty or disobedience of orders which may come under her notice."[92] In addition, no nurse was permitted to leave until after the evening meal and could only be absent after curfew with the permission of the matron.[93] Kilmainham was not alone; nurses at Dr. Steevens Hospital were "not to leave the hospital without the written permission of the Matron."[94] In addition to such restrictions, because they were housed on site, hospitals felt that they could work nurses for long hours. For example, Dr Steevens stated that nurses would work 56 hours per week on day duty or sixty hours a week on night duty.[95] Baggot Street's nurses lived in the hospital, while the probationers resided in a house near the hospital and, as the records note, the women were closely watched and were required to maintain a strict hourly schedule (see Table 5.4). Hospitals took advantage of the fact that by housing these women upon the premises, they were able to control as well as monitor a nurse's movements while she simultaneously worked long hours.

Later in the century, institutions increasingly expected nurses, matrons, and lady superintendents to be unmarried and to retire upon marriage.[96] Nursing schools, too, desired unmarried recruits, although, on occasion, they did give married women special dispensation. Jubilee visiting nurses (to be discussed later), and particularly those in rural districts, were required to resign upon marriage.[97] Rosalind Paget, who would be the first

Table 5.4
1887: Baggot Street Hospital Nurses' Schedule

Time Table for Day Duty

Rise	Breakfast	Wards	Dinner	Wards	Tea	Wards	Supper	Dormitories
6:15a.m.	6:40	7:00	1p.m.	1:30	5:00	5:30	9:00	10:00

Time Table for Night Duty

Rise	Breakfast	Wards	Night Meal	Leave Wards	Dinner	Supper	Dormitories
8p.m.	8:35	9:00	12:30a.m.	8:00a.m.	8:30	12noon	1p.m.

Off Duty Times for Day Nurses and Probationers:

3p.m. to 5:30p.m. one day; 5:30p.m. to 9p.m. next day.

Sundays–either from 10a.m. to 3p.m. or from 3p.m. to 9p.m.

Off-Duty Times for Night Nurses and Probationers:

Every day after their dinner at 8:30a.m., Night Nurses may leave the Hospital for recreation and exercise, returning to their dormitories not later than 1p.m. For those who desire it, a light meal is provided at noon. Once a month, Night Nurses are off duty from 10a.m. to 1p.m. on the following day. Unless they have received special permission from the Lady Superintendent to be absent, they must sleep in the Hospital, reporting themselves at 10p.m.

Source: Davis Coakley, *Baggot Street: A Short History of the Royal City of Dublin Hospital* (Dublin: Royal City of Dublin Hospital, 1995), p. 29; Royal City of Dublin Hospital, May 13, 1887.

superintendent of the Queen Victoria's Jubilee Institute for Nurses and was married, requested that she be paid no salary because she felt that this would make her "even more strict in her observance of the rules and in her attention to duty than if she were dependent on [a salary] for her livelihood."[98]

Such restrictions reflect how reformers believed that nurses must be shown the proper way to behave in order for them to become examples of moral living to their patients. Through restrictions against marriage, reformers believed it would keep these women ignorant of the enticements of male patients. While reformers argued that by housing nurses in the hospital they saved them from moral danger, it is unlikely reformers completely trusted their rank and file nurses, because they believed that the lower classes were inclined toward immoral behavior. Finally, the restrictive nature of mid-nineteenth-century hospital nursing reinforces the argument that middle-class women would not have entered the profession at this early stage. Victorian society restrained the mobility of women of the middle and upper classes, and they could not, without loss of dignity, have lived outside the morally protective domain of their paternal or marital home, nor submitted themselves to a regimen that was so similar to that of a domestic servant.

Some of the most visible women in hospital records were those who were not actually employed by the hospital. It was the ladies' committee and other volunteers who fought to improve conditions within the hospitals for nurses as well as patients. In addition to raising funds, early in the nineteenth century, ladies' committees could wield considerable power, including budgetary expenditures and employment decisions. In addition, these were often the same women who established nursing schools in order to train a better sort of nurse for the hospital.[99]

Although they had a variety of titles, the ladies' committees affiliated with local hospitals all generally handled the same tasks of raising money, working with female staff, and trying to make patients in the hospital more comfortable.[100] Lady visitors, as they were called by Sir Patrick Dun's Hospital, were to see that basic items be supplied for the patients and staff of the hospital in order to improve the quality of life and service of Sir Patrick Dun's. Dun's also hoped that, as these ladies wandered the halls seeing to the smooth running of the institution, they would be models of propriety for staff and patients to emulate.

Baggot Street Hospital's ladies' committee managed many of the hospital's daily activities that concerned the general welfare of patients. In order to enable the ladies to do their work, Baggot Street supplied the ladies' committee with a budget and permitted the committee administrative authority over certain staff.[101] Baggot Street's reliance on the ladies' committee suggests that hospital administrators were not only happy to save the money needed to pay an administrator to do this work, but also that it believed these women to be competent to hold such authority.

In 1866 one lady philanthropist offered Sir Patrick Dun's a new opportunity. Maria Trench contacted Dun's and requested that the Dublin Nurses' Training Institute, which she and her husband, Richard Chenevix Trench, a reforming Protestant archbishop of Dublin, had established, provide trained nurses to the hospital.[102] Dun's board accepted Trench's proposal.[103] While the records of the institute have yet to be located, from the minute books of Sir Patrick Dun's, it appears that upper-class ladies ran the institute, which recruited young women to live in the institute's home and train as nurses in the hospital. While the institute hired a matron to attend to the nurses' needs in the home, it was the ladies of the institute's governing board who both administered the home and had the final say on all decisions.

The Dublin Nurses' Training Institution improved the quality of the nurses who worked for Sir Patrick Dun's. However, like most Irish institutions, the sectarian tensions that infiltrated much of Irish life would eventually be the Training Institution's undoing. Throughout its history, Sir Patrick Dun's records showed that the hospital made extensive efforts to avoid the sectarian conflicts that plagued many of Dublin's local charities and hospitals. For example, Dun's provided the Douai version of the Bible for Roman Catholic patients and ensured that patients received a minister or priest as they desired.[104] In fact, the minutes noted that, in 1873, when the Rev. Thomas Doyle wrote to ask permission for the Association for Visiting Roman Catholics in Hospitals to visit Sir Patrick Dun's, the board of governors responded that they "with pleasure grant the permission sought."[105] Nevertheless, Dun's efforts to remain nonsectarian were put to the test as problems between the hospital and the Training Institution arose.[106] In 1872, the board requested that the institute cease using the hospital's name in its advertisements for nurses, because the institute only sought women who were members of the Church of Ireland and the board believed that "the sectarian character of the advertisement is calculated to be very injurious to the Hospital."[107]

The hospital's problems with the Training Institute culminated on January 23, 1883, when the lady superintendent of Sir Patrick Dun's, Margaret Johnson, wrote to the board to inform them that Miss Maude Trench of the Training Institute "has ordered me to dismiss three of my best probationers and one hospital nurse because they are dissenters."[108] Johnson argued that this would "paralyze" the hospital and revealed that "I have great difficulty just now in securing probationers belonging to the Irish Church, but can get sufficient numbers of highly respectable girls from the North who are Presbyterians."[109] Johnson finished the letter by begging the board not to force her to dismiss these women. The board permitted Johnson to keep both the probationers and the nurse. Then, in a letter to the Training Institution, Sir Patrick Dun's terminated its association and stated that "it is now absolutely necessary for the welfare of the Hospital to throw it open for the training of nurses of all religious denomination[s]."[110] The board noted that it would keep without charge the present probationers and charge for any future probationers that the institute desired to send.

Kirkpatrick defends Trench's Training Institution, arguing that the institute was limited as to whom it could accept because it was founded by a prominent Protestant archbishop and "was likely to be looked on as suspect by a Roman Catholic community, while it would have too much flavor of a Roman Catholic religious order to be acceptable to some Protestants."[111] Because of the sectarian climate of nineteenth-century Dublin, the institute chose to limit itself to Episcopalian[112] recruits, although it explicitly noted that trainees were to be "strictly non-sectarian in the work."[113] As evidence, Kirkpatrick noted that the institute refused to associate itself with the Protestant-only Adelaide Hospital as a sign of its efforts to remain nonsectarian. While the religious restrictions of the Dublin Nurses' Training Institution were not singular for Dublin charities, Dun's policy of nondiscrimination was possibly more practical than charitable, as it allowed the hospital to hire a more diverse population and thereby a better quality of nurse. Regardless, over time, the influence of the ladies of charity waned and, as the records show, it was the matrons and lady superintendents who increasingly wielded the power within the administrative structures of local hospitals.

From its earliest days Dun's gave its matrons and lady superintendents broad authority and extensive responsibility in order to ensure the efficient administration of the hospital. For example, in 1835, the records show that the board of governors ordered the matron to provide a report at each of their meetings and expected her to guarantee "that the nurses by night as well as by day attend upon the sick with diligence."[114] Among many other things, the matron was to ensure the cleanliness of the hospital, the smooth running of the laundry, and a healthy and generous diet for the patients, which, the records noted, required that she watch that the nurses did not sell, waste, or abscond with the food.[115] Dun's matron most likely would have been a woman with a lower- or middle-class background and, as noted earlier, she too faced many challenges when trying to control the behavior of her nurses.

On March 11, 1884 when Sir Patrick Dun's appointed Miss Margaret Huxley and gave her the dual title of lady superintendent and matron, the hospital entered a new era of nursing. Huxley, born in 1856, received her training in London at St. Bartholomew's Hospital and had been matron of the National Eye and Ear Infirmary in Dublin since 1882.[116] One of Huxley's first acts was to change the nurse training program for Sir Patrick Dun's from one year to three. Next she added a final examination and extended to two years the length of time nurses needed to work in the hospital before receiving their diplomas.[117] Finally, Huxley added courses in anatomy and included lectures by Dun's surgeons.[118]

In 1890, Huxley founded a nursing home in Lower Mount Street, a facility that offered private medical and surgical care and employed Dun's probationers.[119] This arrangement was advantageous for the hospital because the surgical home hired one of Sir Patrick Dun's private nurses as matron, for which the hospital received a fee of £30 a year. In addition, Dun's probationers received surgical training in the home.[120] In 1894, Miss Huxley was named honorary secretary of the newly established Dublin Metropolitan School for Nurses. The school supplied nurses to six Dublin hospitals and, as the minutes reveal, provided instruction to both experienced and probationer nurses "in Anatomy, Physiology, Hygiene, Invalid Cookery [and] such other subjects outside hospital training, as may be deemed necessary for the sufficient training of nurses."[121] The Dublin Metropolitan School for Nurses committee rented rooms in the Royal College of Surgeons and eventually established a sophisticated testing and grading system in order to provide the most qualified of candidates.

While the teaching of nurses was another common requirement for lady superintendents, this activity also further enforced a lady superintendent's authority over her nurses. Thus, in 1895, Huxley added her own weekly lectures to the probationers.[122] Miss McGivney, the first matron of the nursing school for the Mater Misericordiae in Dublin, was responsible for teaching nurses. The Baggot Street Hospital required its lady superintendent to administer the hospital's nurses and to "carefully attend to their instruction, and give them all proper opportunities of learning their duties as Nurses."[123] Here again the lady superintendent played the same role as the middle-class lady to her servants. She set a daily agenda for her nurses, taught them how to do their jobs, made sure that they had all the supplies they needed, and was an example of moral behavior. The lady superintendent was a participant in the hospital's culture of surveillance as well as an enforcer of its agenda of social control. She was an additional administrative support within the growing number of panoptic institutions in which employees as well as "inmates" could be watched from all angles.

Interestingly, the stature of Margaret Huxley and the power she wielded may be most evident at the end of her tenure at Sir Patrick Dun's. During all of her years at the hospital, Huxley continued to advance the training of both nurses and midwives. Like the nurses, the midwives had a separate training home and were required to attend labor cases both in the hospital and in private homes. However, as Dun's records show, midwives did not receive the same level of preparation as nurse probationers. In 1900, Miss Huxley discovered that Dun's midwives were advertising themselves as fully qualified private nurses. Huxley argued that this was misleading and dangerous, citing cases of drunkenness and inefficiency and stating that this placed patients' lives in jeopardy. She asked the board to take action. After a full investigation, the board decided to put the midwives under the lady superintendent's control and to mark diplomas clearly for nurses and midwives.[124] Nevertheless, the hospital gynecologist, Dr. Arthur Macan, disagreed. Macan argued that the women who were trained in maternity at Dun's could call themselves nurses. In 1902, Miss Huxley resigned her post in protest. While the board next chose to eliminate the maternity ward of the hospital, Huxley did not rescind her resignation and before the year's end the hospital hired her replacement.[125]

Huxley's refusal to continue with Dun's may have been more out of desire for a professional change than a principled stand. However, while the board's elimination of the maternity ward may have also been a smart fiscal decision, it certainly reflected their desire to retain an administrator as competent as Huxley, a woman who had given years of service to the hospital. Huxley had achieved a great deal of authority at Dun's, as shown by her interaction with the hospital's administration. Nevertheless, after tendering her resignation, she did not lose favor with the hospital, and the board of governors made her its first woman member in 1912, later establishing an award to nurses in her name.[126] Margaret Huxley continued her work with the Dublin Metropolitan School for Nurses and went on to help to establish the Irish Nurses Association, the Dublin Nurses' Club, and the Irish Matron's Association, all while advocating for the registration of Irish nurses. She was matron of the Dublin University Women's Voluntary Aid Detachment Hospital during World War I and, in 1928, Dublin University awarded Huxley an Honorary Master of Arts.[127]

Sir Patrick Dun's continually sought to improve both the nursing and medical care that it provided to the Dublin community. The hospital's minutes from later in the century reveal fewer personnel problems with the nurses and thus suggest the effectiveness of Huxley's leadership as well as reflecting the more professional nature of the nursing staff. Nevertheless, despite improved training and conditions, the hospital continued to implement a restrictive regimen for nurses that inhibited many middle- and upper-class women from joining nursing's ranks. So too, nurses' hours remained long and their pay remained low as their position within the hospital slowly gained respectability. Such respectability came through the standardization of training and registration of nurses, and Huxley and the lady superintendents of the late nineteenth century were at the forefront of this effort. It was through the work of women like Margaret Huxley and Maria Trench that Sir Patrick Dun's Hospital offered middle- and upper-class women the opportunity to become intimately involved in the reform of nursing and the creation of another career for their working-class sisters.

Other local hospitals also sought to improve the quality of their nurse training, and at the end of the nineteenth century the Baggot Street Hospital joined Sir Patrick Dun's in instituting changes. In 1883, Dr. William de Courcy Wheeler, a surgeon with Baggot Street, established the City of Dublin Nursing Institution in order to train nurses for the hospital.[128] The hospital then created the position of lady superintendent. She was to hire and fire all nurses and probationers and to ensure that the nurses, probationers, and wardmaids had everything they needed, from bedding to food. For the patients, she was to guarantee clean sheets, furniture, and other items. She was to make certain that nurses followed all instructions from hospital physicians and that all medication was correctly administered. As her duties clearly indicated, the lady superintendent was an important member of the hospital's administration.

In 1884, Baggot Street hired 31-year-old S. Helena Bewley of Bray to be the hospital's lady superintendent. It appears that Bewley understood her role as a reformer, and she immediately began to restructure the hospital's nursing program.[129] Bewley devised all her changes within the limits of the hospital's budget and implemented a reduction to the nursing staff that ensured that patient care "would be performed in a thoroughly satisfactory manner and by six hospital nurses instead of nine."[130] Under Bewley's plan, the expenditure on probationers and nurses actually decreased. (See Table 5.5.)[131]

Bewley showed herself to be quite a capable manager, something she would have been trained for both in nursing school and as a member of one of Dublin's prominent business families. Helena Bewley was related to the Quaker family whose successful teahouses can still be found on the most fashionable avenues in Dublin. As a youngster growing up in an elite household, it seems that her family probably provided Bewley with a formal education that also trained her to know how to run a home and supervise servants—all of which would have been important to her position as administrator of nurses and wardmaids. In addition, Bewley's membership in the Religious Society of Friends meant that she was part of a religious sect that supported women's public activities. Likely, Bewley's family and close friends encouraged her to pursue nursing's call. Nonetheless, after only a few months on the job, in December of 1884, Bewley tendered her resignation. While the minutes provide no explanation as to why she made such a decision, Friends' records show that a Helena Bewley married George Goodbody in February of 1885.[132] As noted earlier, many hospitals did not want married nurses or lady superintendents, and, whether by choice or not, it appears that Bewley may have left because of her impending marriage. Susan Beresford was hired as Bewley's replacement, and the training of nurses at Baggot Street

Table 5.5
1884: Baggot Street Hospital Proposed Budget for Nurses' Salaries

Current Scale:	
Total Wages of Nurses in 1883	£134
Total Wages of Special Nurses 1883	£14
Total Sum for Gratuities & Holidays	£23
Total	£170
Proposed Scale:	
2 Staff Nurses at £25 Each	£50
2 Night Nurses at £18 Each	£36
1 Fever Nurse at £18	£18
1 Children's Ward Nurse at £16	£16
Total	£138

slowly became more exacting, reflecting the slow but steady shift from vocation to career and the call for nurses to be educated in the science of medicine.

As time progressed, Baggot Street's City of Dublin Nursing Institution sought to make the nursing curriculum more rigorous and in 1886 requested that "no probationer shall be put in night duty until she has been at least three months on day duty . . . and no probationer shall be put on duty in the fever wards until she has had at least six months training."[133] The directors of the Nursing Institution wrote the hospital requesting that the board of governors express to the lady superintendent that it was their desire that each probationer be given four-month stints in the medical, surgical, and fever wards and that each quarter should include one month on night duty.[134] By the turn of the century the hospital had established a rigorous curriculum for nurses that included the medical staff acting as lecturers.[135] Baggot Street Hospital also sent its nurses out to private cases. The charging of fees for their services brought extra profit to the hospital. Nevertheless, knowing that these women would not have all the amenities of a hospital with them, only those nurses who had spent a minimum of two years in the hospital's wards and had passed examinations on all of their courses were sent out.[136] By the end of 1905, the hospital was hiring out 26 nurses as private nurses with 25 others in training.[137] Thus, by the turn of the century, Baggot Street was trying to guarantee that only its best nurses were sent into the public realm. These women, the hospital hoped, with their training and education, had learned to behave both as "ladies" and as professional nurses.

It was during all these changes that the ladies' committees of Baggot Street and Sir Patrick Dun's quietly continued to work to see that their respective hospitals continued to run smoothly. Baggot Street's ladies' committee purchased quilts for the nursery to replace worn ones, suggested improvements in the nurses' diet, and continued to raise money for the hospital.[138] It also worked to enhance the accommodations and standards of its nurses and, eventually, through fund-raisers, "each nurse and probationer [was] provided with a separate bedroom."[139] As the women of philanthropy continued to seek to improve not only nursing conditions but also nurse training and education, they also aspired to break the social binds that restrained upper-class women from entering the profession. By turning nursing into a career, philanthropists were advocating greater credibility for the profession. Gradually, as the Victorian era slowly came to an end and the restraints on upper-class women's mobility subtly decreased, the improved education, training, and reputation of the nurse made it seem possible for more middle-class women to begin to answer nursing's call.

By the end of the nineteenth century, many hospitals had established their own nursing schools and hired nurses with some level of training. Nevertheless, into the twentieth century, nurse preparation was not uniform. For example, in 1890 Dr. Steevens and Baggot Street trained its nurses for two years, while Sir Patrick Dun's and the Mater Misericordiae trained them for three. Over time, education and training improved as the women who took a leadership role in nursing in Ireland, England, and the United States sought to legitimize the profession through regulation and registration of trained nurses.[140] These women hoped to move nursing work away from the subordinate role in which many hospital administrators and doctors sought to maintain it.[141] Among those calling for longer training and more stringent qualifications for nurses were philanthropists and nurse reformers alike, who believed that a nurse was more than a gentle voice and someone with the ability to cook a good meal. They wanted to create a career that would provide women with challenge, responsibility, and personal independence.

A NURSE OF A DIFFERENT SORT: WOMEN PHILANTHROPISTS AND IRELAND'S DISTRICT NURSES

While there are many similarities, the history of the district nurse is different from that of her sisters who worked in hospitals. Ireland's district nurse was much more an independent figure; she had to be. Sometimes the only medical person for miles, these women worked long hours doing both complex and menial jobs for the many persons to whom they gave care. In return, these women gained more respect and authority within the local community. With more training than hospital nurses, district nursing may have been one of the first legitimate professions for women where most of the time they were free of authority, managed their own time, and relied on their own ingenuity to get the job done. Yet, here again, as with hospital reform, we find the women of philanthropy working to improve the training of and working conditions for the district nurse. So too, like the hospital nurse, philanthropists had clear expectations about the type of women they wanted to become Ireland's district nurses.

District nursing was an important part of the nineteenth-century nursing agenda. While Britain's industrialization had led to increasing urbanization, in which larger institutions including hospitals found a home, most countries remained predominantly rural. Except for the northeast, Ireland had not industrialized in the nineteenth century, and the majority of the Irish population was to be found in the countryside or in small towns.[142] Thus, for some, the district nurse staved off hospitalization, while for most, she was their primary and sometimes only contact with the medical world.

In examining the records of Ireland's district nursing organizations, they portray the district nurse as an independent figure with extensive responsibility. The records also show that district nurses were expected to assume a great deal of authority and be prepared to accept an extensive variety of medical tasks, even more than their fellow professionals who nursed in hospitals. The district nurse, if good at her job, could become a trusted authority within the community and a person to whom both men and women went for advice and care.[143] While she was not an upper-class female, she was more likely the daughter of a skilled workman or merchant than the child of an unskilled laborer.

William Rathbone, executive at a Liverpool shipping company, is considered the father of district nursing.[144] In 1859, Rathbone's wife died. During her illness, she had been the patient of a woman who nursed her until her death. Rathbone, who was involved in local philanthropic organizations, recognized the benefits of the great support his late wife had derived from her visiting nurse.[145] Inspired by his wife's experience, Rathbone decided to employ this nurse to visit the sick poor of the local neighborhood. Pleased with how this experiment went, Rathbone established and helped pay for a nurse-training institute associated with the Liverpool Royal Infirmary. The institute provided accommodation and training for women to nurse either for the Royal Infirmary or private families, or act as district nurses to the poor.[146] For these early district nursing programs, lady volunteers worked in committee to raise funds for the training institute as well as keep an "an eye on the nurse's case register and from time to time visiting with her to see that she was doing her work properly."[147] It was, however, working-class women who actually ventured into Liverpool neighborhoods and nursed the poor. Here again, like the class structure in which they lived, ladies believed themselves to be moral role models who, as the guardians of a domestic sphere that included nursing, could best advise their working-class sisters, while the working-class women actually did the work.

Increasingly, philanthropists throughout Great Britain established charities that provided nurses for the sick poor. For example, in London, Ellen Ranyard established the Ranyard Mission in 1857.[148] In 1868, the mission added nursing to its religious missionary work in order to supply Bible women nurses to the poor. The nurses trained for three months as Bible women, three months in a hospital, two weeks in a maternity ward, and worked as probationers for three months before being sent to nurse and mission among the poor. The women that the Ranyard Mission recruited were not "ladies" but instead described as "missing links" or "a good poor woman who would venture into every room as a paid agent of the Bible Society."[149] As these women entered into the homes of their contemporaries, the mission hoped that they would express middle-class desires for working-class respectability. Florence Nightingale wrote that the district nurse was "the great civilizer of the poor, training them as well as nursing them out of ill health into good health, out of drunkenness into self control."[150] The visiting nurse was another agent through which the upper classes sought to discipline the poor. At the same time, through demonstration, reformers hoped that visiting nurses provided the indigent with a prototype of a productive and devout member of the state.

Ireland followed England's example, and in 1874 Irish women philanthropists founded the Belfast Society for Providing Nurses for the Sick Poor, which paid nurses who were directed "under the superintendence of the ladies of the committee."[151] In 1878, the society's records show that nurses worked seven hours a day, six days a week, and were provided room, board, retirement payments, and £34 annually during a five-year contract.[152] In addition, and reminiscent of the upper-class encouragement for those in the working classes to be frugal, the Belfast Society placed "an addition of ten shillings a month, to be lodged in the Savings Bank by the Committee, and paid to her at the end of her engagement, with the interest accruing thereon."[153] The ladies' committee that directed the society expected the nurses to make themselves examples of cleanliness and order to their patients "and to urge upon [them] the importance . . . of the immediate removal of all things offensive both from the bed and room, and care to keep the sick-room clean and tidy."[154] Because most of the nurses were members of the same socioeconomic background as their patients, the Belfast association, like the Ranyard Mission, hoped that the middle-class message of sanitary behavior, hard work, and moral living would be delivered by working-class nurses and thus more easily accepted.

In Dublin, in 1876, Lady Anne Lee Plunket, a very active philanthropist and wife of Lord William Plunket, Archbishop of Dublin, established the St. Patrick's Nurses' Home and Bible Woman Association.[155] This charity's object was, "by means of Bible-Women, Mothers' Meetings, Trained Nurses, District Visiting, Temperance Associations, and similar agencies, to make use of Woman's Work to promote the spiritual and temporal welfare of the poor."[156] While evangelical, the organization noted that it focused on bringing the Word of God to members of the Church of Ireland specifically, although not exclusively. The nurses were to do "all such work as may be required for the patient," while the lady superintendent instructed the nurses, provided examples, and inspected and watched over the nurses, particularly in difficult cases.[157] It does not appear that nurses and Bible women traveled together, although the Bible women, at times, might have also provided nursing services, "which needs only that skill which tenderness and experience gives."[158] Eventually, St. Patrick's became a training facility for the Queen Victoria's Jubilee Institute for Nurses and would cease its missionary activities.

The largest and most well-known district nursing institution in nineteenth-century Britain was the Queen Victoria's Jubilee Institute for Nurses, founded with £82,000 raised as a gift for Queen Victoria on the jubilee anniversary of her coronation.[159] In 1887, under the consultation of both Rathbone and Florence Lees,[160] the Queen Victoria's Jubilee Institute for Nurses, a visiting nurse program, was founded. While this organization was to establish branches in all areas of Great Britain, early in the planning of the Jubilee Institute in Ireland, sectarian problems surfaced when the Catholic archbishop of Dublin, William Walsh, demanded that Roman Catholic nurses live in a separate home from Protestant nurses. Thus, in Dublin, St. Patrick's, created in 1876, and St. Lawrence's, opened in 1891, Protestant and Catholic respectively, became nurse-training homes for Irish Jubilee nurses.[161]

In 1893, Mrs. Charles Martin wrote an article on St. Lawrence's Institute that particularly emphasized that the Catholic sick poor needed to be nursed by sympathetic Roman Catholic women.[162] Martin argued that the nurses would be a great help to the "wretched and ignorant poor, who know nothing of the most elementary rules for either preserving or repairing health."[163] These nurses would be the foot soldiers for middle-class notions of respectability and were expected to enforce the rules of sanitary practice and moral living for the poor. Finally, and interestingly, Martin implied that the nurses working at St. Lawrence's Home should be "ladies." Martin attempted to sell nursing at St. Lawrence's to those women who wanted to volunteer their time without accepting wages or dedicating their lives to God. She stated that nursing "may be looked upon now as a career for women which combines the exercise of the highest Christian Charity with a certain amount of freedom and absence of the solemn obligations of conventual life."[164] Martin reflected many reformers' belief that becoming a nurse was not unlike entering the convent and that nursing was more a vocation than a profession. Thus, a lady remained respectable and fulfilled her caring role, all while still leaving open the option of marriage and motherhood. However, as the Jubilee records showed, due to the nature of the work, most district nurses would not be the upper-class ladies that Martin hoped to recruit.

By 1895, throughout Britain, there were over 500 nurses enrolled on the Jubilee books. Paternal occupations provided by all Jubilee nurses showed that they were generally daughters of farmers and tradesmen.[165] This was true of Ireland's Jubilee nurses as well.[166] Of 107 nurses appointed in Ireland between the years 1897 and 1908, 94 provided their father's occupation (see Table 5.6).

These were women who, due to their socioeconomic status, would, by this time, have had access to an education.[167] This is emphasized by the fact that throughout the nineteenth century, Irish literacy rates for males and females rose. Westminster had inaugurated a national system of schools in Ireland in 1831.[168] While the system had clear problems, by the turn of the century statistics suggest that over 90 percent of Irish emigrants to the United States were literate in English.[169] As the state began to improve the level of education for girls, more women were able to enter higher skilled occupations such as nursing and teaching. Both occupations increasingly required ever more educational and vocational training, thereby further diminishing the ability for the poorest of working-class women to enter either occupation. While the pay scale for such jobs, compared to those still dominated by men, would remain unequal, for district nursing, the provision of room, board, and a small salary did provide

Table 5.6
1897–1908: Jubilee Nurses' Fathers' Occupations

Farmers=	39 %
Religious=	6 %
Merchants/Shopkeepers, etc.=	15%
Military/Police, etc.=	11%
Others=	29%

women with a measure of, at minimum, personal if not financial independence.

The evidence above suggests that district nurses were not members of the poorest classes, as many early hospital nurses were. As Nightingale wrote, a district nurse "must be of a higher class and have fuller training than a hospital nurse, because she has no hospital appliances at hand at all; and because she has to make notes of the case for the doctor, who has no one but her to report to. She is his staff of clinical clerks, dressers, and nurses."[170] Nevertheless, because they were not from the highest economic echelons in society, these women needed the income they earned from nursing.

The Jubilee Nurses' Institute desired well-trained candidates and required that a Jubilee nurse have two years of hospital experience before she could train to be a district nurse. Her education also included lessons on domestic hygiene and information for mothers of young children, including directions regarding the provision of a healthy diet.[171] A woman did not officially become a Jubilee nurse until after a month's trial period, which, if she passed, she could continue with "technical class instruction" for five more months and sign a contract for a year from completion date of training. Finally, unlike some hospital nurses, knowledge of midwifery was essential for a rural district nurse.[172]

Certainly the visiting nurse had a greater diversity of responsibility than most hospital nurses. It appears that such requirements may have made recruitment more difficult as, for example, when the author of St. Patrick's Nurses' Home and Bible Women Association report of 1901 stated that a visiting nurse must possess "both medical and surgical skill, and, in addition, calm judgment and inexhaustible patience to bear with the numberless, nameless trials she has to face in the daily round. Above all, she must have that unfailing tact and courtesy which will in no way ruffle the sensibilities of the poor."[173] The work of the district nurse was very demanding, and, although she was only expected to work six days a week, she was on call 24 hours a day. For her troubles, the Jubilee organization supplied its nurses with salary, room, board, a uniform, bicycles (eventually cars), and a month's holiday.[174]

Once out in the field it would soon become clear that while, at minimum, hospital nursing provided comradeship, this was much less the case for district nurses. Isolation was a particular problem faced by any of Ireland's rural visiting nurses. As one nurse wrote of her experiences in the west of Ireland in 1925, she found "a wild rugged country—nothing but bare rocks, bog and sea to greet the eye . . . the nearest station is 18 miles, and the nearest hospital 25 miles away. The people speak practically nothing but Gaelic, and have no industry beyond turf-saving to support them."[175] The work for women stationed in these desolate counties was made more difficult because the districts in which they nursed were very large. For example, one area in County Galway was "on an island 7 miles from the mainland and 17 miles from the nearest doctor. On this island a Nurse has carried on single handed for over 12 years, for during stormy weather no boat can cross the stretch of water which separates the Island from the mainland . . . the nurse therefore has had to be Doctor, Midwife, Nurse, and Health Visitor to the poor people."[176] In another case, one nurse reported:

> During the past week I have been on duty day and night. A few nights ago when called to a case over six miles away [I] could only get a cart, and apart from being thoroughly shaken I was quite saturated with rain, and my clothes in a dreadful state of mud and dirt. On arrival at case found patient quite alone except for four small children, the oldest not six years. No fire, no water. Baby born in about half an hour, patient in most critical state. After much work and anxiety got things into a satisfactory condition, and remained with patient until following day. I have six midwifery cases at present—one six miles on one side of my district, and one five miles on the other side, others on by-roads two and three miles away.[177]

These recollections show that district nursing could be a lonely occupation; the nurse might be the only person between the patient and death, and these women could find themselves facing the most extreme of medical cases.

While her role was more often a combination of mother, maid, nurse, hygienic counselor, teacher, and therapist, her duties also included those of a domestic servant.[178] The annual report of the Belfast Society for Providing Nurses to the Sick Poor expected that, upon arrival, the nurse would clean the home and ensure proper ventilation.[179] While reformers made great efforts to remove from the hospital nurse's work many housekeeping tasks, they could not have provided the district nurse with this luxury, and a woman entering a home to take the mother's role of nurse would also have been expected to handle all of the woman's duties.[180] As one district nurse wrote of a visit to a family with five small children, she "rubbed and bandaged patient, washed and dressed baby daily and four other children; eldest girl of seven very sore head, which was poulticed and cleansed; little boy with sore eyes attended to; mother's hair cut, head cleansed, her bed made daily, emptied slops, prepared food; washed clothes and cleansed room."[181]

Such hard physical labor required by the district nurses' job was something that few ladies would participate in for fear of placing their respectability in jeopardy. "The district nurse of 1888 would be a 'suitable' woman, not a 'lady,' but one used to rolling up her sleeves and getting down to things. She probably did as much midwifery as general nursing, often staying in the homes of her patients, and becoming cook and housekeeper for a time as well."[182] The lady directed and watched. She guided, provided a good example, and advised. Never, however, could she sully herself by participating in physical labor. A lady taught nurses sanitary techniques and proper domestic administrating skills that would bring the working classes closer to the ultimate upper-class goal: creation of an "honest" laboring poor.[183]

Thus, it was middle-class philanthropists that established a structure into which the daughters of skilled labor, large farmers, and other professionals could enter. It was organizations such as the Ranyard Mission or the St. Patrick's Nurses' Home and Bible Woman Association that created the opportunity for these women to attain greater independence, education, responsibility, and authority than almost any other position open to women. The community to which she ministered sought her out in times of crisis, listened to her advice on maintaining health, and saw her as a font of knowledge that added to the stability and security of the district.[184] Ultimately, these women found that a career as a district nurse could bring this outsider a measure of respectability not otherwise attainable within such rural communities.[185]

The work to reform nursing by lady philanthropists was another part of Victorian upper-class society's agenda of managing the poor. As Foucault argues, another part of the upper-class endeavor at containment of the masses was through medical facilities, which became more institutionalized during the seventeenth and eighteenth centuries.[186] This social control stretched into all areas of the nurse's life, and hospitals' strict daily agendas and refusal to permit married women to nurse were just two of many examples. By using the hospital as a place of containment, the women of philanthropy worked to impose strict rules upon nurses in order to monitor their actions and behavior. Reformers hoped nurses would then bring these lessons to their patients. Nevertheless, as the records clearly show, nurses did not always provide the desired response.

It is ironic that women were considered innately nurses while nineteenth-century nurse training gradually became more technical and increasingly specialized.[187] Whether nurses' skills were innate or developed through training, reformers wanted them to be strong, moral, kind, gentle, personable, diligent, intelligent, womanly, and, above all, obedient. They wanted a woman with upper-class breeding who combined the experience, strength, and familiarity with following orders of a working-class domestic servant. When nursing reformers realized that most of their recruits would be working-class women, they then attempted to shape these women into examples of hard-working, honest, and moral nurses. As social reformer Louisa Twining expressed, "Let us hope that the race of Mrs. Gamps, now dying out, will rapidly become extinct, to be remembered only with shame and confusion of face that we ever suffered them to exist. Even now it is almost impossible to realize that such things once were."[188]

Slowly, increasing numbers of "ladies" applied for nurse training as paying probationers.[189] Early on, most hospitals supplied these women with special privileges such as separate sleeping quarters, separate places in the chapel, different uniforms, and less stringent educational requirements.[190] Dublin's Baggot Street Hospital divided its nurses into paying and articled probationers. Paying probationers were charged 70 guineas and awarded a certificate after two years of training, while articled probationers paid 30 guineas and were required to work two additional years before receiving their certificate.[191]

The entrance of ladies into the profession did not occur with ease. Doctors expressed the fear that these women would have the social standing to allow them to ignore or make demands of doctors. As John Flint South, a doctor associated with the Nightingale training school, warned, the fear was that by admitting ladies, nursing would be placed "in the hands of ladies who will never be content till *they* become the executives of the hospitals."[192] In Dublin, for example, the directors of the medical board at Dublin's Adelaide Hospital noted that they feared "disrepute" if a lady was allowed to enter the nursing school, and they dreaded the loss of total control over staff.[193] However, as this chapter has shown, there was no flood of "ladies" into nursing.[194]

Dublin's hospital records revealed that women philanthropists were integral to the formation of nursing as a career for women both at home and abroad.[195] Early on, the hard work, long hours, low salary, on-site accommodations, and strict regimen argue against nursing being a position entered into by many upper-class women.[196] What hospital records instead show is that a small percentage of upper-class women willingly entered the paid position of lady superintendent. Here, it may be argued, was a position that upper-class women could engage in without loss of social status or personal dignity. First, as the documents reveal, lady superintendents made a much higher salary as compared to their nurses, and second, they maintained their respectability because the hospital provided them with extensive authority. Gradually upper-class women made their mark in Irish hospitals and helped to bring the Irish nurse onto the world stage. Nonetheless, through a strict regimen, restricted freedom, and close surveillance, upper-class reformers attempted to mold a "lady" out of a "woman" and make her into a nurse.

NOTES

1. The hospitals of Ireland have a rich biographical history, and while most include discussion of their nurses, few give more than cursory detail. Pauline Scanlan concentrates on nursing education and gives only the briefest of looks at nursing reform in the years prior to the twentieth century. Pauline Scanlan, *The Irish Nurse: A Study of Nursing in Ireland: History and Education, 1718–1981* (Co. Leitrum, Ireland: Drumlin Publications, 1991). See also Margaret Ó hÓgartaigh,

"Flower Power and 'Mental Grooviness': Nurses and Midwives in Ireland in the Early Twentieth Century," in *Women and Paid Work in Ireland 1500–1930*, ed. Bernadette Whelan (Dublin: Four Courts Press, 2000), pp. 133–47; Margaret Preston, "The Good Nurse: Women Philanthropists and the Evolution of Nursing in Nineteenth-Century Dublin," *New Hibernian Review* (Spring, 1998), pp. 91–110; Maria Luddy, "District Nursing In Ireland, 1815–1974," *Tipperary Historical Journal* (1996), pp. 164–69; Miriam Fallon, "Alice Reeves 1874–1955," *Nursing Review* 10, 3 and 4 (1992), pp. 38–39; Moira Lysaght, "The Evolution of Nursing in Dublin 1820–1970," *St. Vincent's Annual* (1975), pp. 52–56; and Margaret Reidy, "The History of Nursing in Ireland," *International Nursing Review* 18 (1971), pp. 326–33.

2. Susan Armeny, "Organized Nurses, Women Philanthropists, and the Intellectual Bases for Cooperation Among Women, 1898–1920," in *Nursing History: New Perspectives, New Possibilities*, ed. Ellen Condlifee Lagemann (New York: Teachers College Press, 1983), p. 33. Armeny argues that nurses and women in America came together not out of feminist solidarity but due to the Victorian desire for sanitary reform and the push to organize and professionalize nursing.

3. Many Irish hospitals were forced to rely on outside donations. In the eighteenth century, George Handel performed for a number of Irish hospital fundraisers. See J. B. Lyons, *The Quality of Mercer's: The Story of Mercer's Hospital, 1734–1991* (Dublin: Glendale, 1991).

4. It is important to note that the title of lady superintendent was not universal. The matron could also be the woman in charge of nursing responsibilities. If a hospital had both a lady superintendent and a matron, then the lady superintendent was in charge of nursing and the matron managed housekeeping duties. Generally, the matron was subordinate to the lady superintendent. Baggot Street's hospital board reminded its matron that "any communication to any person requiring the services of a nurse . . . on all such occasions it is the duty of the Matron to refer applicants to the Lady Superintendent without any interference or expression of opinion on her own part." Royal City of Dublin Hospital, henceforth RCD (13 February 1885). These records are located in Dublin's Mercer's Library.

5. The higher social status of Dublin's Sir Patrick Dun's Hospital's lady superintendent was emphasized when, in 1878, upon Susan Beresford's departure, the hospital granted her a position on the hospital's ladies' committee. Sir Patrick Dun's, henceforth SPD (25 June 1878). The records for Sir Patrick Dun's Hospital are held in the Royal College of Physicians, and the Governors Minute Books begin in 1822. Susan Beresford moved from Sir Patrick Dun's to become the lady superintendent of Dublin's Baggot Street Hospital where, upon her retirement, she was made honorary president of Baggot Street's ladies' committee. RCD (16 October 1896).

6. In Ireland, for example, Alice Reeves (1874–1955), being the granddaughter of the Lord Bishop of Down Conor and Dromore, would have been considered a woman of middle- to upper-class lineage. Reeves became matron of Dr. Steevens's in 1918 and worked to improve nursing at the hospital. Fallon, "Alice Reeves 1874–1955," pp. 38–39.

7. As quoted by Judith Moore, *A Zeal for Responsibility The Struggle for Professional Nursing in Victorian England, 1868–1883* (Athens: University of Georgia Press, 1988), p. 5.

8. Carol S. Helmstadter, "Doctors and Nurses in the London Teaching Hos-

pitals," *Nursing History Review* 5 (1997), p. 173. See also Carol S. Helmstadter, "Nurse Recruitment and Retention in the Nineteenth Century London Teaching Hospitals," *International History of Nursing Journal* 2, 1 (Autumn 1996), pp. 58–69.

9. The first petition for women's suffrage was sent to the British Parliament in 1866. The National Society for Women's Suffrage was founded in England in 1867. In Ireland, there was the Northern Ireland Society for Women's Suffrage established in 1871 and the Dublin Women's Suffrage Association founded in 1876. Mary Cullen, "Anna Maria Haslam," in *Women, Power and Consciousness in Nineteenth-Century Ireland,* ed. Maria Luddy and Mary O'Dowd (Dublin: Attic Press, 1995), p. 173. See also Sandra Beth Lewenson, *Taking Charge: Nursing, Suffrage and Feminism in America 1873–1920* (New York: NLN Press, 1996).

10. Changes in nursing came swiftly, because "the ladies who sought power in the hospitals moved in the same circles as the committees that ran them." Brian Abel-Smith, *A History of the Nursing Profession* (London: Heineman, 1960), p. 36.

11. RCD (8 February 1884).

12. Mrs. J. N. Higgins, "On the Improvement of Nurses in Country Districts," *Transactions of the National Association for the Promotion of Social Science* 6 (1861), p. 574. See also Mary M. Flad, "Tracing an Irish Widow's Journey: Immigration and Medical Care in the Mid-Nineteenth Century," *Geoforum* 26, 3 (1995), p. 263.

13. See John F. Fleetwood, *The History of Medicine in Ireland* (Dublin: The Skellig Press, 1983).

14. Gregory O'Connor, "Speech on the Royal Hospital, Kilmainham" (Dublin: 1994). I would like to thank Gregory O'Connor, archivist of the National Archives of Ireland, for his extensive assistance with my research and for providing me with a copy of this paper.

15. See Edward McFarland, "The Royal Hospital Kilmainham, Co. Dublin," *Country Life* (9–16 May 1985), n.p.; "The Royal Hospital, Kilmainham," *Dublin University Magazine* 7 (January-June 1836), pp. 222–26; and Major E.S.E. Childers and Robert Stewart, *The Story of the Royal Hospital, Kilmainham* (London: Hutchinson and Co., 1921).

16. The records contain many requests from and granting of financial assistance to the widows and enlisted personnel. O'Connor, "Speech on the Royal Hospital," 1994.

17. See J. D. H. Widdess, *The Richmond, Whitworth & Hardwicke Hospitals Dublin 1772–1972* (Dublin: Beacon Printing, 1972), p. 10.

18. E. Evans, "History of Dublin Hospitals: House of Industry Hospital," *The Irish Builder* 39 (1897), pp. 159–60; and William Thornley Stoker, "The Hospitals of the House of Industry," *Dublin Journal of Medical Science* 80 (December 1885), pp. 469–86.

19. Widdess, *The Richmond, Whitworth & Hardwicke Hospitals,* p. 73.

20. Dr. Steevens Hospital was closed in 1987, but the handsome building, modeled on the Hôtel des Invalides in Paris, now houses the offices of the Eastern Health Board of Ireland. See T. Percy Kirkpatrick, *The History of Doctor Steevens Hospital, Dublin, 1720–1920* (Dublin: University Press, 1924); and Davis Coakley, *Dr. Steevens Hospital:, A Brief History* (Dublin: Dr. Steevens' Hospital Historical Centre, 1992).

21. Coakley, *Dr. Steevens Hospital,* p. 9.

22. See Alan Brown, ed., *Masters, Midwives and Ladies in Waiting: The Rotunda*

Hospital: 1745–1995 (Dublin: A&A Farmar, 1995); and Ian Campbell Ross, ed., *Public Virtue, Public Love: The Early Years of the Dublin Lying-In Hospital* (Dublin: The O'Brien Press, 1986).

23. See *An Address to the Public on the Propriety of Midwives instead of Surgeons practicing Midwifery* (London: Longman Rees & Co., 1828). See also "The Education of Midwives," *Medical Press & Circular* (4 July 1866), p. 26; and J. Maxwell, "Uneducated Midwives," *Medical Press & Circular* (7 March 1866), p. 234.

24. See also J. B. Lyons and Mary O'Doherty, *Accouching the Rotundaties: A Guide to the Rotunda* (Dublin: A&A Farmar, 1995); and Cormac Ó Gráda, "Dublin's Demography in the Early Nineteenth Century: Evidence from the Rotunda," *Population Studies* 45 (1991), pp. 43–54.

25. Sir Patrick Dun had also been the first physician for the Royal Hospital, Kilmainham. See O'Connor, "Speech on the Royal Hospital," 1994.

26. Thomas Gillman Moorhead, *A Short History of Sir Patrick Dun's Hospital* (Dublin: Hodges, Figgis and Co., 1942), pp. 18 and 22. The income of the estate of Sir Patrick Dun and private donations sustained the hospital.

27. The Baggot Street Hospital eventually became the Royal City of Dublin Hospital in 1900. See also Davis Coakley, *Baggot Street: A Short History of the Royal City of Dublin Hospital* (Dublin: Royal City of Dublin Hospital, 1995), p. 7.

28. David Mitchell, *A "Peculiar" Place: The Adelaide Hospital, Dublin: Its Times, Places and Personalities, 1839 to 1989* (Dublin: Blackwater, 1989), p. 88.

29. See Mary Peckham Magray, *The Transforming Power of Nuns: Women, Religion and Cultural Change in Ireland: 1790–1900* (New York: Oxford University Press, 1998); and John Newsinger, "The Catholic Church in Nineteenth-Century Ireland," *European History Quarterly* 25 (1995), pp. 247–67.

30. Catriona Clear, *Nuns in 19th Century Ireland* (Dublin: Gill & MacMillan, 1987), p. 107.

31. F. O. C. Meenan, *St. Vincent's Hospital 1834–1994: An Historical and Social Portrait* (Dublin: Gill & MacMillan, 1995), p. 15. Interestingly, Florence Nightingale went to Dublin in 1852 to see the work of the Sisters of Charity in St. Vincent's Hospital and applied to train with them. However, according to Moira Lysaght, the sisters would only train those women who entered the convent and thus they rejected Nightingale's application. See Reidy, "The History of Nursing in Ireland," p. 327; and Moira Lysaght, "The Evolution of Nursing in Dublin 1820–1970," *St. Vincent's Annual* (1975), p. 55.

32. See Maria Luddy, *Women and Philanthropy in Nineteenth Century Ireland* (New York: Cambridge University Press, 1995), p. 25.

33. An east wing was completed in 1872, and in 1886 the west wing containing rooms for the nuns was finished. The hospital expanded further in the twentieth century, and today the Mater remains an important medical facility for Dublin. See Edward T. Freeman, "Centenary of the Mater Misericordiae Hospital 1861–1961," (n.p., n.d.), pp. 3–40.

34. As Nolan notes, the Mater's matron from 1920–1930, Mother Madeline Sophie McCormack, "had a great respect for rules and regulations which contributed both to self discipline and to good order within the hospital." M. Eugene Nolan, *One Hundred Years: A History of the School of Nursing and of Developments at Mater Misericordiae Hospital 1891–1991* (Dublin: Goldpress Limited, 1991), p. 29.

35. It was not until 1891 that the Mater opened a nursing school that admitted lay women. Nolan, *One Hundred Years,* p. 1.

36. As Margaret Reidy notes, outside of Dublin between 1736 and 1834 there were 79 hospitals established. Reidy, "The History of Nursing in Ireland," p. 326. See also James Kelly, "The Emergence of Scientific and Institutional Practice in Ireland, 1650–1800," in *Medicine, Disease and the State in Ireland, 1650–1940,* ed. Elizabeth Malcolm and Greta Jones (Cork: Cork University Press, 1999).

37. Among the many, see Sir Edward Cook, *The Life of Florence Nightingale,* 2 vols. (London: MacMillan, 1913); Cecil Woodham-Smith, *Florence Nightingale* (London: Constable Publishing, 1960); Judith Calhoun, "The Nightingale Pledge: A Commitment that Survives the Passage of Time," *Nursing & Health Care* 14, 3 (March 1993), pp. 130–36; Irene S. Palmer, "Florence Nightingale and the First Organized Delivery of Nursing Services," *American Association of Colleges and Nursing* (1993), pp. 1–14; and Vern Bullough, Bonnie Bullough, and Marietta P. Stanton, eds., *Florence Nightingale and Her Era: A Collection of New Scholarship* (New York: Garland Publishing, 1990).

38. See Mary Ellen Doona, "Sister Mary Croke: Another Voice from the Crimean War, 1854–1856," *Nursing History Review* 3 (1995), pp. 3–41; Irene S. Palmer, "Florence Nightingale and the First Organized Delivery of Nursing Services," *American Association of Colleges and Nursing* (1993), pp. 1–14; Lois A. Monteiro, "Florence Nightingale on Public Health Nursing," *American Journal of Public Health* 75, 2 (1985), pp. 181–85; Sandra Holten, "Feminine Authority and Social Order: Florence Nightingale's Conception of Nursing and Health Care," *Social Analysis* (August 1984), pp. 59–72; Monica Baly, *Florence Nightingale and the Nursing Legacy* (London: Croom Helm, 1986); and F. B. Smith, *Florence Nightingale: Reputation and Power* (London: Croom Helm, 1982). Smith's study is more an analysis of Nightingale's psyche than her accomplishments. Both Baly and Smith argue that Nightingale was very much aware of her image and was careful to avoid having it blemished.

39. While the Crimean War brought nursing as a profession for women onto the public stage, well before this event, nursing reform had already begun. See Carol Helmstadter, "Robert Bentley Todd, Saint John's House and the Origins of the Modern Trained Nurse," *Bulletin of the History of Medicine* 67 (1993), pp. 282–319; Brian Heeney, *The Women's Movement in the Church of England 1850–1930* (Oxford: Clarendon Press, 1988); Margaret Lonsdale, *Sister Dora* (Boston: Roberts Brothers, 1980); Peter F. Anson, *The Call of the Cloister: Religious Communities and Kindred Bodies in the Anglican Communion* (London: SPCF, 1956); and Agnes E. Pavey, *The Story of the Growth of Nursing as an Art, a Vocation and a Profession* (London: Faber and Faber Ltd., 1938).

40. Charles E. Rosenberg, "Florence Nightingale on Contagion: The Hospital as Moral Universe," in *History and Healing Essays for George Rosen,* ed. Charles E. Rosenberg (New York: Watson Academic Publishing, 1979), p. 117. Joan Lynaugh argues that one problem was that Nightingale saw the hospital as "an ordered moral universe that relied on women of high moral character, organizational ability, and a sense of the connectedness between health, behavior, environment and disease." Joan E. Lynaugh, "Narrow Passageways: Nurses and Physicians in Conflict and Concert Since 1875," in *The Physician as Captain of the Ship: A Critical*

Reappraisal, ed. Nancy M. P. King, Larry R. Churchill, and Alan W. Cross (New York: D. Reidel, 1988), p. 25. See also Smith, *Florence Nightingale*, pp. 165–66.

41. Both before and after the nursing reforms ushered in by the Crimean War, the majority of nurses were women. In 1901 in Britain there were approximately 63,500 female nurses and 5,700 male nurses. See Abel-Smith, *A History of the Nursing Profession*, p. 52. In Dublin, the records of the Kilmainham, Baggot Street, Sir Patrick Dun's, and Dr. Steevens hospitals all make references to having employed male nurses. For example, in 1865 the matron of Sir Patrick Dun's Hospital, Mrs. Stephenson, asked that two male nurses "being much worn by heavy duty" be given a two-week leave of absence. SPD (22 August 1865). In 1892 the Board of Dr. Steevens' Hospital recommended that "there should be a male attendant to assist in nursing in No. 2 ward, to attend operations, [and] to take night duty on alternate weeks. . . ." Dr. Steevens Hospital, henceforth DSH (16 March 1892). See also Kirkpatrick, *The History of Dr. Steevens'*, p. 227.

42. DSH (26 February 1879).

43. RCD (12 January 1879).

44. Anne Summers, "The Mysterious Demise of Sarah Gamp: The Domiciliary Nurse and Her Detractors, 1830–1860," *Victorian Studies* 32 (1989), pp. 365–86; and Katherine Williams, "From Sarah Gamp to Florence Nightingale: A Critical Study of Hospital Nursing Systems from 1840–1897," *Rewriting Nursing History*, ed. Celia Davies (London: Croom Helm, 1980), pp. 41–73.

45. Higgins, "On the Improvement of Nurses in Country Districts," p. 573. See also Anne Summers, "Ministering Angels," *History Today* 39 (February 1989) pp. 31–37; and Helmstadter, "Nurse Recruitment and Retention," p. 48.

46. SPD (28 April 1835). The nurses, however, cannot be singled out for their behavior because in 1835 it was noted that the laundress was fired, and the value of the missing items was deducted from her wages. In 1843, Dun's dismissed the cook, Mary Power. Additionally, in 1848, the matron accused the apothecary, Mr. Tallis, of "improper familiarity with the housemaid." SPD (5 May 1835; 28 February 1843, and 19 September 1848).

47. SPD (12 September 1837).

48. SPD (9 December 1851; 10 August 1852; 2 January 1852).

49. RCD (18 April 1884).

50. Royal Hospital Kilmainham (loose papers), henceforth RHK (25 February 1871). Noted Carte, while recommending Mullins's discharge, "if this statement is correct, Walsh has acted in opposition to one of the most stringent rules of the house." Mullins actually wrote a letter in her own defense but whether she received the recommended discharge is not revealed.

51. RHK (22 February 1875).

52. RHK (30 April 1877 and 23 December 1878).

53. RHK (28 February 1874 and 27 July 1874). In July of that year, the police charged George Turner with rape, although neither the police nor the hospital charged Boileau. Turner was later convicted of assault upon the wife of a staff sergeant employed at the hospital. RHK (24 October 1874). There was an attempt to have Turner removed from the hospital but "the Governors in accordance with English law and justice decline to punish him again for the same offence." RHK (30 December 1874).

54. Boileau was not the only matron to have trouble, and the hospital's ad-

ministration disciplined her successor, Matilda Hurford, after she apparently wrote letters of an inappropriate nature to a fellow employee, Major Cooper. The board warned Hurford that "any renewal of such correspondence on your part will result in the inevitable and immediate deprivation of your appointment as matron." RHK (1 March 1883). Hurford retired in 1883. RHK (28 June 1883).

55. In 1875, a resident, Mr. Pim, was dismissed for his "improper conduct towards one of the probationer nurses." That same year, the registrar was reprimanded for concealing his marriage to one of the nurses in the hospital. SPD (13 April 1875).

56. SPD (12 January 1875; 26 January 1875; 23 February 1875).

57. SPD (12 January 1875; 26 January 1875; 23 February 1875).

58. SPD (11 May 1880).

59. See Sandra Holton, "Feminine Authority and Social Order: Florence Nightingale's Conception of Nursing and Health Care," *Social Analysis* (August 1984), pp. 59–72; and Claire Fagin and Donna Diers, "Nursing as Metaphor," *New England Journal of Medicine* (14 July 1983), pp. 116–17.

60. Mrs. Hanbury, *The Good Nurse or Hints on the Management of the Sick and Lying-In Chamber and the Nursery* (London: Longman, Rees, Orme, Brown and Green, 1828), pp. 65, 67, 68, 72, 76. See also M. Martin, "Hints to Amateur Nurses," *Irish Monthly* 9 (April 1881), pp. 214–17.

61. *A Manual for Midwives and Monthly Nurses* (Dublin: Fannin and Co., 1856), p. 5. See also, Anonymous, "Pauper Nurses in Workhouses," *British Medical Journal* (27 May 1865), p. 551.

62. Charles Henry Hardy, *Introductory Lecture on the Duties of Nurses* (Melbourne: George Robertson, 1881), p. 8.

63. She was "neither for the drawing room nor the kitchen." Susan M. Reverby, *Ordered to Care: The Dilemma of American Nursing, 1850–1945* (Cambridge: Cambridge University Press, 1987), p. 97.

64. Jane Austen, *Persuasion* (New York: Penguin, 1994), p. 153.

65. *A Manual for Midwives*, p. 54. One author warned, "you [are]to keep guard over your tongue . . . *it is an unruly member*," (her emphasis). A Lady, *A Friendly Letter to Under Nurses of the Sick Especially in Unions* (London: A. W. Bennett, 1861), p. 7.

66. *A Manual for Midwives*, p. 52.

67. Florence Nightingale, *Notes on Nursing: What It Is and What It Is Not* (London: Harrison, 1860), p. 86.

68. "Nurses for the Sick Poor," *The Lancet* (7 November 1868), p. 615.

69. Catherine Judd, *Bedside Seductions: Nursing and the Victorian Imagination, 1830–1880* (New York: St. Martin's Press, 1998), p. 40.

70. A Physician, *On the Employment of Trained Nurses Among the Labouring Poor Considered Chiefly in Relation to Sanitary Reform and the Arts of Life* (London: John Churchill, 1860), p. 27.

71. A Physician, *On the Employment of Trained Nurses*, p. 27.

72. Kirkpatrick, *The History of Dr. Steevens*, p. 276.

73. Ibid. Eventually, Dr. Steevens offered its nurses room and board, and by 1883 their wages were only £14 annually. "Said payment also to include cost of boots formerly supplied to the nurses." DSH (March 1842 and 22 March 1883).

74. RHK (30 November 1857). In 1883 the head surgeon was making £500 per annum while the nurses averaged between £19 and £23 per annum.

75. SPD (24 December 1866).

76. RCD (18 April 1884). The Dublin Hospital Sunday Fund, an organization that sought to improve conditions in Dublin's hospitals, stated that, "until nurses are better paid and more comfortabley [*sic*] lodged and fed, better superintended and not so overworked as they are at present, it cannot be expected that a better class of nurses will be obtainable." Ann Wickham "A Better Scheme for Nursing," *International History of Nursing Journal* 6, 2 (2001), p. 28. Helmstadter, "Nurse Recruitment and Retention," p. 60.

77. SPD (23 December 1895). The Adelaide paid its nurses a salary that increased annually, building up from £6 to £20 over three years. See Meetings of the Nursing Committee, Adelaide Hospital, October 1892.

78. SPD (26 December 1865 and 26 February 1867).

79. SPD (3 January 1888).

80. RCD (22 February 1884).

81. "She shall satisfy herself, by all means in her power, as to their character, fitness, capabilities, and progress [of the nurses], and shall report the results, with her own opinion and recommendations, from time to time, to the Directors of the Nursing Institution." RCD (22 February 1884).

82. RCD (16 November 1883).

83. As Daly notes, "information on wage rates is not wholly satisfactory." Mary E. Daly, *Dublin: The Deposed Capital* (Cork: Cork University Press, 1984), p. 67. Numbers from Pat Thane, *The Foundations of the Welfare State* (New York: Longman, 1982), p. 5. See also R. V. Jackson, "The Structure of Pay in Nineteenth Century Britain," *Economic History Review* 40, 4 (1987), pp. 561–70. These were men's wages.

84. This was the equivalent of 9 to 12 shillings per week. Daly states that in Dublin between 1855 and 1914, there was a large gap between the wages of skilled and unskilled males, and wages for women were practically nonexistent. Daly, *Dublin: The Deposed Capital,* pp. 67–69; and Mary E. Daly, "Women in the Irish Workforce from Pre-Industrial to Modern Times," *Soathar* 7 (1981), pp. 74–82.

85. The equivalent of 33 to 14 shillings per week respectively. Daly, *Dublin: The Deposed Capital,* p. 70.

86. This is calculated out to be the equivalent of 36 and 38 shillings per week. John Lynch, *A Tale of Three Cities: Comparative Studies in Working-Class Life* (London: Macmillan, 1998), p. 120; and Daly, *Dublin: The Deposed Capital,* p. 69.

87. Susan McGann, *The Battle of the Nurses* (London: Scutari Press, 1992), p. 150.

88. As Reverby notes, "Low pay and chronic overwork plagued the staff nurse and limited the number of graduates willing to take up the work." Reverby, *Ordered to Care,* p. 107.

89. Given Kilmainham's unique nature it is not a surprise that still late in the century such activities were still in practice, as for example when in 1891, Ann Owens, a nurse in Dublin's Royal Hospital, Kilmainham, sent a letter requesting the hospital to transfer her to the upper house, writing, "I am obliged to take this step on account of my little daughter as I would be able to look after her better as she will be permitted to live with me there." RHK (28 May 1891).

90. Kirkpatrick, *The History of Dr. Steevens',* p. 278.

91. RHK (7 April 1856); and RCD (11 June 1878).

92. RHK (26 April 1875).

93. RHK (26 April 1875).

94. Kirkpatrick, *The History of Doctor Steevens'*, p. 279.

95. DSH. Dr. Steevens Hospital, RCOP, "Regulations for the Training of Nurses," (Pamphlet, n.d., about 1890). At this time Dr. Steevens paid its probationers £14 per year.

96. See Catherine Judd, *Bedside Seductions*, p. 40. Interestingly, while Kilmainham's nurses could be married, the governors of Kilmainham Hospital noted in 1855 that Ann Boileau's appointment as the matron for the hospital would become void if she married. RHK (19 December 1855).

97. Mary Quaine, one of the last Jubilee nurses of Ireland and who at one time was also the nursing superintendent of Ireland, stated that the Jubilee Nurse Organization feared that if the husband moved into the home provided to a district nurse, because he was under no legal obligation to the organization, it would not be able to get the couple out of the home if the nurse retired. Margaret Preston, "Interview with Mary Quaine," (July, 1995); Mary Quaine, "Brief Outline of the History of Jubilee Nursing in Ireland 1876/1968," (n.p., 24 September 1990).

98. Stocks, *A Hundred Years of District Nursing*, p. 81.

99. "It was referred to the Economy Committee, to invite the Lady Visitors, and the Ladies of the Committee of the Dublin Nurses' Training Institution, to cooperate with the Board in establishing the Children's Ward in the Board Room, and to take the necessary steps for its immediate furnishing and decoration." SPD (12 February 1878).

100. The first proposal for trained nurses appeared in an 1852 letter written by Dr. Law, who was with the Institutes of Medicine in Dublin. Law told the Dun's Board that a training institute, similar to that in London, was being established in Dublin and asked if some of these nurses might be permitted to attend Dun's Hospital. Unfortunately no action was taken by the hospital at this time. SPD (22 May 1852).

101. The matron reported to the ladies' committee, and in 1878, the ladies advised to Mrs. Finlay, the matron, that she purchase "uniforms for the nurses and wardmaids, blankets, 370 yards calico for women's night dresses and men's shirts, 2 table cloths for resident pupils use and 2 for the Matron's use also six towels and 60 yards calico for pillow covers." RCD (12 November 1878).

102. The Trench family was quite active in philanthropy. Richard Chenevix Trench was integral to the establishment of Alexandra College (for women) and Jane Trench, Maria's sister, established St. John's House of Rest in 1870 with the help of their sister Frances. See Luddy, *Women and Philanthropy*, p. 197. Records for St. John's House of Rest are held by the organization: Marrion Road, Dublin.

103. SPD (26 February 1867). In 1867, showing further willingness to involve the Dublin Nurses' Training Institution, Dun's invited the Honorable Mrs. Trench, Miss Maria, Trench and Lady Laurence to act as "Lady Visitors and co-operate with the visiting Governors during the year."

104. Moorhead, *A Short History*, p. 148.

105. SPD (11 February 1873).

106. In 1869, while the board "had no cause of complaint" against the head maternity nurse, the ladies' committee from the institute dismissed her for insub-

ordination and maintained that it was "unwilling to give her a permanent engagement [in the hospital]." SPD (13 July 1869).

107. SPD (2 February 1872).

108. SPD (23 January 1883). The probationers were Presbyterians and the nurse a Baptist. In 1865, Dun's had created the position of lady superintendent. While the matron's position remained, she no longer had ultimate authority over the nurses. SPD (26 December 1865).

109. SPD (23 January 1883).

110. SPD (13 March 1883).

111. Kirkpatrick, *The History of Dr. Steevens,* p. 280.

112. Church of England or Ireland.

113. Kirkpatrick, *The History of Dr. Steevens,* p. 280.

114. SPD (24 March 1835).

115. "The nurses scour their wards once a week, mop daily and keep them constantly clean by sweeping." SPD (24 March 1835). The matron's salary at this time is not recorded, but in 1844 she was paid £65 per annum.

116. McGann, *Battle of the Nurses,* pp. 130–31. Huxley was the sixth of eight children of William Thomas Huxley (eldest brother of T. H. Huxley, FRS), and his wife, Esther Hopkins. See also Margaret Preston, "Margaret Rachel Huxley," *Dictionary of Irish Biography* (Cambridge: Cambridge University Press, forthcoming).

117. McGann, *Battle of the Nurses,* p. 133; and Moorhead, *A Short History,* p. 158.

118. Moorhead, *A Short History,* p. 158.

119. Huxley would later name the home Elpis, which is Greek for hope.

120. SPD (8 July 1890).

121. Dublin Metropolitan School for Nurses, Mercer's Library: Minute Book (20 April 1894). See also McGann, *The Battle of the Nurses,* pp. 135–39.

122. SPD (23 December 1895).

123. Nolan, *One Hundred Years,* p. 12; and RCD (22 February 1884). A number of the matrons discussed in McGann's *Battle of the Nurses* were teachers and trainers as well. See also "Lady Superintendents in Irish Hospitals," in *Women in Ireland: A Documentary History 1800–1918,* ed. Maria Luddy (Cork: Cork University Press, 1995), pp. 224–26.

124. Moorhead, *A Short History,* pp. 139–40. SPD (13 June 1900). "The distinction between the title of a general nurse and a maternity nurse be clearly indicated in the diploma or certificate granted to each."

125. McGann, *Battle of the Nurses,* p. 134.

126. Moorhead, *A Short History,* p. 160.

127. McGann, *Battle of the Nurses,* pp. 153–54. Huxley died on January 10, 1940.

128. See"Hospital Nursing in Dublin," *Dublin Medical Press* (15 August 1866), p. 181; RCD (11 May 1883). Eventually this nursing institute was also to supply trained nurses to Mercer's Hospital. RCD (14 December 1888).

129. RCD (18 April 1884). This included relieving some nurses of their duties. "The nurse in charge of the Fever Ward [was given] notice to leave at the end of a fortnight, she left the hospital the same day, the night Nurse on the Male landing also left."

130. RCD (18 April 1884).

131. RCD (18 April 1884).

132. Religious Society of Friends, Swanbrook House, 96/91. Interestingly, the

name Goodbody appears in Baggot Street's records as someone with whom the chairman of the board worked while devising the rules and regulations for the lady superintendent.

133. RCD (12 November 1886).

134. RCD (12 November 1886). The hospital attempted to make further accommodation for the special skills of the nurses as opposed to the housekeepers or porters. In addition, the hospital needed more nurses as it accepted more patients, and by 1897, the nursing committee requested an increase in the number of nurse-probationers from 6 to 22. RCD (8 June 1883).

135. RCD (1905), p. 8. "They attend Lectures in Anatomy, Physiology, Hygiene, Medicine, Surgery, Gynecology, and Ophthalmology. Invalid cooking is also taught, and a certificated cook has been engaged for the purpose. Nine Nurses have this year gained the certificate of the Incorporated Society of Trained Masseuses."

136. National Library, Ireland, henceforth NLI, RCD (1905), p. 8.

137. NLI: RCD (1905), p. 8. All probationers needed to be between the ages of 21 and 32, undergoing a two-month trial period, and they needed to provide their own uniforms.

138. RCD (8 March 1889; 14 January 1887; 14 December 1888). In 1881 the ladies committee requested from the public donations of "20 blankets for the patients use, and for dressing gowns, worn or otherwise both for men and women." RCD (9 December 1881). In 1870 Sir Patrick Dun's board of governors offered thanks to the ladies "for the zeal and charity with which they have collected subscriptions for the hospital." They had raised £273 for the hospital. SPD (27 December 1870).

139. NLI: RCD, (1905), p. 8.

140. The 1898 Local Government (of Ireland) Act included legislation regarding the registration of general nurses, but this was only the first step in a longer process that culminated in the Nurses Registration (Ireland) Act of 1919. See Nolan, *One Hundred Years,* p. 16; and McGann, *Battle of the Nurses,* pp. 139–42 and 151.

141. As Lewenson quotes one doctor who equated compliance with acumen, "Any intelligent, not necessarily educated woman can in short time acquire the skill to carry out with implicit obedience the physician's direction." Lewenson, *Taking Charge,* pp. 46–47.

142. For example, in 1881 Dublin's population was approximately 250,000, while Ireland's population was approximately 5.1 million. See Daly, *Dublin: The Deposed Capital,* p. 3; and Cormac Ó Gráda, *Ireland: A New Economic History 1780–1939* (Oxford: Oxford University Press, 1994), p. 214.

143. Mary Quain noted that as a visiting nurse local women sought her advice, and men respected her opinion and followed her recommendations.

144. Baly, *Florence Nightingale,* p. 83.

145. Rathbone, for example, was a member of the District Provident Society in Liverpool. Monteiro, "Florence Nightingale on Public Health Nursing," p. 181.

146. Stocks, *A Hundred Years of District Nursing,* p. 27. Liverpool was divided into eighteen districts, and nurses and lady superintendents were supplied for each area. See Monteiro, "Florence Nightingale on Public Health Nursing," p. 182.

147. Stocks, *A Hundred Years of District Nursing,* p. 29.

148. F. K. Prochaska, "Body and Soul: Bible Nurses and the Poor in Victorian London," *Historical Research* 60 (1987), pp. 336–48.

149. Stocks, *A Hundred Years of District Nursing*, p. 23. The term "missing link" also appeared in the Bible missions established in Dublin. See St. Patrick's Nurses' Home and Bible-Woman Association, henceforth SPN (March 1883), p. 13.

150. Letter from Florence Nightingale to the Duke of Westminster, 1896 (Jubilee Nurses Box, Royal College of Surgeons). See also Martha Vicinus and B. Nergaard, eds., *Ever Yours: Florence Nightingale Selected Letters* (Cambridge: Harvard University Press, 1990); and Mary Quain, "Brief Outline of the History of Jubilee Nursing In Ireland 1876/1968," (unpublished article September 1990).

151. Belfast Society for Providing Nurses for the Sick Poor, henceforth BSN (1878), p. 3. These records are located at the Public Records Office, Northern Ireland, henceforth P.R.O.N.I.

152. BSN (1878), p. 3.

153. BSN (1878), p. 5. Upon marriage, the nurses of the Belfast Society were to resign.

154. BSN (1878), p. 4.

155. N. M. Falkiner, "The Nurse and the State," *State and Social Inquiry Society of Ireland* 14 (1921), p. 40.

156. SPN (March 1883), p. 5. St. Patrick's was located at 101 St. Stephen's Green. This should indicate the organization's prominent place, because this was one of the most exclusive locales in the city.

157. SPN (March 1883), p. 7.

158. SPN (March 1883), p. 13.

159. Livinia Dock, *A History of Nursing*, 3 vols. (New York: G. P. Putnam's Sons, 1912), p. 23. Victoria ascended to the throne in 1838.

160. Lees was lady superintendent of London's Metropolitan Nursing Association, an organization similar to Rathbone's Liverpool district nursing charity.

161. Stocks, *A Hundred Years of District Nursing*, p. 80; and N. M. Falkiner, "The Nurse and the State," *State and Social Inquiry Society of Ireland* 14 (1921), p. 40. Later, in 1903, Lady Rachel Dudley, wife to Ireland's lord lieutenant, established a fund that helped to pay for district nurses in the rural areas of the west of Ireland and Dudley nurses trained in Jubilee nursing homes. Mary Quain noted that all Dudley nurses were Jubilee nurses but not all Jubilee nurses were Dudley nurses. Margaret Preston, "Interview with Mary Quain" (Summer, 1995). See *Eighth Annual Report of Dudley District Nurses* (n.p., 1912).

162. Mrs. Charles Martin, "St. Lawrence's Catholic Home," *Irish Monthly* 21 (January 1893), p. 14.

163. Martin, "St. Lawrence's Catholic Home," p. 15.

164. Martin, "St. Lawrence's Catholic Home," p. 17.

165. Stocks, *A Hundred Years of District Nursing*, p. 89.

166. The average age of the Jubilee nurse in Ireland was 31, and all the women were either single or widowed. The numbers included here are found in the record books of the Irish Branch of the Queen Victoria's Jubilee Nurses' Records.

167. "The career opportunities opening up for Irish girls 1880–1910 also gave them and their parents a continuing impetus to strive for a recognized educational level." Anne V. O'Connor, "The Revolution in Girls' Secondary Education in Ireland 1860–1910," *Girls Don't Do Honours: Irish Women in Education in the 19th and 20th Centuries*, ed. Mary Cullen (Dublin: Women's Educational Bureau, 1987), p. 50.

168. David Fitzpatrick, " 'A Share of the Honeycomb': Education, Emigration, and Irishwomen," *Continuity and Change* 1, 2 (1986), p. 218.

169. Janet A. Nolan, *Ourselves Alone: Women's Emigration from Ireland 1885–1920* (Lexington: University of Kentucky Press, 1989), p. 69. It is important to note, however, that literate women were more likely to emigrate. Fitzpatrick, "'A Share of the Honeycomb,' " p. 231.

170. Quoted from Monteiro, "Florence Nightingale on Public Health Nursing," p. 183.

171. Alice Cristabel Crowther, "Review of the Work Done by Queen Victoria's Jubilee Institute for Nurses in Ireland," *Dublin Journal of Medical Science* 145 (April 1918), p. 287. (This was an address delivered at the Annual Meeting of St. Patrick's Nurses Home, 22 February 1918).

172. Annie Michel, superintendent of nurses for the Queen Victoria's Jubilee Nursing Institution, noted, "one of the nurses attended 52 confinement cases in twelve months, and delivered most of them herself . . . [there were] 1,064 midwifery cases attended during 1924 by our nurses." Annie Michel, "Some Incidents of the Work of a Jubilee Nurse in Ireland," (n.p., 1925), p. 5. See also Emma D., *Recollections of a Nurse* (London: MacMillan and Co., 1889); and B. N. Hedderman, *Glimpses of My Life in Aran. Some Experiences of a District Nurse in These Remote Islands, off the West Coast of Ireland* (London: John Wright & Sons, Ltd., 1917).

173. SPN (March 1901), p. 5.

174. In the early twentieth century, the Jubilee nurses began to hold fund-raisers in order to build a retirement fund, a greatly needed benefit since many nurses were single when they retired. Unfortunately, it was not established until 1930. If a Jubilee nurse met the requirements of 21 years of service and was over 55 years of age, she would receive £30 annually. Mary Quain, *The Jubilee Nurses Need Your Help* (Dublin: John Falconer, 1955), p. 8.

175. In rural Ireland in the spring, people cut and dry turf to use as fuel the next winter; this is referred to as *turf-saving*. Michel, "Some Incidents," p. 1. For a biography on the life of an island nurse see Leslie Matson, *Méiní the Blasket Nurse* (Cork: Mercier Press, 1995).

176. Michel, "Some Incidents," p. 3.

177. Eighth Annual Report of Dudley District Nurses (n.p., 1912), p. 12. See also the Countess of Mayo, "Trained Nurses for the Rural Districts: The Origin and Growth of Lady Dudley's Project," in *The Voice of Ireland*, ed. William G. Fitzgerald (Dublin: John Heywood, 1924), pp. 362–63.

178. In addition she had to be a social worker able to point out government and philanthropic agencies that could provide aid. Crowther, "Review of the Work," p. 287.

179. BSN (1878), p. 8.

180. For example, when it was learned that nurses were carrying soiled sheets from the operating theater to the laundry, Baggot Street Hospital's Board of Governors deemed that this "was a menial service hitherto done by the Porter." RCD (9 April 1897).

181. BSN (1878), appendix.

182. Marian Stringer, "Ninety Years of District Nursing," *Nursing Mirror* (13 April 1978), p. 63. See also E. Morrison, "A District Nurse Among the Poor," *New Ireland Review* 21 (March 1909), pp. 24–31.

183. BSN (1878), appendix. For Eliza J., the nurse among other things "made her breakfast, carried ashes down to yard, emptied slops, brushed up floor, made her bed every second morning . . . got her clothes washed when needed."

184. For other sources on District Nursing see M. Loane and H. Bowers, *The District Nurse as Health Missioner* (n.p., 1922); Rosalind Gillette Shawe, *Notes for Visiting Nurses* (Philadelphia: P. Blakiston, Son & Co., 1893) and Eliza Priestly, "Nurses A La Mode," *Nineteenth Century* (January 1897), p. 29.

185. Ireland's most famous district nurse may be Annie M. P. Smithson (1873–1948), who went on to write a number of novels on the adventures of a district nurse. On Smithson and her novels see Oonagh Walsh, " 'Her Irish Heritage': Annie M. P. Smithson and Auto/Biography," *Études Irlandaises* (Printemps, 1998), pp. 27–42; Annie M. P. Smithson, *The Walk of the Queen* (Cork: Mercier, 1989); and Annie M. P. Smithson, *The Marriage of Nurse Harding* (Cork: Mercier, 1989).

186. As Foucault wrote, "to help and if necessary constrain them to ensure their own good health. The imperative of health: at once the duty of each and the objective of all." Michel Foucault, *Power/Knowledge: Selected Interviews and Other Writings, 1972–1977*, ed. Colin Gordon (New York: Pantheon Books, 1980) p. 170.

187. Moore, *A Zeal for Responsibility*, p. 4.

188. Louisa Twining, *Nurses for the Sick with a Letter to Young Women* (London: Longman, Green, Longman and Roberts, 1861), p. 19.

189. For example, the ladies' committee noted that in 1878 applications for nurse training from two respectable young women were accepted. RCD (12 November 1878).

190. Abel-Smith, *A History of Nursing*, p. 31. However, he notes that this was done away with in the early part of the twentieth century. In the minutes of Sir Patrick Dun's Hospital, on December 14, 1880, Miss Maria Trench of the Dublin Nurses' Training Institution asked the board to allow two ladies to receive nursing instruction in the hospital during the month of January.

191. They were paid £10 the first year, which gradually rose to £18 by the fourth. See Coakley, *Baggot Street*, p. 31.

192. As quoted by Abel-Smith, *A History of Nursing*, p. 27 (his italics).

193. Mitchell, *A 'Peculiar' Place: The Adelaide Hospital*, p. 79.

194. Helmstadter notes that many ladies who were nursing pupils did not remain in nursing. Helmstadter, "Nursing in London Teaching Hospitals," p. 61. See Celia Davies, "The Health Visitor as Mother's Friend: A Woman's Place in Public Health, 1900–14," *Social History of Medicine* (1988), pp. 39–59.

195. Travers notes that between 1948 and 1951 over 5,000 Irish nurses emigrated to England. Pauric Travers, "Emigration and Gender: The Case of Ireland, 1922–60," in *Chattel, Servant or Citizen: Women's Status in Church, State and Society*, ed. Sabine Wichert and Mary O'Dowd (Belfast: Institute of Irish Studies, 1995), p. 189.

196. Nursing was also hazardous to one's health. Throughout the records of hospitals there is mention of nurses who contracted diseases from their patients. For example, at Sir Patrick Dun's, Miss Johnson, the lady superintendent, died from typhus fever and the board expressed its particular regrets because "her death was the result of illness contracted in the discharge of her duties." SPD (26 June 1883).

Conclusion

Sadly, in many ways nineteenth-century Dublin was the perfect place for the women of philanthropy; the need for assistance was overwhelming. Dublin's poorest were living 10 and 12 to a room in unspeakably unsanitary conditions. Dublin Corporation did not have the resources to alleviate such overwhelming need, and the city relied upon private charities to assist those who slipped through the net cast by the poor law guardians. While taken individually, a single charity had little impact; nevertheless, collectively, Dublin's charitable organizations made a difference.

The focus of this work has been the literal as well as theoretical aspects of philanthropy in the nineteenth century. Victorian moral attitudes strengthened the isolation of women, and the family home became the feminine world separated from that of the public, masculine space. Philanthropy provided middle- and upper-class women entrance into society while not threatening their social respectability, or the public sphere. The work done by Ireland's women philanthropists was similar to that of their sisters in Europe and North America. Irish women worked for comparable causes including charities that aided orphans, prostitutes, distressed gentlewomen, domestic servants, and poor families. While there are many parallels, Irish charity also had unique characteristics, and, in particular, disruptive sectarian divisions hindered cooperation and left some charities open to accusations of proselytism. As records of the charities detailed within this work suggested, the souls of poor children were of particular concern. This was what Margaret Aylward suggested of Catholic orphans when she warned that unless "some one for God's sake had taken them up, they had surely fallen into the snares of heresy."[1]

The industrial revolution had helped to foster a middle class who believed that their financial and social success had earned them entrance into that sphere of social and political power inhabited by the aristocracy. Increasingly, in order to maintain their position, the upper classes needed to establish clear demarcations between themselves and those below them. Ethnography and anthropology contributed to the conflation and confusion of race and class, and the upper classes then suggested that financial, social and political success were measures of human progress.[2] As class took on inherent characteristics, the upper classes then suggested that the working class needed to further evolve. Contributing to this process of social control, philantropists suggested that the poor did not have a fully developed moral sense, and, as such, their sinful nature only deepened their indigence. The message of intrinsic inadequacy becomes clear in the records of Victorian charity. What this research has sought to show is that Irish philanthropists—both Catholic and Protestant—adopted the same language as their British counterparts, and this implied an acceptance of British authority in Ireland.

In their efforts to facilitate the poor's improvement, many charities adopted the practice of visiting the poor in their own homes as a key component of their work, and, once in the home, philanthropists delivered a variety of messages. First, if the poor changed their behavior, they could somewhat improve their circumstances but never leave the class status into which they were born. Certainly, some benefits would come with hard work and honest living, and philanthropists offered themselves as models of moral behavior to be mimicked. Another message that charity workers brought was that cleanliness helped to wash away the sin of poverty, and thus philanthropists sought to teach the poor the many hygienic techniques. Additionally, charities implied that finding a job was part and parcel of becoming a contributing member of the state, and, accordingly, the working poor were particularly worthy of the philanthropists' munificence. Finally, another way out of poverty was through participation in organized religion, and so sure were they of this that philanthropists harangued, harassed, and harried the poor to get them through the church door. In the end, while some relented, others continued to resist.

While philanthropists brought their many messages into homes and hospitals in Ireland, charitable volunteers also faced the festering sectarian divisions that hindered cooperation among charities. In addition to class and race, religion was wrapped up into the conversation regarding the character of the poor, and there were those who believed that Catholicism was another inherent strike against the poor Irish. In addition, there was a vocal group that believed that if Catholics would convert, not only would they reach heaven, but also their position in society could be improved. In particular, proselytizing charities contributed to the tensions that bubbled beneath the surface of Dublin life and erupted, at times, in violent episodes that marred the city's charitable terrain. In the end, fearing accusations of proselytism, most charities limited their aid to those of their own denomination, which meant that the indigent's ability to gain assistance was even further constrained.

While few, there were charities in Ireland that did not discriminate on the basis of religion. The Religious Society of Friends is the most well-known example. While Friends brought the Christian message to those they aided, they did not seek to convert them—particularly Catholics. While the Society's numbers in Ireland were quite small, little more than 2,000 at their highest, they made an important impact upon the nation's charitable landscape. Their innovative techniques and inventive agendas led the way in the provision of charitable aid, and Friends provided assistance to all regardless of creed. In addition, this work also points to philosophical changes in the Society, and while the Friends' message of social justice remained, their earlier radical language softened as members increasingly worked within mainstream society.

Ultimately, for the women of philanthropy, nursing was a predictable choice because it was a key conduit for the sanitary mission. Victorian society ordained that nursing the ill was an innate role for females, and thus caring for the sick poor was clearly the responsibility of the women of philanthropy. Ireland's medical establishment was well developed by the early nineteenth century, and the women of charity quickly realized an opportunity to involve themselves in nursing reform. Through nurse training schools and nursing philanthropies, women reformers were able to influence nursing curriculums while molding nurse apprentices into proper medical missionaries. Not only carried out in local hospitals, nursing reform was also brought into the home. Visiting nurse programs were a natural evolution, because visiting the sick poor had long been a central part of the charitable agenda. Once in the home, the visitor, while providing care for the ill, could also impose important lessons on how to run an efficient, honest, and sanitary household. Increasingly, as Ireland's visiting nurse organizations evolved, the nurse visitor became an important member of the rural community. Whether in the hospital or the home, the women of philanthropy took the lead in seeking to form a profession out of a vocation.

While Irish women philanthropists established charities as various as retirement homes for the elderly, training schools for former prisoners, or infirmaries for the sick, what few sought to understand is why such extensive poverty existed.[3] This work has shown that while there were philanthropists such as Margaret Aylward who suggested a different understanding of the role of sin in poverty, and the Quakers who did criticize government policy, these were in the minority. Few philanthropists questioned the clear disparity that existed between rich and poor or sought to question why such endemic poverty existed. Most suggested that poverty was the result of a combination of inherency and individual choice, and, as some records suggested, philanthropists believed that what the poor needed most was advice on how best to overcome their poverty.

This work has not attempted to tackle all of the questions regarding Irish women's roles in philanthropy, and there remain many other avenues of research. To begin, this study has not focused upon those women who took religious vows, but this certainly does not suggest that their history is complete. Further discussion of the role of the nun in Irish nursing is needed, along with a broader study of nursing in Ireland. Closer investigation of Irish visiting nurses may reveal an important dynamic between the district nurse and the women and men of Ireland's rural communities. It seems that visiting nurses, in particular, found a measure of authority in their role as the medical missionaries to country dwellers. Another avenue for future investigation may be the sectarian divisions alluded to in chapter three. A much broader discussion would help give perspective on how sectarian animosities impacted Ireland, particularly in a social context. So too, this work proposes that the original tenets of the Religious Society of Friends changed over time, influenced by the opportunities that came with financial success. While the Religious Society of Friends had long made Ireland its home, a closer look at its role in Ireland's business economy might further our knowledge of the modifying principles of this Society. Finally, there is still much to be said about the women of charity as we continue to recognize their important contribution to the evolution of our modern social service professions.

Charity permitted middle- and upper-class women access to a world from which they were generally forbidden. While women went into the homes of the poor in order to provide sanitary assistance and medical care, they also entered local hospitals, workhouses, and jails in order to offer inmates spiritual counseling and basic human contact. In addition to Bibles, charitable women doled out a variety of goods such as clothing, blankets, and food to the poor. Visiting became the philanthropic woman's lifeline to the community, and the women chronicled here were pioneers in the evolution of social work. These women not only encountered disease, but also the violence of the streets, as well as ridicule from many to whom they were attempting to bring aid. Margaret Aylward began a visiting association, Ellen Smyly gave public lectures in order to raise money for her orphans, and the women of the Religious Society of Friends were increasingly active in social justice causes beyond the world of philanthropy. The women of charity turned the qualities that the Victorian middle classes presumed they possessed into the keys that opened the locked doors to the world outside their homes.

NOTES

1. LAC (1857), p. 14.

2. "The science of ethnography, in particular succeeded in establishing as 'true' (both among scientific communities and in the popular imagination) the belief that individual, national, and communal identities (or essences) were inherent, and determined by race." Kavita Philip, "Race, Class and the Imperial Politics of Ethnography in India, Ireland and London 1850–1910," *Irish Studies Review* 10, 3 (2002), p. 289.

3. For example, Jane Trench established the St. John's House of Rest in 1870. In 1872, of the inmates included, "twelve were household servants, six nurses from the Dublin Nurses' Training Institution, four were children, and the rest trades people and roomkeepers." Second Annual Report, St. John's House of Rest (1872), pp. 6–7. Jane was sister to Maria Trench, who established the Dublin Nurses' Training Institution as discussed in chapter 5. See also Maria Luddy, *Women and Philanthropy in Nineteenth Century Ireland* (New York: Cambridge University Press, 1995), p. 197.

Select Bibliography

PARLIAMENTARY PAPERS

The Annual Reports of the Poor Law Commissioners, First–Twenty-fifth Annual Reports of the Commissioners for Administering the Laws for Relief of the Poor in Ireland, 1848–1872.

First Report of Inquiry into the Condition of the Poorer Classes in Ireland, 1836.

First Report of the Commissioners for Inquiring into the Condition of the Poorer Classes in Ireland, 1835.

Poor Law Reform Commission Ireland, *Report of the Vice-Regal Commission on Poor Law Reform in Ireland.* Vol. 1. Dublin: Alexander Thom and Co., 1906.

Report Concerning the Admissions to the Dublin Workhouse During the Years 1706–1810. M.S.Z. 3. 11 No. 153, 1710.

Report Concerning the Financial Problems of the Workhouse. Manuscript Z. 3. 11 No. 149, 1726.

Report Concerning the 'Treasurer's Report of the City Workhouse.' M.S.Z.3. 11 No. 146, 1710.

Report from Poor Relief Inquiry Commission. House of Commons (H.C.) 1887, 25, 38.

Report from the Select Committee on Industries Ireland. H.C. 1885, 288, 9.

Report of Royal Commission on Sewerage and Drainage of the City of Dublin. H.C. 1880, 2605, 30.

Report of the Departmental Committee Appointed by the Local Government Board to Inquire into the Public Health of the City of Dublin. H.C. 1900, 301, 6.

Report of the Joint Committee Selected from the Committees of the Duchess of Marlborough Relief Fund and the Dublin Mansion House Fund for Relief of Distress in Ireland. H.C. 1881, 326, 75.

Report of the Select Committee of the House of Lords on the Laws Relating to the Relief of Destitute Poor in Ireland, 1846.

Reports for the Select Committee of the House of Lords Appointed to Inquire into the Operation of the Irish Poor Law and the Expediency of Making any Amendments in Its Enactments. 1849.
Royal Commission on the Housing of the Working Class. House of Lords (H.L.) 1885, 3, 31.
Second Report of the Commissioners for Inquiring into the Condition of the Poorer Classes in Ireland, 1836.
Third Report of the Commissioners for Inquiring into the Condition of the Poorer Classes in Ireland, 1836.

MANUSCRIPT MATERIAL

Atkinson House (Formerly Home for Aged Females)

Minute Books, 1861–1996.

Cottage Home for Little Children

Annual Reports, 1879–1914.

Dublin Roman Catholic Diocesan Archives

Cullen Papers.
McCabe Pamphlets.
McCabe Papers.
Murray Papers.
Walsh Pamphlets.
Walsh Papers.

Harcourt Home

Home for Aged Governesses and Other Unmarried Ladies. Annual Records, 1877–1900.

Holy Faith Convent, Glasnevin

Ladies Association of Charity of St. Vincent De Paul. Annual Reports, 1851–1862.
St. Brigid Orphanage. Payments to Nurses Accounts for St. Brigid's Orphanage, 1869–70 and 1870–74.

Irish Church Missions

Minute Books, 1846–1851.

National Archives

Female Orphan House, Circular Road Dublin, 1866–1878.
Penitent Relief Society, 1835–1874.
Records of Committee Homes for Charitable Societies, 1816–1894.

Records of Protestant Orphan Society, 1840–1843, pp. 49–58.
Registry Books of the North Dublin Union, 1839–1916.
Registry Books of the South Dublin Union, 1840, 1847–1848, 1860–1861, and 1880–1952.

National Library of Ireland

Minutes of Meeting of Governors of St. Mary's Charity Schools, Dublin, 1790–1805.

Religious Society of Friends, Swanbrook House

Annual Minutes, Committee Meetings, 1887–1917, and Nurses Monthly Reports, 1902–1924.
Liberty Infant School, 1827–1897.
Meath Place Mission Papers.
Minutes of Liberty Crèche Committee Meetings, 1892–1896.
Minutes of Women's Friend's Poor Committee, 1843–1873.
Minutes of Women's Meetings for Quakers, 1878–1880.
Sick Poor Institution and Dorset Nourishment Dispensary.
Strand Street Institute Reports, 1868–1900.

Representative Church Body Library

J. D. H. Widdess, *The Magdalen Asylum Dublin, 1766–1966.* N.p., 1966.
Magdalen Asylum Guardians' Minute Books, 1848–1915.
Minutes of Prison Gate Mission, 1881–1900.

St. John's House of Rest

Annual Reports, 1872–1996.

University College Dublin

Report of St. Vincent's Hospital, Dublin, 1842.
Special Collection: The Sisters of Charity, Prospectus of an Institution Intended to be Established in Stephen's Green, Dublin, 1834.

Young Women's Christian Association

Annual Reports, 1887–1994.

MEDICAL RECORDS

"Case for Counsel on Behalf of The Queens Institute of District Nursing." Typescript, 13 July 1948.
"Circularising of Nurses re Marriage Rule." Jubilee Nurses Box, Nursing Board of Ireland. (no date)
"Development of Nursing in Ireland." Jubilee Nurses Box, Nursing Board of Ireland. (no date)
Dr. Steevens' Hospital, National Library of Ireland (NLI): Minute Books and File, 1881–1954.

Dr. Steevens' Hospital, Royal College of Physicians (RCP): "Regulations for the Training of Nurses." Pamphlet, n.d.
Dr. Steevens' Hospital: Rough Proceedings Book. Dr. Steevens', 1843; Fair Proceedings Book, 1876–1892.
Dr. Steevens' Hospital, Trinity College Dublin: Governor's Minute Books, 1802–1846; Rough Committee Minute Book, 27 Aug. 1885–19 Dec. 1899.
Dublin Metropolitan School for Nurses, Mercer's Library: Minute Book, 1893–1952.
House of Industry, Mercer's Library: Proceedings of the Governors of the House of Industry, 1820–1844.
Irish Victoria Jubilee Nursing Institute, Irish Nurses Organization: Minute Books, 1894–1908.
"Letter from Florence Nightingale to the Duke of Westminster, 1896." Jubilee Nurses Box Royal College of Surgeons.
Medical Directory for Ireland. 1853, 1895.
"Queen's Institute of District Nursing." Jubilee Nurses Box Royal College of Surgeons. (c. 1956)
Royal City of Dublin Hospital, Mercer's Library: Minutes, 1878–1900.
Royal Hospital, Kilmainham, National Archives Ireland: Loose Papers; Minute Books, 1833–1895; Physicians: Minute Books of Board of Governors, 1822–1900 (7 July 1808–12 November 1821 missing).
"Some Incidents of the Work of the Jubilee Nurse in Ireland." Jubilee Nurses Box Royal College of Surgeons, c. 1925.
"The Jubilee Nurses Need Your Help." Jubilee Nurses Box Royal College of Surgeons. (1953)

SELECTION OF PAMPHLETS

Dublin Roman Catholic Diocesan Archives

Association for Visiting Hospitals and Workhouses, Dublin, 1878.
Bird's Nest Reports, Kingstown, Dublin, 1882, 1887–1894.
Dublin By Lamplight, 1879.
Dublin Discharged Female Roman Catholic Prisoners Aid Society, 1884.
Dublin Visiting Mission in Connection with the Society for Irish Church, 1883, 1885, 1888–1889, 1894.
Elliott Home for Waifs and Strays (later Elliott Home for Little Children), 1883, 1885, 1888–1889.
Girls Home and Ragged School, 19 Luke St., Dublin, 1885, 1889, 1892.
"Helping Hand" Home, Dublin, 1888, 1892.
The Ragged Boys' Home, Grand Canal Street, Dublin, 1883–1885, 1888–1889.
Schools for Little Ragged Children and Women's Sewing Class, Grand Canal St., Dublin, 1883.
St. John's House of Rest, Merrion, 1879.
St. Patrick's Nurses' Home and Bible-Woman Association, Dublin, 1883.
St. Patrick's Nurses' Home for Supplying Trained Nurses to the Sick Poor in Their Own Homes, 1901, 1960.

Public Records Office, Northern Ireland

Belfast Society for Providing Nurses for the Sick Poor, 1888.

National Archives, Ireland

Report of the Ladies Industrial Society for Ireland for the Encouragement of Remunerative Labour among the Peasantry of Ireland Established in 1847.

The Report of the Ladies Relief Association for Ireland, from December, 1846, to the Closing of the Association, December, 1850.

National Library, Ireland

Dublin Bible Woman Mission, 1877.

Dublin By Lamplight, 1867.

General and First Annual Report of St. Joseph's Reformatory School for Catholic Girls. Dublin: Browne and Nolan, 1862.

Ladies Irish Association for Promoting Religious Instruction of the Native Irish—Partly through the Medium of their Own Language. Dublin, 1887.

Report of the Association for the Suppression of Mendacity in Dublin for the Year 1818. Dublin: A. Thom, 1819.

Report of the Female Orphan House, North Circular Road, Dublin, Founded A.D. 1790 with an Account of Its Origin, Progress and Present Position, 1851.

Report of the Wicklow-Street Late Fishamble Street Sunday Ragged School, December 31, 1862.

Seventh Report of the School for Educating the Daughters of the Irish Clergy, 1849.

Soup Kitchen, 101 St. Stephen's Green, 1878.

Third and Fourth Reports of the Inspector appointed to visit the Reformatory Schools of Ireland. Dublin: Alexander Thom 87 & 88, Abbey Street, 1865.

Third Report of the Training School for Female Servants, 135 Townsend Street; and Industrial School, 2 Mark's Lane, Dublin, 1857.

Twenty-fifth Annual Report and Statement of Accounts of The St. Patrick's Nurses' Home, 101st Stephen's Green, Dublin, for Supplying Trained Nurses to the Sick Poor in Their Own Homes for the Year Ending 31st December 1901. Dublin: C. W. Gibbs & Son, Printers, 1902.

Royal Irish Academy

Association Incorporated for Discountenancing Vice and Promoting the Knowledge and Practice of the Christian Religion, 1832.

The Cure for Ireland by an English Connaught Ranger. Dublin: Hodges and Smith, 1850.

First Report and Statement of Accounts of the Sandymount Loan-Fund Committee, 1832.

Fourteenth Annual Report of the Monkstown Protestant Orphan Society. Dublin: William Espy, 1843.

14th Report Irish Society for Promoting the Education of the Native Irish through the Medium of Their Own Language, 1832.

Fourth Report of the Society for the Encouragement & Improvement of Servants, 1830–1832.
Laws and Regulations of the Penitent Relief Society, 1830.
Letter to Edward Grogran, Esq., M.P., for Presentation to the House of Commons. Dublin 13th of Eleventh Month, 1846.
9th Report Shelter for Females Discharged from Prison, 1833.
Report of the Dingle and Ventry Mission Association County Kerry, Ireland 1847. Dublin: J. Dowling, 1848.
Report of the Mansion-House Relief Committee for the Relief of the Distressed Manufacturers of the City of Dublin and Its Vicinity, 1829.
17th Report Managing Committee of the Association for the Suppression of Mendacity in Dublin, 1833, 1834.
Strangers Friend Society for Visiting and Relieving Distressed Strangers in Dublin and Its Vicinity, 1833.
Third Annual Report of the Protestant Orphan Society founded A.D. 1828, 1832.
Twelfth Report of the Shelter for Females Discharged from Prison. Dublin: P. Dixon Hardy, 1839.

Trinity College Dublin

A Manual for Midwives and Monthly Nurses. Dublin: Fannin and Co., 1856.
On the Employment of Trained Nurses Among the Labouring Poor Considered Chiefly in Relation to Sanitary Reform and the Arts of Life. London: John Churchill, 1860.
Report of the Workhouse Visiting Society upon the Proposed Industrial Home for Young Women and the Correspondence with the Poor Law Board. London: Longman, Brown, Green, Longman & Roberts, 1860.

NEWSPAPERS AND OTHER PERIODICALS

The Catholic Directory
Daily Express
Dublin Builder
Dublin Evening Mail
Freeman's Journal
Irish Catholic
The Irish Independent
The Irish Times
The Lancet
The Nursing Times
Punch
The Times

BOOKS AND ARTICLES

Abel-Smith, Brian. *A History of the Nursing Profession.* London: Heineman, 1960.
Aberdeen, Countess of. "The Sphere of Women in Relation to Public Health." *The Dublin Journal of Medical Science* 22 (1 September 1911), pp. 161–70.

An Address to the Public on the Propriety of Midwives instead of Surgeons Practicing Midwifery. London: Longman Rees & Co., 1828.

Anthias, Floya. "Race and Class Revisted—Conceptualising Race and Racisms." *The Sociological Review* 38 (1 Feb. 1990), pp. 19–42.

Armeny, Susan. "Organized Nurses, Women Philanthropists, and the Intellectual Bases for Cooperation Among Women, 1898–1920." In *Nursing History: New Perspectives, New Possibilities,* ed. Ellen Condlifee Lagemann. New York: Teachers College Press, 1983, pp. 13–45.

Atkinson, Sara, and Ellen Woodlock. "The Irish Poor in Workhouses." *Transactions of the National Association for the Promotion of Social Science* 6 (1861), pp. 645–51.

August, Andrew. "How Separate a Sphere? Poor Women and Paid Work in Late-Victorian London." *Journal of Family History* 19, 3 (1994), pp. 285–309.

Bailey, Peter. " 'Will the Real Bill Banks Please Stand Up?' Towards A Role Analysis of Mid-Victorian Working-Class Respectability." *Journal of Social History* 7 (Spring 1979), pp. 336–53.

Baly, Monica. *Florence Nightingale and the Nursing Legacy.* London: Croom Helm, 1986.

Barrett, Rosa M. *Guide to Dublin Charities.* Dublin: Hodges, Figgis & Co., 1884.

Bayly, Mrs. "Influence of Public Opinion on the Habits of the Working Classes." *Transactions of the Association for the Promotion of Social Science,* 1863, pp. 692–98.

Beckett, J. C. *The Making of Modern Ireland.* London: Faber & Faber, 1981.

Bolt, Christine. *Victorian Attitudes To Race.* London: Routledge & Kegan Paul, 1971.

Bourdieu, Pierre, and John B. Thompson. *Language and Symbolic Power.* Cambridge: Harvard University Press, 1991.

———. *The Protestant Crusade in Ireland, 1800–70: A Study of Protestant-Catholic Relations Between the Act of Union and Disestablishment.* Dublin: Gill & Mac-Millan, 1978.

Bowen, Desmond. *Souperism: Myth or Reality.* Cork: Mercier Press, 1970.

Boyce, D. George. *Nineteenth-Century Ireland: The Search for Stability.* Dublin: Gill & MacMillan, 1990.

Branca, Patricia. *Silent Sisterhood: Middle-Class Women in the Victorian Home.* Pitts-burgh: Carnegie-Mellon University Press, 1975.

Briggs, Asa. "The Language of Class in Early Nineteenth-Century England." In *Essays in Social History,* ed. M. W. Flinn and T. C. Smout. Oxford: Clarendon Press, 1974, pp. 154–77.

Buckley, Anthony D. " 'On the Club': Friendly Societies in Ireland." *Irish Economic and Social History* 24 (1987), pp. 39–58.

Bullough, Vern, Bonnie Bullough, and Marietta P. Stanton, eds. *Florence Nightingale and Her Era: A Collection of New Scholarship.* New York: Garland Publishing, 1990.

Burdett-Coutts, Angela, ed. *Woman's Mission: A Series of Congress Papers on the Philanthropic Work of Women.* London: Sampson, Low, Marson & Co., 1893.

Burke, Helen. *The People and the Poor Law in Nineteenth Century Ireland.* London: George Philip Services, 1987.

Burman, Sandra, ed. *Fit Work For Women.* New York: St. Martin's Press, 1979.

Butel, P., and L. M. Cullen, eds. *Cities and Merchants: French and Irish Perspectives on Urban Development, 1500–1900*. Dublin: Tony Moreau, 1986.

Calhoun, Judith. "The Nightingale Pledge: A Commitment That Survives the Passage of Time." *Nursing & Health Care* 14 (3 March 1993), pp. 130–36.

Cappe, Catherine. *Extracts From Observations or Charity Schools and Other Subjects Connected With the Views of the Ladies Committee*. Dublin: William Watson, 1807.

Carpenter, Mary. "The Application of the Principles of Education to Schools for the Lower Classes of Society." *Transactions of the Association for the Promotion of Social Science*, 1861, pp. 344–51.

———. "The Duty of Government to Aid the Education of Children of the Perishing and Neglected Classes." *Transactions of the National Association for the Promotion of Social Science*, 1864, pp. 436–38.

———. "On the Education of Pauper Girls." *Transactions of the National Association for the Promotion of Social Science*, 1862, pp. 286–92.

———. *On the Supplementary Measures Needed for Reformatories for the Diminution of Juvenile Crime*. London: Emily Faithfull and Co., 1861.

———. "On the Treatment of Female Convicts." *Transactions of the Association for the Promotion of Social Science*, 1863, pp. 415–22.

Cassall, Ronald D. *Medical Charities, Medical Politics: The Irish Dispensary System and the Poor Law, 1836–1872*. Suffolk: Royal Historical Society, 1997.

Chart, D. A. "Unskilled Labour in Dublin: Its Housing and Living Conditions." *Journal of the Statistical & Social Inquiry Society of Ireland*, 1914, pp. 160–75.

Childers, Major E. S. E., and Robert Stewart. *The Story of the Royal Hospital, Kilmainham*. London: Hutchinson and Co., 1921.

Clark, Anna. "The Rhetoric of Chartest Domesticity: Gender, Language, and Class in the 1830s and 1840s." *Journal of British Studies*, 31 January 1992, pp. 62–88.

Clear, Catriona. *Nuns in 19th Century Ireland*. Dublin: Gill & MacMillan, 1987.

Clokey, Robert F. "Irish Emigration from Workhouses." *Journal of the Dublin Statistical Society* 23 (3 April 1863), pp. 416–32.

Coakley, Davis. *Baggot Street: A Short History of the Royal City of Dublin Hospital*. Dublin: Royal City of Dublin Hospital, 1995.

———. *Dr. Steevens' Hospital, A Brief History*. Dublin: Dr. Steevens' Hospital Historical Centre, 1992.

Cole, Alan. "The Quakers and the English Revolution." *Past and Present* 10 (November 1956), pp. 39–54.

Conley, Carolyn A. "No Pedestals: Woman and Violence in Late Nineteenth-Century Ireland." *Journal of Social History*, Summer 1995, pp. 801–18.

Cordery, Simon. "Friendly Societies and the Discourse of Respectability in Britain, 1825–1875." *Journal of British Studies* 34 (January 1995), pp. 35–58.

Craig, Maurice. *Dublin, 1660–1860*. London: Penguin, 1952.

Craven, Mrs. Dacre. *A Guide to District Nursing and Home Nursing*. Dublin: MacMillan & Co., 1889.

Crowley, Margaret, ed. *A Century of Service 1880–1980: The Story of the Development of Nursing in Ireland*. Dublin: Harcourt Printing & Stationary Co., 1980.

Crowther, Alice Cristabel. "Review of Work Done by Queen Victoria's Jubilee

Institute for Nurses in Ireland." *Dublin Journal of Medical Science* 145 (April 1918), pp. 236–40.

Cullen, L. M. *An Economic History of Ireland Since 1660.* London: Barnes & Noble, 1972.

Cullen, Mary, ed. *Girls Don't Do Honours: Irish Women in Education in the 19th and 20th Centuries.* Dublin: Women's Educational Bureau, 1987.

Cullen, Mary. "Women's History in Ireland." In *Writing Women's History: International Perspectives,* ed. Karen Offen, Ruth Pierson, and Jane Randall. Bloomington: Indiana University Press, 1991, pp. 429–42.

Curran, H. "The Workhouse Child." *New Ireland Review,* November 1896, pp. 133–37.

Curtis, L. Perry *Anglo-Saxons and Celts: A Study of Anti-Irish Prejudice in Victorian England.* New York: New York University Press, 1968.

———. *Apes and Angels: The Irishman in Victorian Caricature.* Washington, D.C.: Smithsonian Institution Press, 1997.

Dallas, Alexander R. C. *Continuation of the Story of the Irish Church Missions to the Roman Catholics.* London: J. Nesbit, 1869.

———. *The Story of the Irish Church Missions to the Roman Catholics Part I.* London: Society for the Irish Church Missions, 1867.

Dallas, Mrs. A. *Incidents In the Life and Ministry of the Rev. Alexander R. C. Dallas A. M.* London: J. Nesbit, 1871.

Daly, E. D. "Destitute Children and Imperial Revenue." *The New Ireland Review,* January 1900, pp. 291–300.

———. "Neglected Children and Neglectful Parents." *Journal of the Statistical and Social Inquiry Society of Ireland* 10 (December 1898), pp. 350–66.

Daly, Mary E. *Dublin: The Deposed Capital.* Cork: Cork University Press, 1984.

———. *The Famine in Ireland.* Dundalk: Dundalgan Press, 1986.

———. "Women in the Irish Workforce from Pre-Industrial to Modern Times." *Soathar* 7 (1981), pp. 74–82.

D'Antonio, Patricia O'Brien. "The Legacy of Domesticity: Nursing in Early Nineteenth-Century America." *Nursing History Review* 1 (1993), pp. 229–46.

Davidoff, Leonore, and Catherine Hall. *Family Fortunes: Men and Women of the English Middle Class, 1780–1850.* Chicago: University of Chicago Press, 1987.

Davies, Sarah. *Holly and Ivy: The Story of a Winter Bird's Nest.* Dublin: George Herbert, 1871.

———. *Other Cities Also: The Story of Mission Work in Dublin.* Dublin: George Herbert, 1881.

Davis, Jennifer. "The London Garroting Panic of 1862, A Moral Panic and the Creation of Criminal Class in Mid-Victorian England." In *Crime and Law, The Social History of Crime in Western Europe Since 1500,* eds. V. A. C. Gatrell, Bruce Lenman, and Geoffrey Parker. London: Europa, 1980, pp. 190–213.

———. "A Poor Man's System of Justice: The London Police Courts in the Second Half of the Nineteenth Century." *The Historical Journal* 27, 2 (1984), pp. 309–35.

Dawson, Charles, Esq. "The Dublin Housing Question–Sanitary and Insanitary." *Journal of the Statistical & Social Inquiry Society of Ireland,* 1914, pp. 91–95.

———. "The Valuation of the City of Dublin." *Journal of the Statistical and Social Inquiry Society of Ireland* 10 (December 1897), pp. 320–25.

Day, Susanne R. "The Crime Called Out-Door Relief." *Irish Review,* 2 April 1912, pp. 72–80.

———. "The Workhouse Child." *Irish Review,* 2 June 1912, pp. 169–79.

Dickson, Emily Winfred. "The Need for Women as Poor Law Guardians." *Dublin Journal of Medical Science,* January–June 1895, pp. 309–14.

Diner, Hasia. *Erin's Daughters in America.* Baltimore, Md.: Johns Hopkins University Press, 1983.

"The Distressed Gentlewoman." *University Magazine,* December 1878, pp. 679–85.

Donnelly, James S. *The Great Irish Potato Famine.* London: Sutton Press, 2001.

Doona, Mary Ellen. "Sister Mary Croke: Another Voice from the Crimean War, 1854–1856." *Nursing History Review* 3 (1995), pp. 3–41.

Douglass, Glynn. *Friends and 1798: Quaker Witness to Non-Violence in 18th Century Ireland.* Dublin: Historical Committee of the Religious Society of Friends in Ireland, 1998.

Dublin Mansion House. *The Irish Crisis of 1879–1880: Proceedings of the Relief Committee of 1880.* Dublin: Browne & Nolan, 1881.

Dudley, Rachel. "Lady Dudley's Scheme for the Establishment of District Nurses." N.p., 1912, pp. 1–19.

"The Dwellings of the Poor in Dublin." *Dublin Builder,* 15 October 1863, p. 173.

"The Dwellings of the Poor in Dublin." *Dublin Builder,* 1 November 1863, p. 180.

Eagleton, Terry. *Heathcliff and the Great Hunger: Studies in Irish Culture.* London: Verso, 1995.

"The Education of Midwives," *Medical Press & Circular,* 4 July 1866, p. 26.

Edwards, R. D., and T. D. Williams, eds. *The Great Famine: Studies in Irish History 1845–52.* Dublin: Lilliput Press, 1994.

Enright, Simon. "District Hospitals." *Dublin Medical Press* 1–2 (27 March 1829), p. 189.

Evans, E. "History of Dublin Hospitals: House of Industry Hospital." *The Irish Builder* 39 (1897), pp. 159–60.

Fagin, Claire, and Donna Diers. "Nursing as Metaphor." *New England Journal of Medicine,* 14 July 1983, pp. 116–17.

Falkiner, F. R. "Report on Homes of the Poor." *Journal of the Statistical and Social Inquiry Society of Ireland,* January 1882, pp. 261–71.

Falkiner, N. M. "The Nurse and the State." *State and Social Inquiry Society of Ireland* 14 (1921), pp. 29–60.

Fallon, Miriam. "Alice Reeves 1874–1955." *Nursing Review* 10, 3–4 (1992), pp. 38–39.

Fitzpatrick, David. " 'A Share of the Honeycomb': Education, Emigration, and Irishwomen." *Continuity and Change* 1, 2 (1986), pp. 217–34.

Fitzpatrick, Thomas. "On the Sanitary State of the Labouring Classes in Ireland." *Transactions of the Association for the Promotion of Social Science,* 1861, pp. 504–9.

Flack, Hally. "Nursing in Ireland from Pre-Christian Times to the Middle of the Nineteenth Century." *International Nursing Review* 6 (September 1931), pp. 428–41.

Flad, Mary M. "Tracing an Irish Widow's Journey: Immigration and Medical Care in the Mid-Nineteenth Century." *Geoforum* 26, 3 (1995), pp. 261–72.

Fleetwood, John F. *The History of Medicine in Ireland*. Dublin: The Skellig Press, 1983.

Foley, Tadgh, and Seán Ryder, eds. *Ideology and Ireland in the Nineteenth-Century*. Dublin: Four Courts Press, 1998.

Foster, R. F. *Modern Ireland 1600–1972*. London: Allen Lane, 1988.

———. *Paddy and Mr. Punch: Connections in Irish and English History*. New York: Penguin, 1993.

Foucault, Michel. *The Birth of the Clinic: An Archaeology of Medical Perception*. New York: Pantheon Books, 1973.

———. *Discipline & Punish: The Birth of the Prison*. New York: Vintage Books, 1995.

———. *Power/Knowledge: Selected Interviews and Other Writings, 1972–1977*. Ed. Colin Gordon. New York: Pantheon Books, 1980.

Fowler, John R. "Home Influences on the Children of the Dangerous Classes." *Transactions of the National Association for the Promotion of Social Science* 6 (1861), pp. 455–61.

Fraser, T. G. "Ireland and India." In *An Irish Empire? Aspects of Ireland and the British Empire*, ed. Kieth Jeffery. Manchester: Manchester University Press, 1996, pp. 77–93.

Friends, Society of. *Transactions of the Central Relief Committee of the Society of Friends during the Famine in Ireland 1846–7*. Dublin: Hodges & Smith, 1852.

Gerard, Jessica. "Lady Bountiful: Women of the Landed Classes and Rural Philanthropy." *Victorian Studies* 30 (Winter 1987), pp. 183–210.

Gibbons, Luke. "Race Against Time: Racial Discourse and Irish History." *Oxford Literary Review* 13 (1991), pp. 95–117.

Ginzberg, Lori D. *Women and the Work of Benevolence: Morality, Politics, and Class in the Nineteenth-Century United States*. New Haven, Conn.: Yale University Press, 1990.

Gleeson, Delia. "A Girl Philanthropist." *New Ireland Review* 19 (August 1903), pp. 373–78.

Goodbody, Rob. *A Suitable Channel: Quaker Relief in the Great Famine*. Bray: Pale Publishing, 1995.

Gramsci, Antonio. *Selections from the Prison Notebooks*. Ed. and trans. Quintin Hoare and Geoffrey Nowell Smith. New York: International Publishers, 1975.

Gray, Peter. "Potatoes and Providence: British Government Responses to the Great Famine." *Bullan* 1 (Spring 1994), pp. 75–90.

Grubb, Isabel. *Quakers in Ireland 1654–1900*. London: Longmans, 1927.

Hanbury, Mrs. *The Good Nurse or Hints on the Management of the Sick and Lying-in Chamber and the Nursery*. London: Longman, Rees, Orme, Brown and Green, 1828.

Hancock, W. Neilson. "The Workhouse as a Mode of Relief for Widows and Orphans." *Dublin Statistical Society Journal*, April 1855, pp. 84–92.

Hardy, Charles Henry. *Introductory Lecture on the Duties of Nurses*. Melbourne: George Robertson, 1881.

Harrison, Brian. "Philanthropy and the Victorians." *Victorian Studies* 9, 4 (1966), pp. 353–74.

———. "State Intervention and Moral Reform in Nineteenth-Century England."

In *Pressure From Without in Early Victorian England,* ed. Patricia Hollis. London: Edward Arnold, 1974, pp. 289–317.

Harrison, Richard S. *A Biographical Dictionary of Irish Quakers.* Dublin: Four Courts Press, 1997.

———. "Spiritual Perception and the Evolution of the Irish Quakers." In *The Religion of Irish Dissent 1650–1800,* ed. Kevin Herlihy. Dublin: Four Courts Press, 1996.

Hart, Jennifer. "Religion and Social Control in the Mid-Nineteenth Century." In *Social Control in Nineteenth Century Britain,* ed. A. P. Donajgradzki. London: Croom Helm, 1977, pp. 108–37.

Hatton, Helen. *The Largest Amount of Good: Quaker Relief in Ireland, 1654–1921.* Montreal: McGill-Queens University Press, 1993.

Hearn, Mona. *Below Stairs: Domestic Service Remembered in Dublin and Beyond 1880–1922.* Dublin: Lilliput Press, 1993.

Helmstadter, Carol. "Nurse Recruitment and Retention in the Nineteenth Century London Teaching Hospitals." *International History of Nursing Journal* 2, 1 (1996), pp. 58–69.

———. "Old Nurses and New Nursing in the London Teaching Hospitals before and after the Mid-Nineteenth-Century Reforms." *Nursing History Review* 1 (1993), pp. 43–70.

Higgins, Mrs. J. N. "On the Improvement of Nurses in Country Districts." *Transactions of the National Association for the Promotion of Social Science* 6 (1861), pp. 572–76.

Himmelfarb, Gertrude. *The Idea of Poverty: England In the Early Industrial Age.* London: Alfred A. Knopf, 1984.

———. "Mayhew's Poor: A Problem of Identity." *Victorian Studies,* March 1971, pp. 307–20.

———. *Poverty and Compassion: The Moral Imagination of the Late Victorians.* New York: Vintage Books, 1992.

Holten, Sandra. "Feminine Authority and Social Order: Florence Nightingale's Conception of Nursing and Health Care." *Social Analysis,* August 1984, pp. 59–72.

"Hospital Nursing in Dublin." *Dublin Medical Press,* 15 August 1866, p. 181.

Irish Lady, An. "Suggestions for the Technical Education of Young Irishwomen." *New Ireland Review,* November 1896, pp. 175–76.

Jackson, Pauline. "Women in 19th Century Irish Emigration." *International Migration Review* 18, 4 (1984), pp. 1004–20.

Jackson, R. V. "The Structure of Pay in Nineteenth Century Britain." *Economic History Review* 40, 4 (1987), pp. 561–70.

Jellicoe, Anne. "A Visit to the Female Convict Prison at Mountjoy, Dublin." *Transactions of the National Association for the Promotion of Social Science,* 1862, pp. 437–42.

Johnson, Paul. "Class Law in Victorian England." *Past and Present* 141 (November 1993, pp. 147–69.

Johnson, Richard. "Education, Politics and Social Control in Early Victorian England." *Past and Present* 49 (November 1970), pp. 96–119.

Jones, W. R. "England against the Celtic Fringe: A Study in Cultural Stereotypes." *Journal of World History* 13 (1971), pp. 154–71.

Jordon, Alison. *Who Cared? Charity in Victorian and Edwardian Belfast*. Belfast: Queen's University of Belfast, Institute of Irish Studies, 1993.

Judd, Catherine. *Bedside Seductions: Nursing and the Victorian Imagination, 1830–1880*. New York: St. Martin's Press, 1998.

Kelleher, Margaret. *The Feminization of Famine*. Cork: Cork University Press, 1997.

Kenny, Kevin. *The American Irish*. New York: Longman, 2000.

Kilroy, Phil. "Quaker Women in Ireland, 1660–1740." *Irish Journal of Feminist Studies* 2, 2 (Winter 1997), pp. 1–16.

Kinealy, Christine. *This Great Calamity: The Irish Famine 1845–52*. Dublin: Gill & MacMillan, 1994.

Kirkpatrick, T. Percy. *The History of Dr. Steevens' Hospital, Dublin, 1720–1920*. Dublin: University Press, 1924.

Langland, Elizabeth. *Nobody's Angels: Middle-Class Women and Domestic Ideology in Victorian Culture*. Ithaca, N.Y.: Cornell University Press, 1995.

Larimer, Douglas. " Nature, Racism and Late Victorian Science." *Canadian Journal of History* 25 (December 1990), pp. 369–85.

Larkin, Emmet. "The Devotional Revolution in Ireland." *American History Review* 77 (3 June 1972), pp. 625–52.

Lebow, Richard N. "British Historians and Irish History." *Eire-Ireland* 8, 4 (Winter 1973), pp. 3–38.

———. *White Britain and Black Ireland: The Influence of Stereotypes on Colonial Policy*. Philadelphia: Institute for the Study of Human Issues, 1976.

Leopold, Joan. "British Applications of the Aryan Theory of Race to India, 1850–1870." *The English Historical Review* 83 (1974), pp. 578–603.

Levine, Philippa. *Feminist Lives in Victorian England: Private Roles and Public Commitment*. Oxford: Basil Blackwell, 1990.

Littlewood, Barbara, and Linda Mahood. "Prostitutes, Magdalenes and Wayward Girls: Dangerous Sexualities of Working Class Women in Victorian Scotland." *Gender & History* 3, 2 (Summer 1991), pp. 160–75.

Lorimer, Douglas A. " Nature, Racism, and Late Victorian Science." *Canadian Journal of History* 25 (December 1990), pp. 360–85.

———. "Theoretical Racism in Late Victorian Anthropology, 1870–1900." *Victorian Studies*, Spring, 1988, pp. 405–30.

Luddy, Maria. "An Agenda for Women's History in Ireland 1500–1900." *Irish Historical Studies* 27, 109 (May 1992), pp. 1–37.

———. "District Nursing in Ireland, 1815–1974." *Tipperary Historical Journal*, 1996, pp. 164–70.

———. *Women and Philanthropy in Nineteenth Century Ireland*. New York: Cambridge University Press, 1995.

———, ed. *Women in Ireland: A Documentary History 1800–1918*. Cork: Cork University Press, 1995.

Luddy, Maria, and Cliona Murphy, eds. *Women Surviving: Studies in Irish Women's History in the 19th and 20th Centuries*. Dublin: Poolbeg Press, 1990.

Luddy, Maria, and Mary O'Dowd, eds. *Women, Power and Consciousness in Nineteenth-Century Ireland*. Dublin: Attic Press, 1995.

Lynaugh, Joan E. "Narrow Passageways: Nurses and Physicians in Conflict and Concert Since 1875." In *The Physician as Captain of the Ship: A Critical Re-*

appraisal, ed. Nancy M. P. King, Larry R. Churchill, and Alan W. Cross. New York: D. Reidel, 1988, pp. 23–37.

Lynch, John. *A Tale of Three Cities: Comparative Studies in Working-Class Life*. London: MacMillan, 1998.

Lyons, J. B. *The Quality of Mercer's: The Story of Mercer's Hospital, 1734–1991*. Dublin: Glendale, 1991.

Lysaght, Moira. "The Evolution of Nursing in Dublin 1820–1970." *St. Vincent's Annual*, 1975, pp. 52–56.

MacCurtain, Margaret, and Donncha O'Corrain, eds. *Women in Irish Society: The Historical Dimension*. Westport, Conn.: Greenwood Press, 1978.

"The Magdalens of High Park." *The Irish Rosary*, April 1897, p. 178.

Magray, Mary Peckham. *The Transforming Power of Nuns: Women, Religion and Cultural Change in Ireland, 1750–1900*. New York: Oxford University Press, 1998.

Malcolm, Elizabeth, and Greta Jones. *Medicine, Disease and the State in Ireland, 1650–1940*. Cork: Cork University Press, 1999.

Mandler, Peter, ed. "Poverty and Charity in the Nineteenth-Century Metropolis: An Introduction." In *The Uses of Charity: The Poor on Relief in the Nineteenth-Century Metropolis*. Philadelphia: University of Pennsylvania Press, 1990, pp. 1–37.

A Manual for Midwives and Monthly Nurses. Dublin: Fannin and Co., 1856.

Mapother, E. D. "The Sanitary State of Dublin." *Statistical and Social Inquiry Society of Ireland* 26 (January 1864), pp. 62–76.

Martin, J. H. "The Social Geography of Mid-Nineteenth Century Dublin City." In *Common Ground*, ed. William J. Smythe and Kevin Whelan. Cork: Cork University Press, 1988, pp. 173–88.

Martin, Mrs. Charles, "St Lawrence's Catholic Home." *Irish Monthly* 21 (January 1893), pp. 14–18.

McCarthy, Kathleen D., ed. *Lady Bountiful Revisited: Women, Philanthropy, and Power*. New Brunswick, N.J.: Rutgers University Press, 1990.

McClintock, Anne. *Imperial Leather: Race, Gender, and Sexuality in the Colonial Contest*. New York: Routledge, 1995.

McFarland, Edward. "The Royal Hospital Kilmainham, Co. Dublin." *Country Life*, May 9–16 1985, n.p.

McGann, Susan. *The Battle of the Nurses*. London: Scutari Press, 1992.

McKenna, L., S. J. "Co-Ordination of Charity—A Need and an Example." *The Irish Monthly* 45 (1917), pp. 279–91.

"The Medical Charities of Ireland." *Dublin University Magazine* 20 (July 1842), pp. 88–101.

Mitchell, David. *A "Peculiar" Place: The Adelaide Hospital, Dublin: Its Times, Places and Personalities, 1839 to 1989*. Dublin: Blackwater, 1989.

Monteiro, Lois A. "Florence Nightingale on Public Health Nursing." *American Journal of Public Health* 75, 2 (1985), pp. 181–85.

Moore, Judith. *A Zeal For Responsibility: The Struggle for Professional Nursing in Victorian England, 1868–1883*. Athens: University of Georgia Press, 1988.

Moorhead, Thomas Gillman. *A Short History of Sir Patrick Dun's Hospital*. Dublin: Hodges, Figgis and Co., 1942.

Morrison, E. "A District Nurse Among the Poor." *New Ireland Review* 21 (March 1909), pp. 24–31.

Muldoon, James. "The Indian as Irishman." *Essex Institute Historical Collections*, October 1975, pp. 267–89.

Mulhall, Marion. "Boarding Out Workhouse Children." *New Ireland Review*, November 1896, pp. 133–37.

Neville, Parke. "City of Dublin Sewerage." *Transactions of the National Association for the Promotion of Social Science* 6 (1861), pp. 524–35.

Newsinger, John. "The Catholic Church in Nineteenth-Century Ireland." *European History Quarterly* 25 (1995), pp. 247–67.

Nightingale, Florence. *Notes on Nursing: What It Is, and What It Is Not*. London: Harrison, 1860.

———. "Sanitary Statistics of Native Colonial Schools and Hospitals." *Transactions of the Association for the Promotion of Social Science*, 1863, pp. 475–88.

Nolan, Janet A. *Ourselves Alone: Women's Emigration from Ireland 1885–1920*. Lexington: University of Kentucky Press, 1989.

Nolan, M. Eugene, R. S. M. *One Hundred Years: A History of the School of Nursing and of Developments at Mater Misericordiae Hospital 1891–1991*. Dublin: Goldpress Limited, 1991.

"The Nuisance from the Liffey." *Medical Press & Circular*, 28 March 1866, p. 322.

"Nurses for the Labouring Classes." *The Lancet*, 28 October 1854, pp. 365–66.

"Nurses for the Sick Poor." *The Lancet*, 7 November 1868, pp. 615–16.

O'Brien, Gerard. "The Establishment of Poor-Law Unions in Ireland, 1838–43." *Irish Historical Studies* 13, 90 (November 1982), pp. 97–120.

———. "The New Poor Law in Pre-Famine Ireland: A Case History." *Irish Economic Social History* 12 (1985), pp. 33–49.

O' Brien, Joseph V. *"Dear Dirty Dublin": A City in Distress, 1899–1916*. Berkeley: University of California Press, 1982.

O'Connell, Mrs. Morgan J. "Poor Law Administration As It Affects Women and Children in the Workhouses." *Statistical and Social Inquiry Society of Ireland* 7 (April 1880), pp. 20–31.

O'Connor, John. *The Workhouses of Ireland: The Fate of Ireland's Poor*. Dublin: Anvil Books, 1995.

Ó Gráda, Cormac. *Black '47 and Beyond: The Great Irish Famine in History, Economy and Memory*. Princeton, N.J.: Princeton University Press, 1999.

———. "Dublin's Demography in the Early Nineteenth Century: Evidence from the Rotunda." *Population Studies* 45 (1991), pp. 43–54.

———. *Ireland: A New Economic History 1780–1939*. Oxford: Oxford University Press, 1994.

———. *Ireland before and after the Famine: Explorations in Economic History, 1800–1925*. Dublin: Gill & MacMillan, 1993.

O'Mahony, Nora Tynan. "In a Magdalen Asylum." *Irish Monthly* 34 (7 July 1906), pp. 373–75.

O'Neill, Kevin. " 'Almost a Gentlewoman': Gender and Adolescence in the Diary of Mary Shackleton." In *Chattel, Servant or Citizen: Women's Status in Church, State and Society*, ed. Mary O'Dowd and Sabine Wichert. Belfast: Institute of Irish Studies, 1995, pp. 91–102.

———. "Mary Shackleton Leadbetter: Peaceful Rebel." In *The Women of 1798*, ed. Dáire Keogh and Nicholas Furlong. Dublin: Four Courts Press, 1998, pp. 137–62.

O'Neill, Thomas P. "From Famine to Near Famine 1845–1879." *Studia Hibernica* 14 (1974), pp. 161–71.

———. "The Society of Friends and the Great Famine." *Studies* 39 (1950), pp. 203–13.

O'Sullivan, Patrick, ed. *Irish Women and Irish Migration.* London: Leicester University Press, 1995.

O'Toole, Fintan. "Going Native: The Irish as Blacks and Indians." *Études Irlandaises: L'Irlande Aujourd'hui,* Autumn 1994, pp. 121–31.

Palmer, Irene S. "Florence Nightingale and the First Organized Delivery of Nursing Services." *American Association of Colleges and Nursing,* 1993, pp. 1–14.

Parker, Julia. *Women and Welfare: Ten Victorian Women in Public Social Service.* London: St. Martin's Press, 1989.

"Pauper Nurses in Workhouses." *British Medical Journal,* 27 May 1865, p. 551.

Philip, Kavita. "Race, Class and the Imperial Politics of Ethnography in India, Ireland and London 1850–1910." *Irish Studies Review* 10, 3 (2002), pp. 289–302.

Phillipps, K. C. *Language and Class in Victorian England.* Oxford: Basil Blackwell, 1984.

Physician, A. *On the Employment of Trained Nurses Among the Labouring Poor Considered Chiefly in Relation to Sanitary Reform and the Arts of Life.* London: John Churchill, 1860.

Platt, Elspeth. *The Story of the Ranyard Mission 1857–1937.* London: Hodder & Stoughton, 1937.

Plunkett, Isabel. *Words of Help for Working Women; or Short Addresses for Mothers' Meetings.* London: Gall & Inglis, 1877.

Póirtéir, Cathal, ed. *The Great Irish Famine.* Dublin: Mercier Press, 1995.

Priestly, Eliza. "Nurses a la Mode." *Nineteenth Century,* January 1897, pp. 28–37.

Prochaska, F. K. "Charity Bazaars in Nineteenth-Century England." *Journal of British Studies* 16, 2 (Spring 1977), pp. 62–84.

———. "A Mother's Country: Mothers' Meetings and Family Welfare in Britain, 1850–1950." *History* 74 (October 1989), pp. 379–99.

———. *Women and Philanthropy in 19th Century England.* Oxford: Oxford University Press, 1980.

Prunty, Jacinta. *Dublin Slums 1800–1925.* Dublin: Irish Academic Press, 1997.

———. *Lady of Charity, Sister of Faith: Margaret Aylward, 1810–1889.* Dublin, Irish Academic Press, 1999.

Reidy, Margaret. "The History of Nursing in Ireland." *International Nursing Review* 18 (1971), pp. 326–33.

Reverby, Susan M. *Ordered to Care: The Dilemma of American Nursing, 1850–1945.* Cambridge: Cambridge University Press, 1987.

Rhodes, Rita M. *Women and the Family in Post-Famine Ireland: Status and Opportunity in a Patriarchal Society.* New York: Garland Publishing, 1992.

Rich, Paul B. *Race and Empire in British Politics.* Cambridge: Cambridge University Press, 1986.

Roberts, Henry, F. S. A. "On the Sanitary Instruction of the Laboring Classes, and Their Training in Those Domiciliary Habits Which Conduce to Physical and Moral Well-Being." *Transactions of the Association for the Promotion of Social Science,* 1862, pp. 750–57.

Robins, Joseph. *The Lost Children: A Study of Charity Children in Ireland 1700–1900.* Dublin: Institute of Public Administration, 1980.

Robinson, Nugent. *Homes of the Working Poor.* Dublin: Goodwin, Son and Nethercott, 1862.

Rose, Sonya. *Limited Livelihoods: Gender and Class in Nineteenth-Century England.* Berkeley: University of California Press, 1993.

Rosenberg, Charles E. "Florence Nightingale on Contagion: The Hospital as Moral Universe." *History and Healing: Essays for George Rosen,* ed. Charles E. Rosenberg. New York: Watson Academic Publishing, 1979, pp. 116–36.

Ross, Ellen. *Love and Toil: Motherhood in Outcast London, 1870–1918.* New York: Oxford University Press, 1993.

Ross, Ian Campbell, ed. *Public Virtue, Public Love: The Early Years of the Dublin Lying-In Hospital.* Dublin: The O'Brien Press, 1986.

"The Royal Hospital, Kilmainham." *Dublin University Magazine* 7 (January–June 1836), pp. 222–26.

Scanlan, Pauline. *The Irish Nurse: A Study of Nursing in Ireland: History and Education 1718–1981.* Co. Leitrum, Ireland: Drumlin Publications, 1991.

Schupf, H. W. "Single Women and Social Reform in the Mid-Nineteenth Century: The Case of Mary Carpenter." *Victorian Studies* 27 (1974), pp. 301–17.

Shaw, Edith M. "How Poor Ladies Might Live: An Answer from the Workhouse." *Nineteenth Century,* April 1897, pp. 620–27.

Shawe, Rosalind Gillette. *Notes for Visiting Nurses.* Philadelphia: P. Blakiston, Son & Co., 1893.

Shinman, Lillian Lewis. "The Band of Hope Movement: Respectable Recreation for Working-Class Children." *Victorian Studies,* September 1973, pp. 49–74.

Showalter, Elaine. "Florence Nightingale's Feminist Complaint: Women, Religion and Suggestions for Thought." *Signs* 6 (Spring 1981), pp. 395–412.

Smith, Beverly A. "The Female Prisoner in Ireland 1855–1878." *Federal Probation,* December 1990, pp. 69–81.

Smith, Olivia. *The Politics of Language, 1791–1819.* Oxford: Clarendon Press, 1984.

Stedman Jones, Gareth. *Languages of Class: Studies in English Working Class History.* Cambridge: Cambridge University Press, 1984.

———. *Outcast London: A Study in the Relationship between Classes in Victorian Society.* London: Penguin, 1984.

———. "Working-Class Culture and Working-Class Politics in London, 1870–1900: Notes on the Remaking of a Working Class." *Journal of Social History* 7 (1974), pp. 460–508.

Stepan, Nancy. *The Idea of Race in Science: Great Britain 1800–1960.* Oxford: Oxford University Press, 1981.

Stocks, Mary. *A Hundred Years of District Nursing.* London: George Allen & Unwin Ltd., 1960.

Stoker, William Thornley. "The Hospitals of the House of Industry." *Dublin Journal of Medical Science* 80 (December 1885), pp. 469–86.

Stringer, Marian. "Ninety Years of District Nursing," *Nursing Mirror,* 13 April 1978, pp. 63–66.

Summers, Anne. "Ministering Angels." *History Today* 39 (February 1989), pp. 31–37.

———. "The Mysterious Demise of Sarah Gamp: The Domiciliary Nurse and Her Detractors, 1830–1860." *Victorian Studies* 32 (1989), pp. 365–86.

Symes, Langford. "On the Mortality of Children in Ireland." *Dublin Journal of Medical Science,* May 1898, pp. 479–86.

Thompson, E. P. *The Making of the English Working Class.* New York: Pantheon Books, 1963.

———. "Patrician Society, Plebeian Culture," *Journal of Social History* 7 (1974), pp. 382–405.

Tod, Isabella. "Boarding-out of Pauper Children." *Statistical and Social Inquiry Society of Ireland* 7, 5 (August 1878), pp. 298–99.

Twining, Louisa. "Workhouse Education." *Transactions of the National Association for the Promotion of Social Science* 6 (1861), pp. 331–37.

Valiulis, Maryann Gialanella, and Mary O'Dowd, eds. *Women & Irish History.* Dublin: Wolfhound Press, 1997.

Vaughn, W. E., and A. J. Fitzpatrick, *Irish Historical Statistics Population 1821–1871.* Dublin: Royal Irish Academy, 1978.

Vicinus, Martha. *Independent Women: Work and Community For Single Women, 1850–1920.* Chicago: University of Chicago Press, 1985.

———. *A Widening Sphere: Changing Roles of Victorian Women.* Bloomington: Indiana University Press, 1977.

Walvin, James. *The Quakers: Money and Morals.* London: John Murray Publishing, 1997.

Warburton, J., J. Whitelaw, and R. Walsh. *History of the City of Dublin,* Vol 1. London: T. Cadell and Davies, 1818.

Ware, Vron. *Beyond the Pale.* London: Verso, 1992.

Waters, Hazel. "The Great Famine and the Rise of Anti-Irish Racism." *Race & Class* 37, 1 (1995), pp. 95–108.

Welter, Barbara. "The Cult of True Womanhood, 1820–1860." *American Quarterly* 18 (Summer 1966), pp. 151–74.

Whelan, Bernadette. *Women and Paid Work in Ireland 1500–1930.* Dublin: Four Courts Press, 2000.

Whelan, Kevin. "Pre- and Post-Famine Landscape Change." In *The Great Famine,* ed. Cathal Póitéier. Dublin: Mercier, 1995, pp. 19–33.

White, Francis. *Report and Observations on the State of the Poor of Dublin.* Dublin: J. Porter, 1833.

White, Rosemary. *Social Change and the Development of the Nursing Profession: A Study of the Poor Law Nursing Service 1848–1948.* London: Henry Kimpton Publishers, 1976.

"Why Not Become a Queen's Nurse—a Worthwhile Career." London: Queen's Institute of District Nursing. N.d., n.p.

Widdess, J. D. H. *The Richmond, Whitworth and Hardwicke Hospitals Dublin 1772–1972.* Dublin: Beacon Printing, 1972.

Wigham, Maurice J. *The Irish Quakers: A Short History of the Religious Society of Friends in Ireland.* Dublin: Historical Committee of the Religious Society of Friends in Ireland, 1992.

Williams, George C., ed. *Dublin Charities: A Handbook.* Dublin: Association of Dublin Charities, 1902.

Williams, Katherine. "From Sarah Gamp to Florence Nightingale: A Critical Study

of Hospital Nursing Systems from 1840–1897." In *Rewriting Nursing History*, ed. Celia Davies. London: Croom Helm, 1980, pp. 41–73.
"Women and Work." *Dublin University Magazine*, December 1872, pp. 670–82.
Woodcock, George. "Henry Mayhew and the Undiscovered Country of the Poor." *The Sewanee Review* 92 (Fall 1984), pp. 556–73.
Woodroofe, Kathleen. *From Charity to Social Work in England and the United States.* London: Routledge and Paul, 1966.

UNPUBLISHED WORKS

Cremin, Vicky. *The Liberty Crèche 1893–1993*. Dublin, 1993.
Freeman, Edward T. "Centenary of the Mater Misericordiae Hospital 1861–1961." N.d., pp. 3–40.
Magray, Mary Peckham. "The Strange Case of Mary Mathews: Religion, Gender & the Construction of Irish Catholic Identity." Presented at the American Conference for Irish Studies, Albany, New York: 1997.
McMahon, Dorren. "The Irish Quaker Community 1870–1925." M.A. thesis, University College Dublin, 1985.
O'Connor, Gregory. "Speech on the Royal Hospital, Kilmainham." Dublin, 1994.
Preston, Margaret. "Interview with Mary Quain." Dublin, July 1995.
Quaine, Mary. "Brief Outline of the History of Jubilee Nursing in Ireland 1876/1968." 24 September 1990.
Smyly, Vivian. "The Early History of Mrs. Smyly's Homes and Schools." Speech Given to the Smyly Home Reunion, 1976.
Tatten, Assisi, Sr. "A Brief Account of the Life and Work of Margaret Aylward Foundress of Sisters of the Holy Faith." Holy Faith Convent, Glasnevin, n.d.

Index

Act of Union, 105
Adelaide Institution and Protestant Hospital, 113, 132, 135, 147, 160
Aikenhead, Mary, 132–33. *See also* St. Vincent's Hospital
Anthropology, 41, 176
Association for the Suppression of Mendacity in Dublin, 5, 43, 49, 51–52
Association for Visiting Roman Catholics in Hospitals, 73, 146
Asylum for Aged and Infirm Female Servants, 5
Atkinson House, 70
Austin, Jane, 138–39
Aylward, Margaret, 6–7, 17, 52, 68–69, 74, 80, 82–92, 175, 177–78. *See also* Ladies Association of Charity of St. Vincent de Paul

Baggot Street Hospital, 130, 132, 134, 136, 140–43, 145, 148, 150–52, 160
Ballitore, County Kidare, 104
Barrett, Rosa, 25, 50, 67, 73–74. *See also Guide to Dublin Charities*
Belfast Society for Providing Nurses for the Sick Poor, 154, 158
Beresford, Susan, 130, 150
Bewley, Helena S., 136, 150
Bewley, Joseph, 106
Bible women, 83, 154–55
Bird's Nest, 75–76, 79

Carpenter, Mary, 41, 48, 115
Catholic Rotunda Girls Aid Society, 73
Charity. *See* philanthropy
City of Dublin Nursing Institution, 135, 150–51
Class, 2, 4, 42–43, 49–50, 68, 109–13, 128–30, 157, 159–60
Clergy Daughters School, 5
Coercion. *See* religious coercion
Committee of the Catholic Ragged Schools, 53
Corn Laws, 17, 106
Cottage Home for Little Children, 50, 73
Cromwell, Oliver, 103
Cullen, Paul, 88

Dallas, Alexander, 54, 80–81
Darwin, Charles, 4, 44
Daughters of Saint Brigid, 88

Davies, Sarah, 54, 78–81; *Erin's Hope,* 80
Dickens, Charles, 136; *Martin Chuzzlewit,* 136; Sarah Gamp, 136, 139, 159
Dingle and Ventry Mission, 53
District nursing, 3, 7, 131, 152–59, 177; duties of, 157–59; isolation, 157–58; paternal occupation, 156–57; work schedules, 157
Dr. Steevens' Hospital, 131, 134, 135, 140, 143
Dublin, 5–6, 13–14, 19–30, 70, 84, 130, 175; diet, 112; Dublin Corporation, 23, 25–26, 30, 70, 175; employment, 13–15, 30, 43, 48; housing, 13–14, 22–26, 28–30; medical infrastructure, 130–35; mortality, 26–27; population, 28, 108; religious denominations, 68, 74; sanitation, 23–24; skilled and unskilled laborers, 26, 78, 142–43
Dublin By Lamplight, 5
Dublin Charities: A Handbook, 26, 67, 73, 113. *See also* George C. Williams
Dublin Discharged Female Roman Catholic Prisoners' Aid Society, 48–49, 52, 73
Dublin Female Orphan House, 51
Dublin Female Penitent Asylum, 52
Dublin Female Penitentiary, 48–49, 115
Dublin Metropolitan Technical School for Nurses, 135, 148–49
Dublin Nurses' Training Institution, 135, 140, 146–47
Dublin Visiting Mission in Connection with the Society for Irish Church Missions, 45, 53–54
Dublin Women's Suffrage Association, 116
Dudley District Nurses, 131

Edmundson, Mary, 113. *See also* Prison Gate Mission
Education, 14, 41, 71–72, 75, 84–87, 109
Elizabeth I, 16, 69, 130
Elliot Home for Waifs and Strays, 28–29, 75–76, 79
Emigration, 21, 156
Ethnography, 41, 176

Famine, 15, 17–22, 81, 105–8, 134. *See also* Irish Famine
Female Penitent Asylum, 73
Fowler, John R., 43
Foster parents, 87
Foucault, Michel, 42 n.8, 159
Fox, George, 102, 104, 108
Friendly societies, 42
Fundraising, 2, 128, 152

Gamp, Sarah. *See* Charles Dickens
Gandon, James, 14
Girls and Infants' Ragged School, 75, 78
Girls' Training Home, 3, 115
Gleeson, Delia, 43
Grangegorman Street Prison, 113
Griffith, Robert, 28, 30; Griffith's valuation, 28
Guide to Dublin Charities, 25, 50, 67, 73–74. *See also* Rosa Barrett

Haslam, Anna, 116–17
"Helping Hand" Home, 75, 78–79
Hill, Matthew Davenport, 1
Home for Aged Governesses and Other Unmarried Ladies, 73
Home for Big Lads, 75
House of Industry, 131
House of Protection for Distressed Young Women of Unblemished Character, 48, 53
House of Refuge for Industrious and Distressed Females of Good Character, 49
Huxley, Margaret, 140–41, 147–50

India, 45–46
Ireland, 15–16, 69
Irish Church Missions, 54, 80–81, 85, 88
Irish Famine, 15, 17–22, 81, 105–8, 134. *See also* famine

Irish Society for Promoting the Education of the Native Irish through the Medium of Their Own Language, 54

Jubilee Institute for Nurses, 145, 155–57

Kirkpatrick, T. Percy, 140, 147

Ladies Association of Charity of St. Vincent de Paul, 6, 14, 52, 73, 82–86. *See also* Margaret Aylward
Ladies Committees, 128–29, 137–38, 145–46, 152
Ladies Irish Association for Promoting the Religious Instruction of the Native Irish, Partially Through the Medium of Their Own Language, 54
Lady Superintendent, 128, 138, 147; responsibilities, 142, 147; salary, 141; teaching, 148
Landlord absenteeism, 106
Language, 4–5, 6, 42–43, 46–50, 52–55, 68, 82, 89–92, 106–7, 111, 115
Leadbeater, Mary, 104–5

Magdalen Asylum, 50, 73, 115
Managing Committee for the Association of Suppression of Mendacity in Dublin, 5, 43, 49, 51–52
Martin, Mrs. Charles, 155–56
Mater Misericordiae Hospital, 133, 135, 148, 152
Matthews, Maria, 87–88
Matthews, Mary, 87–88
McAuley, Catherine, 133. *See also* Mater Misericordiae Hospital
McCabe, Edward, 52, 79
Meath Place Mission, 26, 109; Dorset Nourishment Dispensary, 109; Friends Ragged School, 109; Liberty Crèche, 110; Sick Poor Institute, 109
Medical dispensaries, 109
Mercer, Mary, 72
Mercer's Endowed Boarding School for Girls, 72
Mercer's Hospital, 131, 135
Midwifery, 131, 138, 141, 149, 157–58
Moore, George, 13
Mosse, Bartholomew, 131
Mother's Meetings, 2

Napoleonic Wars, 15, 105
Nicholson, Aesnith, 17–18
Nightingale, Florence, 127–28, 134, 136, 139, 154, 157
North Dublin Union, 6, 18–21, 24, 69–72; guardians, 18–21; numbers of inmates, 20; as sanitary authority, 24
Nuns, 132–33
Nursing, 3–4, 7, 10, 130, 134; character of, 138–40; compensation, 140–43, 148, 151, 154, 160; marriage, 143, 145, 150; misconduct, 136–38; on-site accommodation, 143, 145, 155, 159; reform, 128–30; training, 136, 151, 152, 159, 177; vocation vs. career, 3, 127–28, 130, 134, 149, 152–53, 155–56, 159–60; work schedules, 143–44, 157

O'Connell, Daniel, 42

Peel, Robert, 17
Penal laws, 69
Philanthropic Society, 42, 47, 51
Philanthropy, 1–3, 5, 22, 27, 30, 73, 127, 175; aristocratic sponsorship, 28–30, 114–15; fundraising, 2, 128, 152
Pim, Jonathan, 102, 106–7
Plunket, Anne Lee, 155. *See also* St. Patrick's Nurses' Home and Bible Woman Association
Poor Law, 16; Irish Poor Relief Act (1838), 16, 50, 107, 131; poor law unions, 16–17, 19; public works, 18; Temporary Relief Act (1847), 19
Population, 15. *See also* Dublin
Poverty, 1, 5, 17, 19, 23, 55, 89–91, 101;

deserving poor, 47–51; intrinsic nature, 4, 41–49, 52–55, 89–91, 101; undeserving poor, 51–52
Prison Gate Mission, 113–16
Proselytism. *See* Sectarianism
Protestant Orphan Society, 3, 70, 115
Prostitution, 42, 48–50, 116
Providence (Row) Night Refuge and Home, 50
Punch, 44–45

Quakers. *See* Society of Friends
Queen Victoria Jubilee Institute for Nurses, 145, 155–57

Race, 4, 41–49, 52–55, 89–91, 101, 176
Ragged Boys Home, 75–79
Ranyard, Ellen, 154
Ranyard Mission, 154
Rathbone, William, 153–54
Rebellion of 1798, 104–5
Religious coercion, 83–84, 176
Religious conversion, 52–55, 79–82, 84–89, 108, 176; kidnapping, 79–80, 87–88. *See also* sectarianism
Report of the Ladies Irish Association, 54
Rescue Mission Home, 5
Rotunda Hospital, 131, 135
Royal City of Dublin Hospital. *See* Baggot Street Hospital
Royal College of Physicians, 132, 135
Royal College of Surgeons, 130, 135
Royal Hospital Kilmainham, 131, 135–37, 140, 143

Saint Brigid's Orphanage, 86–88
Sanitary reform, 1, 84, 127–28, 154, 158, 176–77
Seaton Association Fund, 5
Sectarianism, 4, 6, 43, 52–55, 67–73, 79–82, 84–88, 91, 108–9, 117, 146–47, 155, 175–77. *See also* religious conversion
Separate spheres, 2, 154, 175
Sir Patrick Dun's Hospital, 130–32, 134, 136–37, 140–41, 145–50; midwives, 148–50
Sisters of Charity, 132–33. *See also* Mary Aikenhead
Sisters of the Holy Faith, 88; Sister M. Agatha, 88. *See also* Margaret Aylward
Sisters of Mercy, 133. *See also* Catherine McAuley
Smith, Adam, 15
Smyly, Ellen, 6, 67–69, 74–82, 90–92, 178; Smyly schools, 85, 88
Society of Friends, 7, 26, 101–16, 177, 178; Central Relief Committee, 106–7; famine relief, 107–8; in industry, 103, 117, 150; population, 108; Rebellion of 1798, 104–5; *Transactions of the Central Relief Committee of the Society of Friends During the Famine in Ireland 1846–7*, 106–8; women, 102, 116–17
Souperism, 72
South Dublin Union, 20, 26
Steevens' Hospital, 131, 134, 135, 140, 143, 152
St. Joseph's Reformatory School for Catholic Girls, 47, 53, 73
St. Lawrence's Institute, 155–56
St. Mary's Industrial Institute, 51
St. Patrick's Nurses' Home and Bible Woman Association, 115, 155, 157, 159
Strand Street Institute, 110–13; Mothers Meeting Committee, 111; ragged school, 112; Young Men's Association, 112–13; Young Women's Association, 112
Strangers' Friend Society for Visiting and Relieving Distressed Strangers and Resident Sick Poor, 51
St. Vincent's Hospital, 133, 135
Suffrage, 116–17, 129–30

Temperance, 111
Tod, Isabella, 47
Training School for Female Servants, 28–29
Trench, Maria, 146–47, 149. *See also* Dublin Nurses' Training Institution
Trevelyan, Charles, 16
Trinity College, 130, 132

Tuke, James Hack, 105
Twining, Louisa, 159

United Irishmen, 104

Visiting the poor, 4, 113, 176, 178

Webb, Beatrice, 44
Webb, Sidney, 44
Wheeler, William de Courcy, 150. *See also* City of Dublin Nursing Institution
White, Francis, 13 n.3, 25, 51
Williams, George C., 26, 67, 73, 113. *See also Dublin Charities: A Handbook*
Women: employment, 26, 114, 156; incarceration, 48–49, 113–14

About the Author

MARGARET H. PRESTON is Assistant Professor of History at Augustana College in Sioux Falls, South Dakota. She is a social and economic historian who also focuses on issues of gender in modern Ireland, Britain, and India.